ABIDE AND GO

The Didsbury Lectures
Series Preface

The Didsbury Lectures, delivered annually at Nazarene Theological College, Manchester, are now a well-established feature on the theological calendar in Britain. The lectures are planned primarily for the academic and church community in Manchester but through their publication have reached a global readership.

The name "Didsbury Lectures" was chosen for its double significance. Didsbury is the location of Nazarene Theological College, but it was also the location of Didsbury College (sometimes known as Didsbury Wesleyan College), established in 1842 for training Wesleyan Methodist ministers.

The Didsbury Lectures were inaugurated in 1979 by Professor F. F. Bruce. He was followed annually by highly regarded scholars who established the series' standard. All have been notable for making high calibre scholarship accessible to interested and informed listeners.

The lectures give a platform for leading thinkers within the historic Christian faith to address topics of current relevance. While each lecturer is given freedom in choice of topic, the series is intended to address topics that traditionally would fall into the category of "Divinity." Beyond that, the college does not set parameters. Didsbury lecturers, in turn, have relished the privilege of engaging in the dialogue between church and academy.

Most Didsbury lecturers have been well-known scholars in the United Kingdom. From the start, the college envisaged the series as a means by which it could contribute to theological discourse between the church and the academic community more widely in Britain and abroad. The publication is an important part of fulfilling that goal. It remains the hope and prayer of the College that each volume will have a lasting and positive impact on the life of the church, and in the service of the gospel of Christ.

<table>
<tr><td>1979</td><td>Professor F. F. Bruce†</td><td>Men and Movements in the Primitive Church</td></tr>
<tr><td>1980</td><td>The Revd Professor I. Howard Marshall</td><td>Last Supper and Lord's Supper</td></tr>
<tr><td>1981</td><td>The Revd Professor James Atkinson†</td><td>Martin Luther: Prophet to the Church Catholic</td></tr>
<tr><td>1982</td><td>The Very Revd Professor T. F. Torrance†</td><td>The Mediation of Christ</td></tr>
<tr><td>1983</td><td>The Revd Professor C. K. Barrett†</td><td>Church, Ministry and Sacraments in the New Testament</td></tr>
<tr><td>1984</td><td>The Revd Dr A. R. G. Deasley</td><td>The Shape of Qumran Theology</td></tr>
</table>

Abide and Go

Missional Theosis in the Gospel of John

THE DIDSBURY LECTURES 2016

MICHAEL J. GORMAN

CASCADE *Books* · Eugene, Oregon

ABIDE AND GO
Missional Theosis in the Gospel of John

Didsbury Lectures Series

Cascade Books
An Imprint of Wipf and Stock Publishers
199 W. 8th Ave., Suite 3
Eugene, OR 97401

www.wipfandstock.com

PAPERBACK ISBN: 978-1-5326-1545-0
HARDCOVER ISBN: 978-1-5326-1547-4
EBOOK ISBN: 978-1-5326-1546-7

Cataloguing-in-Publication data:

Names: Gorman, Michael J., 1955–author.

Title: Abide and go : missional theosis in the Gospel of John / Michael J. Gorman.

Description: Eugene, OR: Cascade Books, 2018 | Series: Didsbury Lectures Series | Includes bibliographical references and index.

Identifiers: ISBN 978-1-5326-1545-0 (paperback) | ISBN 978-1-5326-1547-4 (hardcover) | ISBN 978-1-5326-1546-7 (ebook)

Subjects: LCSH: Bible. John—Criticism, interpretation, etc. | Deification (Christianity) | Missions—Biblical teaching | Mission of the church—Biblical teaching

Classification: BS2615.52 G676 2018 (print) | BS2615.52 (ebook)

07/24/18

For Nancy

and with gratitude to Bob Leavitt,
who asked the REB chair when there
would be a book on John

Contents

Acknowledgments

This book contains the revised and expanded Didsbury Lectures, "Missional Theosis in the Gospel of John," delivered at Nazarene Theological College (NTC) in Manchester, England in October of 2016 (chapters 1–5), as well as the address given to the Ehrhardt Biblical Seminar at the University of Manchester during my stay at NTC (chapter 6). I am grateful to the entire NTC faculty and administration for the invitation to deliver these lectures, and to the entire community for their hospitality. It is a great privilege and responsibility to participate in the Didsbury Lectures, following a significant and inspiring cloud of witnesses. Special thanks go to Kent Brower for his role in planning and facilitating the lectures. But I would be remiss not to mention, as well, NTC principal Deirdre Brower Latz, Svetlana Khobnya, Julie Lunn, Peter Rae, and Dwight Swanson for their kindnesses. I am grateful as well to Todd Klutz and Peter Oakes of the University for their invitation to the Seminar and for their hospitality.

The lectures have been expanded in three main ways for publication. First, the text of some of the original footnotes to the lectures has been brought into the body of the chapters themselves, while some footnotes have been expanded and many others added, as is appropriate for a scholarly monograph. Second, parts of other lectures on similar topics, delivered before or after the Didsburys, have been added to the lectures to supplement some of the points of the Didsbury Lectures. Third, some additional research and reflection have also added to the substance of the book.

Portions of these chapters were also presented as the Payton Lectures at Fuller Theological Seminary in April 2016, under the theme of "Reading John Missionally," and as the keynote lecture at the Theology Conference of

Northeastern Seminary in Rochester, New York in March 2016, with the title "John: The Non-Sectarian, Missional Gospel." I am grateful to my friends, Dean Joel Green at Fuller and Professor Richard Middleton at Northeastern, for the invitations to those lectureships. It was a special privilege and responsibility to participate in these two events, too, and in the case of the Payton Lectures, once again to stand in a distinguished line of scholars. I am very thankful as well to Professors Keon-Sang An and Marianne Meye Thompson at Fuller for their incisive and helpful responses to my lectures, which contributed to making the Didsbury Lectures and this book better than they otherwise would have been. In addition, while at Fuller I benefitted from fruitful conversations with faculty members in both intercultural studies and biblical studies, and with doctoral students in New Testament.

An overview of my thesis was presented to the New Testament seminar at Ridley Hall, Cambridge, England in October 2016. My thanks go to Michael Thompson and Richard Bauckham for the invitation to participate in their group. Parts of this book were also delivered as addresses at conferences for pastors in the fall of 2017, first at Rochester College (Michigan) and then at my alma mater, Gordon College (Massachusetts). I am grateful to Mark Love and to Steve Hunt, respectively, for their invitations and hospitality.

A version of chapter 6 has appeared also in *Johannine Ethics: The Moral World of the Gospel and Epistles of John*, edited by Sherri Brown and Christopher W. Skinner and published by Fortress Press in late 2017, as "John's Implicit Ethic of Enemy-Love." I express my deep gratitude to the editors and publishers to include it here, in slightly revised form.

I am extremely grateful as well to the various Christian communities and ministries I visited while doing the research for and writing of this book: in Durham, North Carolina; Baltimore, Maryland; Chicago, Illinois; Taizé, France; and Worthing, England. I especially wish to thank Jonathan and Leah Wilson-Hartgrove, Sarah Jobe, Colin Miller, Douglas and Rachel Campbell, and Brian Diekman in Durham; Sarah Batley in Baltimore; Charlotte Lehman, Greg Clark, Allan Howe, David Janzen, David Fitch, Josiah Daniels, Wayne Gordon, and Cherith Fee Nordling in Chicago; Brother John at Taizé; and Larry and Stephanie Kraft in England. The reflections in chapter 7 stem in part from visits with these wonderful people.

As I was completing the manuscript for this book, Andy Byers published his excellent dissertation on Johannine theosis, *Ecclesiology and Theosis in the Gospel of John* (Cambridge University Press, 2017). I am grateful to Andy and the publisher for sharing his text with me prior to its publication. Similarly, Cornelis Bennema published his book *Mimesis in the Johannine Literature: A Study in Johannine Ethics* (T. & T. Clark, 2017) as I was finishing the manuscript. I appreciate Cor's willingness to share the book with me. And, at the last minute, Andrew Lincoln kindly sent me the pre-publication version of his essay "The Johannine Vision of the Church."

As readers will note, in this book I am in dialogue with multiple interpreters of John, both those living on earth and those living in glory. Among the latter, I express special appreciation to and for the late Raymond E. Brown, who began his academic career where I have taught for more than a quarter-century and whose chair, so to speak, I now occupy. Among the former, I express special gratitude to Cor Bennema, Sherri Brown, Andy Byers, Ross Hastings, Craig Keener, Craig Koester, Andrew Lincoln, Frank Moloney, Chris Skinner, Jan van der Watt, and (once again) Marianne Meye Thompson—most of whom I am also privileged to count as friends. A special thank-you goes out to Frank, Marianne, and Chris, who read part (Marianne) or all (Frank and Chris) of the manuscript and provided valuable feedback. Moreover, my good friend and colleague Andy Johnson, of Nazarene Seminary, has—once more—made my work better by reading parts of it carefully. I of course remain responsible for all remaining shortcomings.

I cannot mention my academic home without expressing gratitude to St. Mary's Seminary & University, and particularly to those who supported the research and writing of this book in various ways: Tom Hurst, Phil Brown, Tom Burke, and Brent Laytham. In addition, a special word of thanks goes to my research assistants during this process: Gary Staszak, himself a budding Johannine scholar, and especially Michelle Rader, another budding New Testament scholar. Gary promoted the lectures in video form, using them in a class he taught, and provided valuable feedback on the content. He also helped with some editorial tasks. Michelle checked many Scripture references, compiled the indexes, and performed multiple other tasks to prepare the book for publication. My colleagues and students at St. Mary's have heard or read (or both) some of the ideas articulated in this book, and I appreciate their interest and feedback, especially that of Brent Laytham and that of the members of my "Currents in Johannine Theology" seminar in the spring of 2018: Jesus Anguiano, John Baab, John Morrison, Marty Nocchi, and Gary Staszak. Last but not least, I am indebted to Bob Leavitt for his frequent reminders that the holder of the Raymond E. Brown chair should write a book on John.

As for publication, I am once again grateful to my friends at Wipf and Stock, and particularly in this case to Robin Parry for his keen editorial insight.

Finally, my debt of gratitude to the Henry Luce Foundation and the Association of Theological Schools in North America (ATS) is immense.

Acknowledgments

As a Luce Fellow for 2015–16, with a fellowship in the category of "the Bible and the church," I had the great opportunity of spending an entire sabbatical year reading, thinking, writing, and lecturing about the Gospel of John, mission, and related topics. The results of much of that research appear in this book, which further explains why the original lectures have been expanded (without losing their main, original claims). I mention in particular Stephen Graham of ATS and (yet again) Marianne Meye Thompson of Fuller Seminary for their encouragement and feedback. Chapter 7 is a revision of a presentation made to the ATS, the Luce Foundation, and other Luce Fellows in November of 2016.

Finally, I am happy to acknowledge the person to whom this book is dedicated: my wife Nancy. In many ways, for many years, she has embodied the thesis of this book.

My original proposal to ATS included the following words:

> The question driving this proposed project is "What is the relationship between a biblically grounded spirituality of theosis (deification), or participation in the life of the Triune God, and the mission of the church?" This question is significant for the church in North America (and elsewhere) if the church is going to appropriately hold together two aspects of its life that are often separated: spirituality and mission. Thus the project aims to bring together the fields of biblical studies, spirituality, and missiology in order to assist in the construction of an answer to the driving question. The recent renewed interest in theosis has become highly significant for systematic and ecumenical theology, and it has begun to impact New Testament studies as well. But because theosis is traditionally associated with contemplation and personal spirituality, few people have attempted to connect it directly to the church's mission.

The Didsbury Lectures and other events associated with the Luce Grant have been part of my attempt to incarnate this proposal. The work continues.

Maundy/Holy Thursday 2018
Mandatum novum do vobis . . .
(I give you a new commandment . . .)

John . . . makes use of the strongest expressions for union with God that contemporary religious language provided, in order to assure his readers that he does seriously mean what he says: that through faith in Christ we may enter into a personal community of life with the eternal God, which has the character of ἀγάπη [agapē], which is essentially supernatural and not of this world, and yet plants its feet firmly in this world, not only because real ἀγάπη cannot but express itself in practical conduct, but also because the crucial act of ἀγάπη was actually performed in history, on an April day about A.D. 30, at a supper-table in Jerusalem, in a garden across the Kidron valley, in the headquarters of Pontius Pilate, and on a Roman cross at Golgotha. So concrete, so actual, is the nature of the divine ἀγάπη; yet none the less for that, by entering into the relation of ἀγάπη thus opened up for [humanity], we may dwell in God and He in us.

—C. H. Dodd, *The Interpretation of the Fourth Gospel*, 199–200

Getting Started

In this book I reflect on reading the Gospel of John *missionally*. Specifically, I will argue that the Fourth Gospel is *a missional* gospel with a *missional* spirituality, and that these two aspects of the Gospel have profound relevance for the contemporary church. Still more specifically, I will argue that John has a particular missional structure and theme that manifest its understanding of the *missio Dei*—the mission of God—and that its missional spirituality is a spirituality of participation in the very life and life-giving mission of God, by which Jesus' disciples demonstrate their likeness to God and become more and more like God.

I will refer to this missional spirituality as "missional theosis," theosis (also known as deification or divinization) being one of the Christian tradition's words for transformative participation in the life of the Triune God.[1] John's Gospel, both as a whole and some key texts within it (such as 1:12–13; 3:3–8; and 10:34–35, quoting Ps 82:6 [LXX 81:6]), was a key source for the Christian doctrine of theosis. It has been an equally important source for Christian mission (e.g., "As the Father has sent me, so I send you" in 20:21[2]). Accordingly, joining these two dimensions of the Gospel makes perfect sense. The primary focus of the book is the second half of John's Gospel, where these two dimensions are most explicitly present and most explicitly joined together.

1. Matthew Sousa, a doctoral student at Fuller Seminary writing on theosis in John, suggested to me that "missional theosis" is a redundant term because theosis is inherently missional. While I agree, I am not certain that the Christian tradition has always fully recognized that reality, or that contemporary readers would necessarily embrace it.

2. Unless otherwise indicated, scriptural quotations are taken from the NRSV.

The book is divided into seven chapters. Chapter 1 outlines my understanding of missional hermeneutics and of theosis as the basis for my approach to reading the Gospel of John missionally and theotically (i.e., in terms of mission and theosis). Chapter 2 is an overview of the Gospel's structure and theme, stressing these two dimensions, as well as a consideration of some missional and theotic aspects of the first half of the Gospel. Chapters 3 through 5 look at missional theosis in John 13–16, John 17, and John 20–21, respectively. Chapter 6 steps back and considers the Gospel as a whole, focusing on the extreme missional and theotic theme of enemy-love. Chapter 7, the final chapter, offers conclusions, theological reflections, and observations about how contemporary Christian communities are embodying the Gospel's vision of missional theosis.

As a book in the field of what is now called "missional hermeneutics," this study is primarily interested in what John says about mission and missional spirituality. My primary goal is to read and interpret the text carefully. Yet I acknowledge that a fully missional reading can only be done in the context of the people of God "on the ground," so to speak. My ultimate hope, then, is that this book will stimulate such localized readings of the Fourth Gospel in order that its readers will be better able to discern and participate in the *missio Dei* wherever they happen to be.

A final introductory word: words and phrases like "mission" and "Christian mission" and even *missio Dei* understandably trouble some people. Whether this trouble is generated by associating mission with colonialism and its siblings (e.g., nationalism, exceptionalism, and ethnocentrism), by assuming that mission implies an intolerant, totalizing metanarrative, or by other intellectual concerns and/or personal experiences, the burden of this book is, in part, to suggest that Christian mission—as participation in the life and activity of the Triune God—does not underwrite such colonizing and controlling of human bodies and minds. Rather, mission is about life and love, even love of enemies, and it is this liberating, life-giving notion of mission that we find in the Gospel of John.

> *A note to readers*: This book is intended for both the academy and the church. The argument of the book is carried in the body of the text. The footnotes include documentation, interaction with other interpreters, and the like. The book may be profitably read with or without referring to all the notes.

1

Reading John Missionally and Theotically

You put two things together that have not been put together before. And the world is changed.[1]

What is the Gospel of John? What are its chief features, purposes, and theological claims? These are questions that have both charmed and baffled hearers and readers of the Fourth Gospel for the better part of two millennia.[2]

The particular approach of this book is to read the Gospel of John *missionally* and *theotically*. Essentially, this means we will consider this Gospel as a document that has a robust missional focus and contains an equally robust theology of theosis (a foreign word to many people), or transformative participation in the life of God. Indeed, this book sees mission and theosis as inseparable in the Fourth Gospel, and their union as its theological and spiritual soul. Hence the book's title: *Abide and Go*. By putting these two things together (theosis and mission, abide and go), perhaps this book will effect a bit of change in Johannine studies, in the church, and in the world that—according to John—God loves.

In this first chapter we consider what reading Scripture, and particularly the Fourth Gospel, missionally and theotically (that is, to repeat, in terms of mission and theosis) means. This will serve as preparation for actually

1. Julian Barnes, *Levels of Life*, 2nd ed. (London: Vintage, 2014), 3, cited in Bauckham, *Gospel of Glory*, 131.

2. For helpful guides to many of the main issues (historical, literary, and theological), see Anderson, *Riddles of the Fourth Gospel*, and, more briefly, van der Watt, *Introduction*, who helpfully pays attention to mission. For John's theology, see especially Koester, *Word of Life*.

reading John in terms of mission and theosis in subsequent chapters. We begin with a brief overview of the topic of reading Scripture missionally, or missional *hermeneutics*, before turning to the thornier question of missional *theosis*, or becoming like God by sharing in the missional life of God.[3]

Missional Hermeneutics

Hermeneutics is the art of interpretation, in this case the art of interpreting Scripture. The present book is an exercise in *missional* hermeneutics, the art of interpreting Scripture missionally. Missional hermeneutics is a type of theological interpretation of Scripture, that is, a type of interpretation in and for the life of the church.[4] It brings together the fields of biblical studies, hermeneutics, and missiology. Simply put, missional hermeneutics is "reading texts through a missional lens."[5] This simple definition suggests that missional hermeneutics consists of a set of perspectives, purposes, and practices.

As a relatively new sub-discipline of theology, missional hermeneutics is still a work in progress. For our purposes, it can be summarized briefly as grounded in three theological assumptions:

1. that God, who is love, is missional and therefore has a mission, the *missio Dei*;[6]

3. For additional discussions of missional theosis, arising from my work in Paul, see my *Becoming the Gospel* and "Paul's Corporate, Cruciform, Missional Theosis."

4. "Theological interpretation" is itself a field with a variety of descriptions and definitions. Perhaps simplicity is the best way to achieve some generally agreed-upon understanding. Hence, Steve Fowl's description of theological interpretation as interpretation that "keeps theological concerns primary" is both good and useful (see most recently Fowl, "Theological Interpretation of Scripture and Its Future," 677). "Interpretation in and for the life of the church," with "life of the church" to be understood very broadly (inclusive of mission), is meant as a gloss on Fowl's description.

5. Barram, *Missional Economics*, 24. For more in-depth definitions and discussions, see, e.g., Barram, "Bible, Mission, and Social Location"; McKinzie, "Missional Hermeneutics."

6. A succinct, classic statement of the term *missio Dei* and its development is Bosch, *Transforming Mission*, 398–402. At the 1952 Willingen Conference of the International Missionary Council, Bosch says, "Mission was understood as being derived from the very nature of God. It was thus put in the context of the doctrine of the Trinity, not of ecclesiology or soteriology" (399). The focus on mission as *God's* mission, Bosch continues, "represents a crucial breakthrough in respect of the preceding centuries" (402). See further Holmes, "Trinitarian Missiology" and Flett, *The Witness of God*. (I am grateful to Keon-Sang An of Fuller Seminary for theological and bibliographical insights about this matter.) Holmes writes that if we merely claim that God *has* a mission, "mission may be incidental, disconnected from who God is," but if we claim that

2. that Scripture bears witness to God's mission; and

3. that the church is called and sent to participate in that mission in God-like, or God-shaped, ways.[7]

It is important not to separate being and act in God, which is why I begin with stating both that God *is* missional and that God *has* a mission; that is, because God is love, God *acts* missionally, or purposefully, toward humans and the rest of creation in love. For Christians, of course, all references to God in the three theological assumptions noted above are references to the triune God of Christian faith. The claim that God is missional needs to be rooted, therefore, in the Christian—and Johannine—theological affirmations that God exists as a triadic community of Father, Son, and Spirit, and that "God is love" (1 John 4:8, 16).[8] It is to this God that Scripture

---

God *is* missionary, "mission is one of the perfections of God, as adequate a description" of who God is as "love, omnipotence or eternity" ("Trinitarian Missiology," 89). Not all theologians will agree that "missionary-ness" (to coin a word) is an inherent divine attribute as fundamental as love or eternality. Flett writes that "[t]he problem of how human beings can witness to God is a problem of God, and it is answered because the witness of God is first God himself in his eternal life of fellowship from and to all eternity. . . . God is a missionary God because he has determined himself to be for and with the human. . . . Fellowship is the nature of God's life" (*The Witness of God*, 288). In other words, ultimately, God is missional because God is love, indeed, a communion of self-giving love. My own view is similar to that of Flett. It is appropriate to call God "missional" or "missionary," but to see this as a derivative attribute of the more essential and inherent attribute of love.

7. Commenting on the Willingen Conference, Bosch succinctly states the main point (*Transforming Mission*, 399): "The classical doctrine on the *missio Dei* as God the Father sending the Son, and God the Father and the Son sending the Spirit was expanded to include yet another 'movement': Father, Son, and Holy Spirit sending the church into the world." Further, "To participate in mission is to participate in the movement of God's love toward people, since God is a fountain of sending love" (400). Holmes ("Trinitarian Missiology," 75) says that "by the Spirit, the church participates in the continuing working out of the (already eschatologically complete) mission given to Christ by the Father" and that the shape of such missional activity will be theoform and therefore cruciform: "Just as purposeful, cruciform, self-sacrificial sending is intrinsic to God's own life, being sent in a cruciform, purposeful and self-sacrificial way must be intrinsic to the church being the church" (89). In many ways this quote sums up the major claims of the present book.

8. No book of the New Testament has a fully developed doctrine of the Trinity in the conceptuality or language of later Christian theology. Nevertheless, parts of the New Testament, including especially the letters of Paul and the Johannine writings, pushed the church in this theological direction. In retrospect, therefore, we can use terms like "Trinity" and "triune" to refer to this triadic community of divine actors in John—Father, Son, and Spirit/Paraclete—without implying that all of the later understandings of the Trinity are explicit in the Johannine writings. Moloney (*John*, 21) uses similar language of three "'characters in the story' [who] are clearly in relationship." Moloney (20–21) stresses the relational rather than the (later) metaphysical theology we find in

in general, and John in particular, bears witness, and it is in the mission of this God—the *missio Dei*—that the church is invited to participate.[9] As I have written elsewhere, the term *missio Dei*

> summarizes the conviction that the Scriptures of both Testaments bear witness to a God who, as creator and redeemer of the world, is already on a mission. Indeed, God is by nature a missional God, who is seeking not just to save "souls" to take to heaven some day, but to restore and save the created order: individuals, communities, nations, the environment, the world, the cosmos. This God calls the people of God assembled in the name of Christ—who was the incarnation of the divine mission—to participate in this *missio Dei,* to discern what God is up to in the world, and to join in.[10]

Missional hermeneutics, then, is reading Scripture to discern and participate in what God is doing in Christ by the Spirit in general, and in a particular time and place.[11] Or, as Joel Green puts it, "Missional hermeneutics locates the Bible and its interpretation within the arc of God's mission (the *missio Dei*) as this is articulated in Scripture; it also inquires into how the Bible might shape the church's contemporary identity and mission."[12] To read Scripture in this way requires an act of faith and commitment that

---

John. Interestingly, the salvation of God described in Ezekiel 34, an important text for John, is the work of three dramatis personae: God as the good shepherd, God's anointed one (the Davidic messiah-figure) as the good shepherd as well, and God's life-giving Spirit. Could John be influenced by this prophetic triad?

9. "A participatory understanding [of mission] opens up a highly reciprocal view of the God-world-church relationship, in which the church shares in the Triune God's own vulnerable engagement with the world" (Van Gelder and Zscheile, *The Missional Church in Perspective*, 111).

10. Gorman, *Elements of Biblical Exegesis*, 155.

11. Of course, all reading of Scripture is done in a particular time and place ("social location"), and thus also all discerning of the *missio Dei*. In this I concur with the work of Michael Barram and the general direction of Greg McKinzie in his important article "Missional Hermeneutics." Nonetheless, it is part of the task of biblical studies, particularly biblical scholarship, to discern within the text of Scripture the contours of the *missio Dei* and thus to provide a canonical framework within which to discern and understand the *missio Dei* in a particular location. So, for instance, a text like 2 Cor 5:19—"in Christ God was reconciling the world to himself, not counting their trespasses against them, and entrusting the message of reconciliation to us"—bears witness to God's overarching work of reconciliation, which then takes shape in particular locales. Moreover, close readings of scriptural texts that pay attention to the particular "social location" (original context) of those texts themselves helps provide the basis for contemporary contextualized readings that work on the principle of analogy, or "spotting the rhyme," to use William Spohn's words (*Go and Do Likewise*, 54–55, 63, 152).

12. Green, "Modern and Postmodern Methods," 201.

is itself a way of sharing in the *missio Dei*: to see Scripture as witness and summons, and to seek to be an attentive participant in the very reality being studied.[13] Missional hermeneutics, like all theological interpretation, is inherently self-involving.

Missional hermeneutics does not ignore the standard ways of engaging in close readings of biblical texts. But it does expand the contexts of scriptural interpretation beyond the text's historical and literary contexts, beyond its canonical context, and even beyond its ecclesial context narrowly construed (i.e., in terms of reception history and theological interpretation) to include the context of the *missio Dei*. (This is no small goal, since discerning the *missio Dei* itself involves scriptural interpretation.) A single theological word for that divine mission would be "salvation" or, in more specifically Johannine idiom, "life" or "eternal life." Unpacking what this means requires careful exegesis of both the text and the world—the particular place in history and space in which the missional reading of Scripture takes place.

Accordingly, missional hermeneutics is something of a hermeneutical circle inasmuch as (1) the *missio Dei* is discerned in Scripture and (2) participation in the *missio Dei* is necessary for a right reading of Scripture as witness to the *missio Dei*.[14] (This is similar to the claim of Stanley Hauerwas that only those who practice the Sermon on the Mount can rightly understand it.[15]) That is, as theological exegesis, missional exegesis is inherently participatory.[16] This in turn means, therefore, that participation in the *mis-*

13. Cf. McKinzie's claim ("Missional Hermeneutics," 164): "In order to read the text of the Bible as Scripture, the church should be theologically committed to a trinitarian understanding of God's mission, and this theological commitment *is* embodied participation in God's mission."

14. See especially McKinzie, "Missional Hermeneutics."

15. See, e.g., Hauerwas, *Unleashing the Scripture*, 63–72.

16. Barram (e.g., "Reflections on the Practice," 10) proposes the "sentness" of the church as the *sine qua non* of ecclesial hermeneutics; McKinzie ("Missional Hermeneutics," 165) calls participation in the *missio Dei* itself, and hence a concrete social embodiment, a *sine qua non* of all theological interpretation, including missional hermeneutics. McKinzie also borrows from the hermeneutics of liberation theology to propose that missional hermeneutics should be understood as "*works seeking understanding*" (esp. 178–79). He cites Brian Russell (*(re)Aligning with God*, 180) with approval: "*Missional* reading of Scripture needs to arise out of our *missional praxis*. . . . There is something of a hermeneutical circle in the process. A missional reading ought to fuel the actual practice of mission; the practice of mission brings the Church back to the Scriptures." Although McKinzie briefly acknowledges the hermeneutical circle operative in the formation of good scriptural readers (170), his emphasis on works seeking understanding does not display the hermeneutical balance we see in the Russell quote. An important question for McKinzie would be this: What criteria, apart from Scripture, do we have for determining that certain works are or are not manifestations of the *missio Dei*? For instance, as with liberation theology, is violent revolution to be

sio Dei in a specific context is necessary for truly good missional hermeneutics. At the same time, however, one can at least attempt to investigate "the arc of God's mission . . . as this is articulated in Scripture" (in Joel Green's words cited above) as a form of careful scriptural interpretation without being bound to connect that to a highly specific, localized context.

This claim fits in with the general polyvalent shape that missional hermeneutics as a discipline of academic theology has taken. There are various "streams" of, or approaches to, missional hermeneutics; my particular approach is heavily text-centered, in this case focused on the missional purposes, theology, and especially spirituality of one biblical book.[17] At the same time, in order to avoid separating text from context, I have found it useful to think of missional hermeneutics as involving two sets of related questions, one more exegetical of the text, one more exegetical of our particular context, as follows:

General Questions	Specific, Contextual Questions
What does this text say about the *missio Dei*?	What does this text say about the *missio Dei here and now*?
What does this text say about the condition of humanity and the world, about the need for God's saving mission?	What does this text say about the specific condition and need of humanity and the world *here and now*, in our context?
What does this text say about the nature and mission of God's people as participants in the *missio Dei*?	What does this text say to us about the call of God on us to participate in the *missio Dei here and now*?

---

understood as the work of God, even if a close reading of the New Testament offers little or no support for such a view?

17. George Hunsberger has studied the contributions of practitioners of missional hermeneutics, identifying four "streams" of emphasis in, or basic approaches to, missional hermeneutics. Emphasis may be placed on (1) the missional direction of the biblical narrative as a whole; (2) the missional purpose of the individual writings (my particular approach here); (3) the missional location of the Christian community; and (4) the missional engagement with cultures. See Hunsberger, "Proposals for a Missional Hermeneutic." James Brownson adds a possible fifth stream, or at least a rider to the third and fourth: "that missional encounters between people are, almost by definition, *cross-cultural* encounters." See Brownson, "A Response at SBL," delivered at the annual meeting of the GOCN Forum on Missional Hermeneutics in November 2008. Somewhat similar is Tim Carriker's application to missional hermeneutics of Paul Ricoeur's interpretive categories of reading behind, within, and in front of the text. See Carriker, "The Bible as Text for Mission." My approach is largely one of attending to "mission within the text," though I make some explicit, and many implicit, suggestions about "mission in front of the text."

It should be clear from the nature of these questions that to interrogate Scripture in such a way is simultaneously to allow Scripture to question—and ultimately shape—those posing the questions.

There are of course other, more specific questions, that could and should be asked, as I and others have noted elsewhere. But given the topic of this book, missional theosis, these basic questions will serve us well as a framework.[18]

For the purposes of the book, our focus will be on the more general questions in the table, although in the last chapter some aspects of the specific, contextual questions will be considered as we reflect theologically and briefly discuss missional theosis in concrete communities.[19] Our primary questions will be those in the left-hand column above: What does the Gospel of John say about the *missio Dei*, about humanity and the world, and especially—for this is the focus of the book—the participation of Jesus' disciples in the *missio Dei*? Ultimately the two sets of questions in the table cannot and should not be separated since (to repeat) all missional hermeneutics is, by definition, contextual. Yet the role of biblical scholars engaging in missional readings of Scripture is, in part, to discover aspects of the text that might not be discernible either by scholars uncommitted to theological/missional approaches or by lay people without expertise in the academic study of Scripture and theology.

It needs to be noted that these questions posed by practitioners of missional hermeneutics are decidedly different from one of the traditional questions interpreters have asked about the genre of the Gospel of John: Is it an evangelistic text or a document intended to nurture existing Christians and one or more Christian communities? These alternatives have

---

18. For other kinds of missional hermeneutics questions, see my *Elements of Biblical Exegesis*, 156–57; two of the questions there are How does this text relate to the larger scriptural witness, in both testaments, to the *missio Dei* and the mission of God's people? and How does this text call us as God's people to be both different from and involved in the world? See also Barram, *Missional Economics*, 36–37. Barram's questions are specifically contextually oriented and include, among others, the following: Does our reading of the text challenge or baptize our assumptions and blind spots? In what ways are we tempted to "spiritualize" the concrete implications of the gospel as articulated in this text? In what ways does this text proclaim good news to the poor and release to the captives, and how might our own social locations make it difficult to hear that news as good? Does our reading of the text reflect a tendency to bifurcate evangelism and justice? In what ways does the text challenge us to rethink our often cozy relationships with power and privilege?

19. For more on missional hermeneutics, see, e.g., my *Elements of Biblical Exegesis*, 155–58, and *Becoming the Gospel*, 50–57; Barram, *Missional Economics*, 19–38; Brownson, *Speaking the Truth in Love*; Goheen, *Reading the Bible Missionally*; plus the literature cited in these works.

sometimes been captured in two Germans words, *Missionsschrift* (missionary text) versus *Gemeindeschrift* (community text). In fact, these are probably false alternatives,[20] for John is a missionary text at least in part by virtue of its being a community-forming text. But the question of John's genre (in this theological sense) is not our primary concern. Our premise is that the Gospel of John, like all Scripture, bears witness to the *missio Dei* and calls all people to respond to and participate in that *missio*.[21]

We turn now to the question of what participation in the *missio Dei* might mean, and specifically to the term "missional theosis" that is in the subtitle of this book. What does it mean to read John not only missionally but also *theotically*?

Missional Theosis

This book's basic claim about John's Gospel is this:[22]

> Johannine spirituality fundamentally consists in the *mutual indwelling* of the Triune God (Father, Son, and Spirit) and Jesus' disciples such that disciples *participate* in the divine love and life, and therefore in the life-giving mission of God, thereby both *demonstrating their likeness to God as God's children* and *becoming more and more like God as they become like his Son by the work of the Spirit*. This spirituality can be summarized in the phrase "abide and go," based on John 15.[23]

20. See, e.g., Okure, *Johannine Approach to Mission*.

21. We will see that this *missio Dei* cannot be simplistically reduced to "eternal life," narrowly understood, or to eliciting belief, narrowly construed; nor, therefore, can evangelism—participating in the *missio* by sharing the good news—be narrowly understood as bearing *verbal* witness to a solely future, heavenly experience. We will return to this matter both below and in chapter 2.

22. As already indicated, in this thesis statement and throughout the book, I use the language of the Triune God as shorthand for what I understand to be John's presentation of the unity of Father, Son, and Spirit/Paraclete as three divine actors (or "persons," to use later theological language) constituting the one true God, the God of Israel. This does not mean that I believe John had "worked out" all the details and nuances of later trinitarian theology. It does mean, however, that later trinitarian theology was a logical, appropriate articulation of Johannine theology.

23. David Rensberger ("Spirituality and Christology," 184) insightfully and succinctly puts it this way: "'Abiding' implies persistence, but not stasis." Rensberger, however, largely limits the "journey" that is the opposite of stasis to love for the community of disciples, though he offers hints of a broader vision of "identification with those whom the world despises" (186).

The phrase "abide and go"—or "stay put and depart"—indicates the creative theological paradox in John's Gospel that unites spirituality ("abide") and mission ("go").[24] I will refer to this marriage of mission and spirituality as "missional theosis," but if at first readers are hesitant about the word "theosis," they should feel free to call it "missional transformative participation" or even "participatory missional sanctification"—at least for now.[25]

This approach to the Fourth Gospel will surprise some readers, since John is often perceived as the Gospel that reflects and perpetuates a community of disciples turned in on themselves, loving one another but not others—"sectarian," as some have charged. (We will consider this accusation more fully in chapter 2.) The interpretation of Johannine spirituality, and of the Gospel more broadly, in the following pages is a strongly anti-sectarian reading of John.

We begin our discussion of John's missional spirituality with the term "spirituality" itself. It is back in the news, so to speak, in academic biblical circles, increasingly a respectable term and concept.[26]

Renewed attention to Johannine spirituality and to participation/theosis

One standard definition of Christian spirituality is "the lived experience of Christian belief" or "of Christian faith and discipleship."[27] Another description is "a transformative relationship with God."[28] This sort of understanding of spirituality is not divorced from "the real world." As I have argued

24. Independently, Andrew Lincoln has come to a very similar conclusion in his analysis of missional discipleship in John: "The metaphors attached to discipleship include, paradoxically, not only being on the move by following Jesus but also staying put by abiding with or, even more intimately, in him" ("Johannine Vision," 109).

25. Cornelis Bennema focuses on the notion of mimesis, or imitation, in his study of John, yet his definition of mimesis has at least some similarity with this book's thesis: "person B represents or emulates person A in activity or state X [in order to become like person A]" (*Mimesis*, 25, 34). As we will see, and as Bennema also says (26), imitation of Jesus requires the power of Jesus himself by virtue of relationship with him and the work of the Spirit. Accordingly, Bennema frequently uses the language of participation as critical to John's theology (66, 97, 115, 130, 132n.64, 135, 146, 152, 154, 155–61, 164, 168, 173–74) even as he stresses that the disciples' mission is more than participation as it is focused on imitation (e.g., 52, 84n.3, 86, 90–91)

26. See, for example, Lincoln, McConville, and Pietersen, *The Bible and Spirituality*; also, De Villiers and Pietersen, *The Spirit That Inspires*.

27. The operative definition in Holder, *Blackwell Companion to Christian Spirituality*. See Holder, "Introduction," 1, 5.

28. See especially Waaijman, *Spirituality*, 305–591.

elsewhere, New Testament spirituality can be characterized as a "this-worldly other-worldly spirituality."[29] (This is no less true of John than of other New Testament documents.) In this book, we will want to combine these basic understandings of spirituality with *mission*. But first, what is distinctive about spirituality in John?

One cannot read the Fourth Gospel without sensing its profound spirituality,[30] a spirituality that can be summarized in these words about the mutual indwelling between believers and Jesus: "Abide in me as I abide in you" (15:4).[31] (As we will see later, the technical term for this relationship of mutual indwelling is perichoresis, and it is grounded in the mutual indwelling of the persons of the Trinity.)[32] But when readers encounter this Johannine spirituality of mutual indwelling, this "mystical union of awesome intimacy,"[33] they often disconnect it from concrete existence in the world, and specifically disconnect it from *mission* in one way or another, even if they do not outright *deny* mission. Several recent and otherwise excellent scholarly works manifest this problem.[34]

29. Gorman, "The This-Worldliness of the New Testament's Other-Worldly Spirituality."

30. It was above all the pioneering work of Sandra Schneiders (*Written That You May Believe*; *Jesus Risen in Our Midst*) that made the study of spirituality and the Fourth Gospel a serious enterprise in recent academic theology. See also Lee, *Hallowed in Truth and Love*, who rightly argues (esp. 133–66) that spirituality and discipleship are essentially synonymous for John.

31. The means of sustaining this relationship of abiding may be connected in John to both sacrament (6:56; "Those who eat my flesh and drink my blood abide in me, and I in them") and word (15:7a, 10a; "If you abide in me, and my words abide in you. . . . If you keep my commandments, you will abide in my love").

32. Peter Leithart's *Traces of the Trinity* is an elegant exposition of the claim that mutual indwelling, or perichoresis, is the fundamental "deep structure of the real world, of human life, and of experience" (129). For Leithart, "We live in a perichoretically shaped world" that reflects the nature of the Triune God, about whose perichoresis we learn especially in the Gospel of John" (137).

33. Ashton, *Understanding the Fourth Gospel*, 441.

34. Mary Coloe's *Dwelling in the Household of God* claims early on (3) that temple imagery includes not only Jesus' mission but also that of the disciples, yet the book attends only to Jesus' mission. Andrew Byers, in his significant book *Ecclesiology and Theosis*, argues strongly for John as a narrative of corporate (ecclesial) filiation, participation, and deification, and rightly wants to avoid reducing this unity to shared activity/mission (e.g., 144, 152, 198–99). But in doing so, he underestimates, or at least under-explores, the significance of mission to theosis in John. There is no mission in David Crump's article "Re-examining the Johannine Trinity," although he rightly speaks of perichoretic salvation and deification in John. Grant Macaskill (*Union with Christ*, 251–64) hints at a fuller understanding of mission in terms of participating in the divine love and continuing the works of Jesus (esp. 264), but does not develop these aspects of participation at length. I would suggest that a robust sense of Johannine

There are, however, counter-voices to this bifurcation of spirituality and mission in John. One short but significant example is the work of the French scholar-missionary Lucien Legrand. Legrand says this about John:

> [John's] "mystical" image of mission is an invitation to broaden and deepen our way of seeing and to transcend our unhappy dichotomies between action and contemplation, grace and human responsibility, interiority and other-directedness, spiritual experience and social commitment, theocentrism and anthropocentrism, monastic and missionary calling.[35]

More recent is the work of Sandra Schneiders, for instance in her book *Jesus Risen in Our Midst*. That title sounds like participation, to be sure, and it clearly implies that the risen, present Jesus is doing something. Thus, the second half of her book focuses especially on the forgiveness of sins as the present reconciling work of Christ and the Spirit in and through the church, which is the means of "the ongoing presence and action of Jesus in the world."[36] Schneiders therefore refers to the church's participation in the present saving work of Jesus in the world.[37] Other examples of this interest in John and both mission and participation could be offered.[38]

Theological and spiritual interest in participation (or in mission) is not limited to students of the Fourth Gospel. There is a particular cultural moment that may account, at least in part, especially for this interest in participation. Cynthia Peters Anderson begins her book *Reclaiming Participation: Christ as God's Life for All* with these words:

> The transformation of human life, the concept of humans becoming more than they currently are, has occupied pagan and religious thought for thousands of years. The captivating idea that humans are destined for something different, something more, is certainly not confined to the past. From modern and post-modern philosophy and science to an array of popular novels and films, this theme of a metamorphosis of human life

---

spirituality and mission will also be connected to a robust Johannine "political" sensibility. On the counter-imperial dimensions of John, see, for example, Carter, *John and Empire* and Thatcher, *Greater than Caesar*—though at times their claims are perhaps a bit exaggerated.

35. Legrand, *Unity and Plurality*, 144–45. The original French title of Legrand's book was *Le Dieu qui vient*, meaning "the God who comes."

36. Schneiders, *Jesus Risen*, 118.

37. See Schneiders, *Jesus Risen*, esp. xx–xxi, 150, 158.

38. See, e.g., Hastings, *Missional God*; much shorter but highly insightful is Lincoln, "Johannine Vision."

pulsates deeply through western culture's veins despite the increasing secularization of western society.

It is a particularly poignant yearning in a postmodern landscape littered with the violent ravages of the twentieth century and the ongoing clashes of the twenty-first. . . . In this landscape, the Christian affirmation of human participation in the life of God's truth, beauty, and goodness offers hope and meaning for humanity that is secured by God's participation in human life through Jesus Christ. However, particularly in light of the vast array of neo-gnostic interpretations of deification that riddle popular culture with the idea that we are gods of our own making, it is crucial that Christianity recover an authentic conception of what it means for humanity to participate in God's life—one that accounts for a full transformation of human life through the grace of Jesus Christ, while retaining the real distinction between God and human.[39]

Anderson argues that "[t]his vision of human life as a participation in the life of God made possible by Jesus Christ through the power of the Holy Spirit offers postmodernity a counter-ontology of transformed humanity made possible by the sheer gift of God's grace and urges us to purposeful and holy living as God's people."[40] Theologians who think and write similarly, she says, "call us to place on the horizon once again the classical Christian conception of real and true participation in the life of God."[41] Speaking today of participation, then, is an act of reappropriation, or ressourcement.

"Participation" is one thing, but the conversation become more complicated when we introduce a word like "deification" or its synonyms "divinization" and "theosis."[42] These words are foreign or unknown terms to most Western Christians, and sometimes frightening to those who know them. Theosis (or deification), then, is a controversial term. Cynthia Peters Anderson's introduction of the topic is given the heading "Is Deification Even Christian?"[43] Kent Brower remarks, "The notion of a mutual indwelling of believers *in God* [versus in Christ] . . . is almost beyond our comprehension. It sounds suspicious, almost pantheistic or new age."[44]

---

39. Anderson, *Reclaiming Participation*, 2.

40. Anderson, *Reclaiming Participation*, 13.

41. Anderson, *Reclaiming Participation*, 13.

42. Some people prefer one term over the others and/or distinguish among them; I use them interchangeably, but prefer theosis.

43. Anderson, *Reclaiming Participation*, 19.

44. Brower, *Holiness in the Gospels*, 64.

Some have accused deification of being fundamentally (ontologically) Platonic rather than Christian.[45]

Defining theosis

There is no single, universal definition of theosis or deification. In fact, a number of scholars have attempted to classify various types of deification in the Christian tradition.[46] At heart, however, it has been perhaps most simply expressed by the early theologians Irenaeus and Athanasius, whose perspective can be summarized in these words:

> God [or Christ] became what we are so that we could become what he is.[47]

The first person to actually define the term, Pseudo-Dionysius, offers a simple description:

> Theosis is the attaining of likeness to God and union with him so far as possible.[48]

Rowan Williams elaborates on this understanding, saying that deification in the patristic period has two main, mutually complementary "strands": "a

45. This may of course be a false either-or, as certain aspects of Platonic thinking were adapted by several key ancient theologians, especially in Alexandria, and perhaps even by the writer of Hebrews. But Khaled Anatolios makes an important point about deification according to Athanasius that may be relevant here: "Ultimately, what is at stake [in Athanasius' understanding of deification] is not some abstract 'Hellenistic' doctrine of divine ontology, but the good news of the intimate 'nearness' of God to the world in Jesus Christ" (*Athanasius*, 210). If we substitute "Platonic" for "Hellenistic," a parallel claim is—correctly, in my view—made.

46. For a survey of some recent attempts at classification, see Keating, "Typologies." For expositions of some of the variety, see Christensen and Wittung, *Partakers of the Divine Nature*, parts III–V; Litwa, *Becoming Divine*. Interestingly, the figures common to these two books, to whom each volume devotes a chapter, are the apostle Paul and Martin Luther. For recent introductions to theosis, in addition to the essays in Christensen and Wittung's collection, see Collins, *Partaking in Divine Nature*; Russell, *Fellow Workers with God*; Keating, *Deification and Grace*; and Finlan and Kharlamov, *Theōsis: Deification in Christian Theology*. For works of Orthodox theology in which theosis is prominent in various ways, see Behr, *The Mystery of Christ*; Zizioulas, *Being as Communion*; Nellas, *Deification in Christ*; and Lossky, *The Mystical Theology of the Eastern Church*.

47. This is something of a compilation of various specific quotes. In *Against Heresies* 5.Preface.1, Irenaeus says, "on account of his immense love [Christ] was made what we are to make us what he himself is." See also Athanasius, *Incarnation of the Word* 54. The two authors express the same basic theological conviction in various ways.

48. Pseudo-Dionysisus, *Ecclesiastical History* 1.3, translated by and cited in Russell, *The Doctrine of Deification*, 248.

communication of divine attributes" and "participating in an intra-divine relationship."[49]

Norman Russell summarizes early Christian teaching on theosis, specifically that of the Alexandrian school, as having four main features, three of which are important for our purposes as they build upon the analysis of Rowan Williams:

- **Christ the paradigm:** the person of Christ as the union of transcendence and immanence, the first person to unite them and the pattern for all who are in Christ.

- **Transformative participation:** believers' increasing "dynamic" participation in the divine nature by the working of the Spirit—while remaining human.

- **Community context:** a move away from asceticism and contemplation toward the practice of the virtues and the reception of the Eucharist in the church.[50]

Russell also provides his own rather generic definition of theosis, arguing that all aspects of it were present in the Christian understanding by the fourth century:

> Theosis is our restoration as persons to integrity and wholeness by participation in Christ through the Holy Spirit, in a process which is initiated in this world through our life of ecclesial communion and moral striving and finds ultimate fulfillment in our union with the Father—all within the broad context of the divine economy.[51]

Orthodox priest and historian John McGuckin offers this definition of "the Greek Christian understanding" of theosis, yet in language more attuned to Western sensitivities:

> the process of sanctification of Christians whereby they become progressively conformed to God; a conformation that is ultimately demonstrated in the glorious transfiguration of the "just" in the heavenly kingdom, when immortality and a more perfect

---

49. Williams, "Deification," 106.

50. Russell, *The Doctrine of Deification in the Greek Patristic Tradition*, 203–4. (The boldface descriptors are my own.) The other feature is the rejection of attempts to bridge the divine-human gap by positing "an inferior level of deity" rather than mediation occurring by humans participating in the exalting of Christ's humanity.

51. Russell, *Fellow Workers*, 21. This and the following definition by McGuckin are cited also in Keating, "Typologies," 280.

vision (and knowledge and experience) of God are clearly manifested in the glorification (δόξα [*doxa*]) of the faithful.[52]

Of particular note in this definition are more familiar (in the West) terms like sanctification, conformation, transfiguration, immortality, and glorification.

Daniel Keating proposes three "core elements" of a theology of deification:

1. Grounding in Scripture—not merely texts, but the entire biblical narrative from Adam to Christ;

2. Incorporation into Christian doctrine, confession, and liturgy as the norm of Christian existence, with a rich trinitarian theology, including attention to the indwelling Spirit, and a spirituality of grace-enabled human cooperation (this suggests both unity and diversity in various articulations of theosis);

3. A clear distinction between Creature and creator combined with a genuine sense of real participation in God that does not compromise that distinction ("non-competitive participation in the divine life").[53]

While the elements of scriptural basis and attention to both correct theology and the work of the Spirit are important, especially critical here is Keating's focus on the absolute distinction between creature and Creator.

My own general description of theosis, echoing the early and basic position of Irenaeus and Athanasius, may also be helpful:

> [T]he fundamental theological axiom of theosis is the formulation by church fathers such as Irenaeus and Athanasius that God (or Christ), out of his great love, became what we are so that we might become what God (or Christ) is. . . . As a spiritual theology, theosis is predicated as well on the Pauline and Johannine experience of Christ's indwelling (see, e.g., Gal 2:19–20; Eph 3:17; Col 1:27; Rom 8:1–17; John 15; 17:20–23).[54]

For Athanasius—and, I would argue, for both Paul and John—the possibility of our deification depends fully on a "high" Christology; that is, the Son actually shares in the divine nature, meaning the divine love and grace, or *philanthrōpia*. Thus in his incarnation (in which he "appropriates" our condition) and death, Christ actually *embodies* that divine *philanthrōpia*,

---

52. McGuckin, "The Strategic Adaptation of Deification," 95.
53. Keating, "Typologies," 281–82 (final quotation from 282).
54. Adapted from Gorman, *Becoming the Gospel*, 3–4n.9.

that "divine posture" of self-involving, condescending beneficence so that we in turn may share in God's nature by becoming like Christ and thus becoming the humans we were created to be.[55] "Christification" and "Christosis" are therefore other words for deification in the Christian tradition.[56] Indeed, as I have written elsewhere, "Christification is divinization, and divinization is humanization."[57]

In Johannine language we might say, "The Word, who was God, became flesh so that those born of the flesh might be born of the Spirit to become children of God and disciples of the Word." Richard Bauckham puts it this way, commenting on the so-called dualisms in John: "The Son, who has eternal life in himself, becomes flesh in order to give flesh eternal life."[58] More succinctly, Martin Luther used this Johannine idiom of "Word" and "flesh" to restate Irenaeus: "just as the Word of God was made flesh, so certainly ought the flesh also become Word."[59] It is significant and appropriate, then, that Marianne Meye Thompson quotes Irenaeus' words in her exposition of John 1:14–18.[60]

As Keating (see above) and many others emphasize, theosis, or deification, does not mean that the line between Creator and creature is blurred or crossed; humans do not become God in that sense; rather, they become *like* God by participating in the divine life. The seventh-century Byzantine theologian Maximus the Confessor helpfully illustrated theosis by comparing it

---

55. Among many helpful accounts of this correlation between Christology and soteriology in Athanasius, see especially Anatolios, *Athanasius*, 50–56. Anatolios rightly says, "In Athanasius' theological vision, Trinitarian theology and a kenotic Christology are closely intertwined and mutually correlative; both are consistent with a core emphasis on the divine posture toward humanity as one of *philanthropia*, the divine love that bridges the transcendent natural inaccessibility of the divine essence" (55–56). To which we can only add that therefore the deified person will be characterized by *philanthrōpia*.

56. See, e.g., Cooper, *Christification*; Blackwell, *Christosis*.

57. Gorman, *Inhabiting the Cruciform God*, 37.

58. Bauckham, *Gospel of Glory*, 125.

59. This was in his 1514 Christmas sermon, in which he clarified that humans do not become "God (*deus*) . . . but divine (*divini*)" (*WA* 1 28.25–28, 34, cited in Litwa, *Becoming Divine*, 172–73). In his commentary on Galatians from the 1530s, Luther wrote, "Thus God is made flesh before flesh is made God. So it ought to be in all things that God first be incarnated before they are divinized (*indivinari*) in God" (*WA* 57 94.11–13, cited on 173n.4). The emphasis on divine initiative is highly significant.

60. Thompson, *John*, 32: "John's formulation certainly finds its resonance in Irenaeus, who famously wrote that 'the Word of God, our Lord Jesus Christ [did] through his transcendent love, become what we are, that he might bring us to be what he is himself'" (Irenaeus, *Adv. Haer.* 5, Preface). See also Thompson's positive references to the Eastern Fathers in her exposition of 17:3 (*John*, 349–50).

to the placing of an iron sword in a fire, such that it remains an iron sword but also takes on certain properties of the fire—light and heat—by "participating" in it.[61] According to some interpreters, theosis is a *relational*, not an *ontological*, participation in God, a relational rather than an ontological form of deification, even though we are actually transformed—we are made more fully human and simultaneously more Godlike by being remade in the image and likeness of God as manifested in his Son Jesus.[62] Humans become by *grace* that which Christ is by *nature*. The biblical, specifically the Pauline and Johannine, notions of adoption and filiation—becoming children of God—are thus normally included in any robust account of theosis.

Because we never become God, says Keating, "*all* accounts of deification must speak in terms of analogy."[63] Or, as Russell puts it, deification is "a metaphor, a poetic figure of speech," but one that "expresses a real and intimate relationship with God."[64] It is a relationship of participation and transformation.

Possible objections to theosis

Despite a growing interest in theosis from across the theological spectrum and across theological traditions, objections to it have been raised. I will mention some of these and briefly respond to them; more in-depth responses would require another chapter, or perhaps another book.

1. ***Theosis breaches the sharp line between humanity and deity.*** This objection takes two forms:

    a. Theosis means human beings become ontologically divine.

---

61. Maximus, *Ambiguum* 7; cf. Opuscule 16 (cited in Blackwell, "Immortal Glory," 304–5).

62. For the distinction between relational and ontological theosis, see Blackwell, *Christosis*, 103–5. For the language of unity and indwelling in John, discussed throughout this book, Bennema speaks of "relational ontology" that signifies "a dynamic, transformative communion or relationship" (*Mimesis*, 126). Bennema, however, does not find the ontological transformation to be appropriately called theosis or deification (156). But his particular understanding of these terms (believers being "literally . . . divine"; 127, 130, 132, 156) may be the cause of this reticence. Bennema does actually allow for use of the term in a sense similar to that proposed in this book (132n.164): "If one wants to use the term 'theosis' for the believer's transformation, it should perhaps be understood in terms of participation in God's life and character in order to become like God (*homoiousios*) rather than participation in God's essence in order to become God (*homoousios*)."

63. Keating, "Typologies," 271–72.

64. Russell, *Fellow Workers*, 25–26.

b. Theosis means human beings become absorbed into God.

As we have already noted several times, this concern is simply a fundamental misunderstanding of terms like theosis, deification, and divinization as they are used in the various orthodox (including Orthodox) Christian traditions. The theology expressed in these words never compromises the distinction between God and humanity, or between Christ the eternal Son of God and Christians as adopted children. In fact, "the Christian doctrine of deification not only maintains the distinction between God and the created order, but is premised on it."[65] Humans "become gods" in Christian theology only in the sense of becoming *like* God in certain limited ways. Theosis, as noted above, is the language of analogy. "Participation" is thus a more accurate description of the reality than "absorption" because human beings retain their distinctive and differentiated personhood. And even this participation is to be understood as relational, as with the persons of the Trinity: "a *relational* union in which persons of irreducible identity mutually indwell one another in an interpenetrated way without loss of personal identity."[66]

2. ***Theosis is not biblical, either in terms of language or in terms of theological substance.***

The absence of the word "theosis" from the Bible does not invalidate the claim that its substance is there. The same sort of situation obtains with a word like "incarnation" or "Trinity"; the absence of such words does not mean that the concepts or realities they signify are missing from Scripture. The philosopher and literary critic Mikhail Bakhtin argued that "semantic phenomena can exist in concealed form, potentially, and be revealed only in semantic cultural contexts of subsequent epochs that are favourable for such disclosure."[67] This is an absolutely critical—and correct—claim, one that justifies the use of terms like theosis, deification, and even perichoresis, even if the terms are absent from John or even were unknown at the time it was written.

3. ***Theosis attributes too much to human activity in the process of salvation (synergism).***

---

65. Keating, *Deification and Grace*, 92. Similarly, Cooper: "the language of participation itself would imply a distinction between creature and Creator that is not to be confused" (*Christification*, 122). This concern is, however, at the root of many people's resistance to theosis; see, e.g., Bennema, *Mimesis*, esp. 132.

66. Hastings, *Missional God*, 273.

67. Bakhtin, *Speech Genres*, 5.

This concern underestimates the role of grace in theosis. One way to summarize theosis is in the claim, noted above, that we become *by grace* what Christ is by nature. To become like Christ is a work of grace, but it does require human consent and cooperation, for God is not a coercive God. But this is nothing essentially different from Paul's words about working out our salvation because God is at work within, or among, us (Phil 2:13).

4. ***Theosis is a peculiarly (Eastern) Orthodox doctrine.***

Although theosis has frequently been associated primarily, or even exclusively, with the (Eastern) Orthodox tradition, it is increasingly recognized as an ecumenical, or catholic, theological motif that appears not only in the Eastern church fathers and their direct heirs, but also in Western church fathers such as Augustine; in Luther, Calvin, and some of their recent interpreters; in the Wesleyan tradition; in the Roman Catholic catechism; and even in contemporary evangelicalism—to name but some of the evidence for its doctrinal catholicity. This is not to say that all theologians or theological traditions accept theosis, or interpret it in precisely the same ways, but only that it is pervasive and ecumenical, not limited to one branch of the Christian church.[68]

5. ***Theosis borders on the "cultic," i.e., that which is taught by (popular versions of) Mormonism.***

To be sure, there are varieties of theosis or deification in the history and contemporary practice of religion throughout the world, some of which are therefore obviously either non-Christian in form and substance, and others—despite having some connection to the Christian tradition—are sub-Christian from the perspective of Christian orthodoxy.[69] This does not negate the importance or meaning of theosis any more than sub- or non-Christian understandings of God or of salvation negate the significance of those terms for Christianity.

Theosis in Summary: A Missional Perspective

In light of this discussion and the diversity of perspectives, it is probably best to think of theosis as a general—albeit major—theological and spiritual theme, rather than as an elaborate doctrine, though for some people it is the

---

68. In addition to the variety of works noted above, see, for example, Mosser, "Greatest Possible Blessing"; Rakestraw, "Becoming Like God" (an evangelical perspective); Habets, "Walking" (a theology of theosis inspired by C. S. Lewis).

69. For some of the great variety, see Litwa, *Becoming Divine*.

latter.[70] The divine traits that I find most commonly shared with humanity in theosis, according to Scripture and the tradition, are two: (1) holiness (sometimes stated as goodness, love, or righteousness/justice) and (2) immortality.[71] In this life, we may of course only attain (some degree of) holiness, and (once again, for purposes of emphasis) we always remain human. But in participating in God's holiness/goodness/love, we are participating in God's life.[72] Yet we must stress that deification means true transformation. At the same time, to repeat with emphasis, the line between humanity and God is *never* breached. The reality of deification is often articulated as becoming children of God—"sonship" or "childship"; the technical term is "filiation."[73] But this filiation is always childship by grace, not by nature (in contrast to Christ the eternal Son).[74] To bring into the conversation another analogy, we know that children receive the parental DNA and thus are like the parent, and also can become more and more like the parent in certain ways, sharing that parental similarity with their siblings, other biological children of the

70. For the distinction between theme and doctrine, see Hallonsten, "*Theosis* in Recent Research," esp. 283–84, 287. I do not concur fully with Hallonsten's essay, but the distinction is helpful. Keating ("Typologies," 273–77) finds the distinction problematic in several ways, suggesting that the language of a theology of theosis is appropriate to a wide range of authors. I would still maintain that some writers with theotic themes in their work have a far less developed theological position than other writers, as even Keating does (278). For another defense of theosis as a (more general and diverse) theme as well as a developed doctrine, see Habets, "Theosis, Yes; Deification, No." By "deification," Habets means understandings of theosis that blur the distinction between humanity and God.

71. See, for example, the significant figure Cyril of Alexandria: "In Cyril's thought, the most obvious way God gives himself to humanity is by his sharing his incorruption (and consequent immortality) and his holiness" (Fairbairn, *Grace and Christology*, 74). Much of Cyril's theology is based in his reading of John and of Paul.

72. Some would also add that we are participating in God's *being*. See, for example, McGuckin ("Strategic Adaptation"): "[P]articipation in sanctity [is], in fact, participation in true being" (107). McGuckin grounds this claim in Gregory of Nyssa's *Life of Moses*. The person "who pursues true virtue participates in nothing other than God," wrote Gregory, "because God is perfect virtue" (*Life of Moses* 1.7–8, cited in McGuckin, "Strategic Adaptation," 106). "At a stroke," McGuckin comments, "the distinction between morality and ontology in the case of a divinely graced creature, became a false one" (107). My own view is closer to that of Athanasius as understood by Anatolios; while deification means real transformation, at the same time, as Athanasius especially emphasizes, "what is received by creation through its participation in God is not identical with its being, but rather constitutes an 'addition' 'from outside'" (Anatolios, *Athanasius*, 108).

73. A third, and equally important, aspect of the divine self-giving in Cyril, for instance, is (adopted) sonship (Fairbairn, *Grace and Christology*, 76–99). Once again, Cyril draws on both John and Paul for this image.

74. See, e.g., Chrysostom, *Homilies on John* 3.2; *Homilies on Romans* 15.1–2.

same parent. But no child ever becomes the parent. Theosis is therefore in part a matter of family communion, in part a matter of family resemblance by receiving (metaphorically speaking) the divine DNA.[75]

If theosis means becoming like God by participating in the life and mission of God, and thus in God, then we must ask two basic questions. The first is this: Who is the God in whose life and mission we participate, and what is this God like? This is a critical question in general because there are versions of God/gods, and of theosis, in many religious traditions.[76] It is a critical question for the Gospel of John because the Gospel's God of self-giving love stands in contrast to other ancient options, such as the (allegedly) divine Roman emperor and other deities like Artemis, and, by implication, any and all other supposed deities or misconstruals of the one true God.[77]

The second question is this: How do we participate in the life of this God? That is, "What is the *means* or *mode* of transformation?"[78] One possible answer is simply "faith."[79] Another is the sacraments—what Protestants often call "the means of grace." So, for instance, Cyril of Alexandria especially stressed baptism and Eucharist.[80] This does not, however, limit the experience of transformation to the moments of sacramental experience, for in baptism believers receive the Holy Spirit, whose work is to transform the human spirit, which "was remodeled by him [the Spirit] to make it conform more closely to God, impressing upon us his own stamp and transforming

---

75. On this metaphor of the divine DNA, to which we will return, see especially Bennett, *Labor of God*. Interestingly, the CEB translates 1 John 3:9a as follows: "Those born of God don't practice sin because God's DNA [alt. trans.: "genetic character" or "nature"; Gk. *sperma*] remains in them" (cf. NRSV: "Those who have been born of God do not sin, because God's seed abides in them"). For Johannine "ethics" as family behavior, see especially van der Watt, *Family of the King*; Bennema, *Mimesis*. Bennema does not use the DNA metaphor, but argues that family membership implies identity and behavior.

76. For an interpretation of some Western versions, both Christian and non-Christian, see, Litwa, *Becoming Divine*.

77. On the contrast reflected in John, see Carter, *John and Empire* and Thatcher, *Greater than Caesar*, though both scholars may over-state their cases about the presence of anti-imperial themes in John. I mention Artemis specifically because of her importance at Ephesus, which may have been the provenance of the Gospel. For a full articulation of the God revealed in John's Gospel, see Thompson, *God of the Gospel*.

78. Every Christian type of deification is rooted in a theology of grace. The question here is, assuming the work of grace and of the Spirit: Which practice(s) increase(s) growth in Christlike Godlikeness?

79. So, e.g., Luther (see Litwa, *Becoming Divine*, 182), though this is inseparable from love of neighbor (183).

80. Russell, *Cyril of Alexandria*, 19–21.

our understanding, as it were, to his own quality."[81] As the work of the Spirit, theosis is effected in part by the Spirit-infused sacraments, but is not limited to them. Other possible means of participation and transformation include contemplation, asceticism, and (striving for) virtue.

By advocating for the term "missional theosis," I too am attempting to articulate the *mode* of theosis, positioning it in non-exclusive contrast to what we might term sacramental, ascetic, contemplative, mystical, liturgical, or virtue theosis. These "types" of theosis focus on specific kinds of practices as the primary mode of transformation and union with God: self-denial and control of the passions, prayer and meditation, transcendent experiences, participation especially in the Eucharist, worship, love of God,[82] or moral practices, respectively. I do not want to deny the transformative and participatory significance of any of these, and in fact these practices sometimes occurred, and occur, in tandem.[83] The last one, virtue theosis, is certainly close to what I am calling missional theosis.[84] Furthermore, for almost any proponent of theosis, holiness—which in many cases, at least, implies virtue vis-à-vis others—is part of the *telos* of the transformation, with immortality its final end.[85]

---

81. Cyril, *Commentary on John*, cited in Russell, *Cyril of Alexandria*, 20; cf. 211n.35. Cyril is commenting on John 3:6, "What is born of the flesh is flesh, and what is born of the Spirit is spirit."

82. Augustine: "By loving God, we are made gods" (*Serm.* 121.1, cited in Litwa, *Becoming Divine*, 183).

83. Gregory of Palamas advocated prayer, contemplation, control of the passions, virtue, and love (Litwa, *Becoming Divine*, 6, 238; cf. 155–71).

84. For Luther, deification was also effected through love for others (Litwa, *Becoming Divine*, 183–84; 238), though because this love comes from grace, it is "the result of justification, not its cause" (238). See further below.

85. Concern for others is probably also implied in many versions of ascetic, contemplative, and mystical theosis. Norman Russell, in some places (e.g., *Fellow Workers with God*, 25–26), classifies all forms of theosis as either "realistic," meaning sacramental/Eucharistic, or "ethical," which essentially means "imitation," the moral effort to be like God, and includes all of the other categories I have listed (ascetic, contemplative, etc.). He insists that these are not really separate but belong together, each needing the other, and notes that the imitation of Christ is enabled by the Spirit (27). Keating goes further, rightly emphasizing that the two are not merely connected but are "ordered together in a particular way," for the "ethical sense of deification . . . must be founded on the realistic sense of deification and ever draw on what Christ has done (and is doing), due to the real indwelling of the Spirit (and so of the Triune God) in the believers" (Keating, "Typologies," 272). Another approach to joining contemplation and mission would be to take the notion of union/communion as friendship with God and loving intimacy with God (as in Cassian; see Fairbairn, *Grace and Christology*, 160–62), to define friendship and love as inclusive of shared interests, and articulate the divine interests in terms of love for the world and hence mission, the *missio Dei*.

My emphasis, however, based on what I see in the New Testament generally and in John particularly, is on participation in the ongoing divine activity of salvation—the *missio Dei*—as the means of transformation. "My Father is glorified by this, that you bear much fruit and become my disciples" (15:8). Participation in God's mission effects transformation. As we will see, however, this does not mean that human beings accomplish their own salvation or deification; participation means, at least for John (as for Paul), a mutual indwelling of the triune God and believers that entails the empowering and transforming work of God, by the Spirit, in and on believers individually and as a community. As we will see, to participate in the Son's union with the Father will be to participate in the Father's (missional) activity in and through the Son. By grace we become children of God and thus participate in the communion and activity that the Son, by nature, shares with the Father.[86]

By *missional* theosis, then, I mean that participating in the life of God means participating in the *missional* life of God because the God we know in Christ is missional—the sending Father—who is of course the loving Father. Luther said, "We are gods through love, which makes us do good to our neighbors. For divine nature is nothing else than beneficence plain and simple."[87] That is, God is love, as 1 John puts it (1 John 4:8, 16). Accordingly, as noted earlier (in "Getting Started"), the addition of "missional" before "theosis" is redundant. But in many circles words like "participation" and "theosis," and even "spirituality," are disconnected from mission, especially among Protestants (a major point of missiologist Scott Sunquist's work),[88] so we will keep them together.

It is, however, possible to do a very sophisticated analysis of theosis in John without stressing its inherent missional component. This is the case, for instance, with the highly insightful work of Andrew Byers, as noted above.[89] His book has

---

86. Rossé succinctly and rightly claims that Jesus as the revealer in John "reveals God to be a communion of persons" (*Spirituality of Communion*, 44).

87. *WA* 10 I 100.13–20, cited in Litwa, *Becoming Divine*, 184.

88. Sunquist, *Understanding Christian Mission*, 173, 396–411.

89. Byers, *Ecclesiology and Theosis*. A similar lack of missional emphasis occurs in the classic study of Matthew Vellanickal, *The Divine Sonship of Christians in the Johannine Writings*. For Vellanickal, drawing on both the Gospel and the Epistles, righteousness, sinlessness, and love for the (Christian) family ("brotherly love") are the criterion (227–63), fruit (265–94), and expression (295–315) of divine sonship, but none of these possesses a missional component, at least not beyond the community. Vellanickal does not, however, use words such as theosis, deification, or divinization to describe what he means by sonship (in fact, he rejects an alleged similarity to Hellenistic "divinization through vision"; 344–45), though his work is often (rightly) interpreted as an

two overarching claims: 1) the Fourth Gospel's ecclesiology envisions the formation and ongoing life of a human community participating in the divine interrelation of the Father and Son; and 2) this relational participation is regularly depicted as filiation and requires a profound ontological transformation largely consonant with what later theologians would call theosis. The diverse evidence of these two claims is so embedded within the Gospel story and wields such force in the shaping of its plotline that John can be regarded as a "deification narrative."[90]

But what does this "ontological transformation" entail and how does it occur? In some respects, Byers' goal is laudable; he retains participation in the divine mission/activity as part of what theosis (and thus transformation and its means) signifies in John, but insists that theosis is *more than* such participation:

> The oneness of the disciples in John 17 certainly entails a participation in Jesus' mission and activity. But the theological basis of the Shema behind the term "one," the expansion of the boundaries of divinity pressed by Psalm 82, and the participation of

exposition of Johannine theosis, for he stresses participation/communion, transformation ("becoming"), and ethical similarity between Christians and Christ/God.

90. Byers, *Ecclesiology and Theosis*, 237. Byers further summarizes his work on the Fourth Gospel in the closing, synthetic chapter in eleven points (238–41): (1) ecclesiology is "of paramount importance" (238); (2) it is a narrative ecclesiology; (3) "the plurality characterizing divinity according to the fourth evangelist generates a participatory ecclesiology," meaning that "the divine identity comprises a community; and the interrelation of Father and Son is inclusive of humans who believe in Jesus and consequently undergo an ontological reconfiguration" (238); (4) "Participation is effected by the Divine-Human exchange of the Incarnation and expressed as filiation" (238), resulting in a participatory ecclesiology expressed as family membership; (5) the Prologue sets into motion an "'ecclesial narrative script' of resocialization that governs the plotline of the entire Gospel" (239); (6) "the Johannine oneness motif is grounded in the Scriptures of Israel," specifically the Shema of Deut 6:4 and the "messianic and nationalistic" hopes of Ezekiel 34 and 37 (239–40); (7) "the prayer 'that they may be one, as we are one' (John 17) expresses an ecclesiology of divine association as the Johannine believers, at odds with their religious heritage, are coordinated with the 'one' God of Israel" (240); (8) that same prayer "also envisions an ecclesiology of divine *participation* as believers enter the Father-Son interrelation as family members newly generated and in the process of divinization" for "Oneness is deification as well as divine association" (fulfilling Psalm 82:6—"you are gods"; 240); (9) "Johannine theosis is Jewish, narrative, and communal" (240); (10) "Johannine theosis is illustrated in the narrative through the characterization of specific figures and groups," and human similarity to the divine ("ecclesial reciprocity") is "roughly voiced through the formula *just as Jesus, so also the believers*" (241); (11) "Johannine theosis is actualized beyond the narrative through the work of the Spirit-Paraclete whose characterization within the Gospel renders triadic the Prologue's dyadic theology" (241).

mortals in the divine and heavenly glory of Jesus all require an understanding of oneness that extends beyond a call to social harmony or a functional imitation of Jesus' earthly ministry. The oneness of John 17 calls for the communal deification of those who have received and will receive the divine revelation of the Word of God.[91]

Byers is arguing against a minimalist interpretation of participation in the divine glory (represented by Herman Ridderbos[92]) that restricts participation to missional activity, and Byers is right to do so. But in arguing against this minimalist view, Byers does not stress some of the more clearly missional dimensions of theosis that we explore in this book. Thus words like "activity," "mission," and "ministry" play fundamentally no role in the extended eleven-point summary of his book (see note above).[93]

On the other hand, in his book *Missional God, Missional Church*, Ross Hastings suggests that *missional* theosis is especially present in the Gospel of John.[94] The entire book is a "theological exposition" of John 20:19–23.[95] Hastings' in-depth consideration of theosis starts with a consideration of John 14, in which Jesus speaks of such themes as his intimate union with the Father and with his disciples, as well as the future coming of the Father, the Son, and the Spirit to the disciples.[96] Building on the language of union/participation in that chapter, connecting it above all to the inbreathing of the Spirit in John 20, Hastings speaks of our "participation in the Son's sentness by the Spirit" as the essence of a pneumatic, missional spirituality, which he also calls theosis.[97] The chapter in which this discussion is found is

91. Byers, *Ecclesiology and Theosis*, 198–99.

92. Byers, *Ecclesiology and Theosis*, 197n.85.

93. Byers does speak of the literary device of "inclusive parallelism" in John (*Ecclesiology and Theosis*, 200–223)—instances when "divine actions or words of Jesus become mirrored in particular human characters or character groups" (200) as representing participation and theosis, and this includes various forms of participation in the divine activity/mission. His discussion of this topic is partly illuminating and partly less than fully convincing, but (once again) mission is less stressed than it could be.

94. Hastings suggests that the mission of the church as participation in the life and mission of God is essentially twofold: discovering *shalom* and disseminating *shalom*, drawn from what he perceives as the two aspects of John 20:19–23 (*Missional God*, 26). After four introductory chapters, he structures the book into two parts, four chapters in part one, "Discovering Shalom" (chs. 5–8, corresponding to John 20:19–20) and four in part two, "Disseminating Shalom" (chs. 9–12, corresponding to John 20:21–23).

95. Hastings, *Missional God*, 16.

96. Hastings, *Missional God*, 268–70.

97. Hastings, *Missional God*, 271–92.

thus called "Mission as Theosis."[98] Hastings contends that this understanding of theosis is in seamless continuity with the doctrine of the incarnation, such that a Johannine-inspired missiology will be one of "incarnational and pneumatic theosis."[99] Two subsequent chapters focus on the missional implications of the gift of the Spirit as it is narrated in John 20.

Conclusion

Ross Hastings writes as a pastoral theologian, rather than as an exegete or biblical theologian per se, yet much of what he perceives in John's Gospel is in sync with what this book will argue. We will also find significant resonances with the work of Andrew Byers and Cornelis Bennema (each mentioned in this chapter), despite differences with their work, and of course with numerous other interpreters. John is a gospel of profound spirituality and expansive mission. It is the gospel whose motto is "abide and go."

And so to John we turn, beginning with the potential problem this gospel poses for missional hermeneutics and missional spirituality, or missional theosis.

---

98. Hastings, *Missional God*, ch. 10 (268–92).

99. Hastings, *Missional God*, 285–92. The main elements of this understanding of theosis, according to Hastings, are (1) speaking what the sending Father says; (2) doing what the sending Father does; (3) judgment; (4) servanthood and sacrifice; (5) intimate communion with the Father; (6) reflecting the likeness of the Sender through communion as contemplation and imitation; (7) being sanctified; and (8) being one with the Father and with one another (276–84).

2

Missional Theosis in John

Structure, Theme, and Chapters 1–12

A few pages in, the previous chapter stated the thesis of this book: Johannine spirituality fundamentally consists in the mutual indwelling of the Triune God (Father, Son, and Spirit) and Jesus' disciples such that disciples participate in the divine love and life, and therefore in the life-giving mission of God, thereby both demonstrating their likeness to God as God's children and becoming more and more like God as they become like his Son by the work of the Spirit. The chapter summarized this thesis by saying that this understanding of John can be captured in the phrase "missional theosis."

Accordingly, the chapter also examined in some depth what I mean by such language, focusing first on the basic idea of reading Scripture missionally before considering the notions of participation and theosis, particularly *missional* theosis. The chapter also briefly began the process of examining the Gospel of John itself missionally and theotically, hinting at some of the themes that the remainder of the book will develop. The phrase "abide and go," the book's title, was offered as a summary of John's paradoxical missional spirituality.

But there is a problem: Is John really a gospel of mission and missional spirituality, or missional theosis? This is not a simple, or settled, matter, so we begin our discussion with a look at this basic issue. After arguing for an affirmative answer to the question, we proceed in the rest of the chapter to look at the Gospel of John as a whole literary work, and then at chapters 1 to 12, the first half of the Gospel.

The Problem

Apart from the presence of the word "theosis" in the thesis statement proposed in chapter 1 and restated above, it may seem that I am arguing the obvious. Careful students of John are well aware of the pervasiveness of the verb "send" (Gk. *apostellō* and *pempō*) in the Gospel, especially its significance in portraying Jesus as the "sent one" from the Father.[1] And nearly every reader of the Gospel knows that Jesus tells the disciples, "As the Father has sent me, so I send you" (20:21), after speaking similar words to his Father in prayer (17:18): "As you [Father] have sent me into the world, so I have sent them into the world." To these we could add other missional elements of the Gospel, not least the following:

- The very activity of Jesus as he interacts and dialogues with various figures and groups, such as Nicodemus, the Samaritan woman, the man born blind, and "the Jews."[2]

- The frequent use of words like "signs" as well as "work" and "works" to describe a major dimension of Jesus' activity.

- The frequent references to coming to faith, and the summary of the Gospel's purpose in 20:31—"these [signs] are written so that you may come to believe that Jesus is the Messiah, the Son of God, and that through believing you may have life in his name."[3]

1. McPolin, "Mission in the Fourth Gospel," notes four characters in John who are sent: John the Baptist, Jesus, the Paraclete, and the disciples. With respect to Johannine Christology, whatever else is true of Jesus, he is clearly the agent of God the Father, the one sent from "above." The verbs *apostellō* and *pempō* are used (interchangeably, according to most scholars) of this sending-sent relationship in the following texts: for *apostellō*, see 3:17 (cf. 3:28), 34; 5:36, 38; 6:29, 57; 7:29; 8:42; 10:36; 11:42; 17:3, 8, 18, 21, 23, 25; 20:21; for *pempō*, see 4:34; 5:23, 24, 30, 37; 6:38, 39, 44; 7:16, 18, 28, 33; 8:16, 18, 26, 29; 9:4; 12:44, 45, 49; 13:16, 20; 14:24; 15:21; 16:5. (See Keener, *John*, 1:317 for this list of texts.)

2. I put the phrase "the Jews" in quotation marks to indicate that it seems to have a particular referent, or set of referents, in John but the identity of the referent(s) is debated. There is a brief discussion in chapter 6 of the strong language, understood there as prophetic speech, used of "the Jews" in some places in this gospel. However one understands those in the first century to whom "the Jews" refers, there is no place for anti-Jewish attitudes on the part of contemporary interpreters of John.

3. Due in part to variations in the ancient manuscripts (such that the verse might be translated "so that you might come to believe" [NRSV] or "so that you might continue to believe" [NLT]), there has been considerable debate about what 20:31 reveals about the Gospel's purpose. Is it evangelistic ("come to believe") or pastoral ("continue to believe")? That is, does it intend to *elicit* Christian faith or *nurture* it? This is an unnecessary either-or that cannot be decided by the verb alone, but only by a careful reading of the Gospel. Many translations wisely render the phrase in question "that you

- The role of witnesses and witnessing, ascribed to the disciples (beginning already in chapter 1), who are the beneficiaries of Jesus' activity, and to the Spirit.

- The miniature mission discourse in 4:34–38.

- The fishing scene in 21:1–14, similar in character to the scenes of Jesus calling disciples to fish for people in the Synoptics.

Geoffrey Harris therefore understandably claims that of the four Gospels, John "provides us with the most developed theological understanding of mission."[4] John appears to be a missional gospel.

Moreover, Christians have called John the "spiritual" gospel (*pneumatikon euangelion*) since at least the time of Clement of Alexandria in the second century.[5] Although this characterization means different things to different people, it at least means, first of all, that John highlights Jesus' "signs" and gets beyond the "surface" meaning of Jesus' words and deeds to their deepest significance. It also means, for many, that this gospel speaks of a deep, intimate relationship between Jesus and his followers, his sheep who know his voice (10:3–4, 16, 27; cf. 20:16), his dear "friends" (15:13–15) who abide in him and in whom he likewise abides (15:1–11), and who are to share in his mission.

So . . . in view of what appears to be two very clear dimensions of the Fourth Gospel (mission and spirituality), what could be more obvious than characterizing John as a Gospel of mission and missional spirituality?

The obvious is not, however, always so obvious. David Bosch's classic and highly influential 1991 work on Christian mission, *Transforming Mission*, does not contain a treatment of the Gospel of John—while there are entire chapters on Matthew, Luke, and Paul.[6] Although Bosch does not have space to consider the entire New Testament, and claims that these three authors are representative of the New Testament's overall missional ethos,

---

may [or "will"] believe" (e.g., CEB, NET, RSV). John Stube's comment is appropriate (*Graeco-Roman Rhetorical Reading*, 220): "Regardless of how the verb is translated in 20.31, the purpose of the Gospel cannot be understood as an either/or. Those who are nurtured, nurture in turn. . . . [B]oth evangelistic and nurturing concerns are present." See also the brief description in chapter 1 about John's "genre" as both missionary *and* community-forming text.

4. Harris, *Mission in the Gospels*, 223. Harris find three key missional motifs in John: God's mission (*missio Dei*), incarnation (including inculturation), and love and service (224–35).

5. According to Eusebius, *Ecclesiastical History* 6.14.7.

6. Bosch, *Transforming Mission: Paradigm Shifts in Theology of Mission*.

this lack of attention to John may have been significant for missiology during the last quarter-century.[7]

This indirect neglect of John is probably less critical, however, than the direct indictments rendered by some significant Johannine scholars who have concluded that John reflects and fosters a *sectarian* community turned in on itself, without ethical or missional concern for others. For instance, the great Yale scholar Wayne Meeks once wrote that this gospel

> defines and vindicates the existence of the community that evidently sees itself as unique, alien from its world, under attack, misunderstood, but living in unity with Christ and through him with God. It could hardly be regarded as a missionary tract. . . . It provided a symbolic universe which gave religious legitimacy, a theodicy, to the group's actual isolation from the larger society.[8]

In other words, according to Meeks, we have in John a profound spirituality of *participation* but not any *mission*. Years later, unrepentant, Meeks wrote that the "only [ethical] rule [of the Johannine Jesus] is 'love one another,' and that rule is both vague in its application and narrowly circumscribed, being limited solely to those who are firmly within the Johannine circle."[9] In fact, according to Meeks, the notion of Johannine ethics and moral formation is "oxymoronic" and sub-Christian.[10]

Harsher still are the words of Jack Sanders, who famously and disparagingly compared John with certain kinds of modern evangelistically minded Christian groups:

> Precisely because such groups, however, now exist in sufficient abundance to be visible, perhaps the *weakness and moral bankruptcy* of the Johannine ethics can be seen more clearly. Here is not a Christianity that considers that loving is the same as fulfilling the law (Paul) or that the good Samaritan parable represents a demand (Luke) to stop and render even first aid to the man who has been robbed, beaten, and left there for dead. Johannine Christianity is interested only in whether he believes. "Are you saved, brother?" the Johannine Christian asks the man

---

7. Not only is there no extended treatment of John in the book, there are only a few index references to the Fourth Gospel (seventeen—versus scores for Matthew and Luke), and only to John 3:16, 10:10, 12:32, and 20:21–23.

8. Meeks, "Man from Heaven," 70. On John's sectarianism, assessed positively, see also Gundry, *Jesus the Word according to John the Sectarian.*

9. Meeks, "The Ethics of the Fourth Evangelist," 318.

10. Meeks, "The Ethics of the Fourth Evangelist," 317.

bleeding to death on the side of the road. "Are you concerned
about your soul?" "Do you believe that Jesus is the one who
came down from God?" "If you believe, you will have eternal
life," promises the Johannine Christian, while the dying man's
blood stains the ground.[11]

Sanders clearly thought that John is a *missional* gospel, but also that its mission is so narrowly construed and so bereft of true spirituality that, implicitly, it does not deserve the label "Christian."

These sample texts emerged from and represent a cluster of conclusions about the Fourth Gospel that we cannot explore at length here. In sum, they build on a general critical consensus about the Johannine community that emerged in the second half of the twentieth century under the influence of J. Louis Martyn, Raymond Brown, Wayne Meeks, and others.[12] That consensus depicted the Johannine community, either as the Gospel was being produced or at the time of its final redaction, as a community that had experienced conflict with, and likely expulsion from, the synagogue (*aposynagōgos*; 9:22; 12:42; 16:2) for its confession of Jesus' being equal to God. The result was a community turned in on itself, a sect in survival mode, at odds with "the world"—whether that world was non-believing Jews, and/or other Christians, and/or everyone—"outsiders." Hence the Gospel's concern for internal cohesion and mutual love, and its (alleged) lack of concern for neighbors and enemies.[13]

My obvious thesis, then, is not so obvious. *John may be neither truly missional nor truly spiritual.*

To be sure, few interpreters of John would fully follow Sanders down his dark Johannine alley, but his stark formulation of the issue helps us see what is at stake in how we read this gospel. If the mission of Jesus in John is simply, "Believe in me," or, as Bultmann argued, "Believe that I am the Revealer,"[14] and if the ethic of John is simply, "Love one another and (implicitly) forget about the needs of the world," then the mission of the disciples is fundamentally, and narrowly, "Believe in Jesus so that you can have a personal encounter with God and join our sweet, holy huddle."

11. Sanders, *Ethics in the New Testament*, 99–100 (emphasis added).

12. See, e.g., Martyn, *History and Theology*; Brown, *Community of the Beloved Disciple*; and Meeks, "Man from Heaven."

13. Not everyone who accepts this sort of historical reconstruction used or uses the word "sect." Raymond Brown ultimately did not, because he did not believe the Johannine community broke fellowship with other Christians (*Community of the Beloved Disciple*, 88–91).

14. "Thus it turns out in the end that Jesus as the Revealer of God *reveals nothing but that he is the Revealer*" (Bultmann, *Theology of the New Testament*, 2.66).

I want to argue that such readings by Meeks, Sanders, Bultmann, and a host of other formal and informal interpreters of John, are misguided. John is the gospel of abundant life, of God's life shared with humanity. That is what Jesus brings, and that is the life into which his disciples are drawn and from which they are dispersed into the world. It is a robustly *missional* gospel.

Movement in a missional direction

There is already movement from others in the direction this book seeks to go. In the introduction to a recent important work on recovering the ethics of John, Christopher Skinner suggests that there are three approaches to Johannine ethics:[15] (1) they don't exist;[16] (2) they are "sectarian, exclusive, negative, or oppositional"[17] (the majority view, I would suggest); and (3) they are robust but largely implicit—the emerging view of a number of scholars, led especially by Jan van der Watt, Susanne Luther, Ruben Zimmerman, Kobus Kok, and now Sherri Brown and Chris Skinner.[18]

Regarding option (2), Skinner says that recent studies of John have produced "countless . . . denunciations of Johannine ethics"[19] similar to those of Meeks and Sanders noted above. Regarding option (3), Skinner points specifically to a representative article by Kobus Kok arguing for a "missional-incarnational ethos" in the narrative of John.[20] Like many studies of mission in John, Kok's study begins in John 4 and widens out. He concludes that this missional-incarnational ethos

15. Skinner, "Introduction," in Brown and Skinner, *Johannine Ethics*, xvii–xxx.

16. Which sometimes actually means they are sectarian. See, e.g., John Meier ("Love in Q and John," 47–48): "Apart from the love that imitates Jesus' love for his own, John's Gospel is practically *amoral*. We look in vain for the equivalents of Jesus' teaching on divorce, oaths and vows, almsgiving, prayer, fasting, or the multitude of other specific moral directives strewn across the pages of Matthew's Gospel. Everything comes down to imitating Jesus' love for his disciples; what concrete and specific actions should flow from this love are largely left unspoken."

17. Skinner, "Introduction," in Brown and Skinner, *Johannine Ethics*, xxi.

18. See, e.g., various essays in van der Watt, *Identity, Ethics, and Ethos in the New Testament* and in Zimmerman, van der Watt, and Luther, *Moral Language in the New Testament*; and the entirety of van der Watt and Zimmerman, *Rethinking the Ethics of John* as well as much of Brown and Skinner, *Johannine Ethics*.

19. Skinner, "Introduction," xxv.

20. Skinner, "Introduction," xxvi. Kok's approach ("As the Father Has Sent Me") is similar to that of Hastings in *Missional God, Missional Church*, discussed at the end of the previous chapter.

will transcend all boundaries (cultural, social, economical, racial, etc.) to show love and be accepting of everyone. . . . [T]he narrative of Jesus and the Samaritan woman should be integrated not only with the sending motive and ethos of the Son, but also with the imperative of the missional ethos of the followers of Jesus (cf. John 20:21). Together these elements form an inclusive moral language or ethical paradigm of mission and give the reader a full and integrated picture of the essence of behavior in following the way of Jesus.[21]

Yet if we transition from the word "ethics" (used by Skinner and others) to the word "mission," or use both, as does Kok, we will still hear many interpreters repeat the sectarian sentiments. For instance, Alan Le Grys, in his book on early Christian mission, claims that the Johannine community is the "introverted community."[22] The so-called Farewell Discourse (chapters 13–17) is "designed to offer reassurance to a community facing an uncertain changing world," bearing witness to a community that "turns in on itself to retreat from this external threat."[23] Mission comes eventually, in 20:21, but "only at the tail-end" of a process of the community members "com[ing] to terms with their new social environment" after the "unwelcome experience of regrouping" after Jesus' death. This was a community "rather fearful" of mission to the gentiles.[24]

Even among significant, sympathetic readers of the Fourth Gospel, however, mission has often been under-appreciated. Dean Flemming claims that "[m]ost recent treatments of the theology of John's Gospel give little attention to the theme of mission."[25] As evidence, he points to two significant works, D. Moody Smith's *Theology of the Gospel of John* and Richard Bauckham's and Carl Mosser's edited volume *The Gospel of John and Christian Theology*. We could add Craig R. Koester, *The Word of Life: A Theology of John's Gospel*. This is not to take away from the value of these excellent works, but simply to note their relative inattention to mission.

It should be noted here that just as focusing on the Gospel's theology does not guarantee attention to mission, not all studies of John that focus on historical reconstruction dismiss the notion of mission, either historically, with reference to the first century, or theologically, with reference to today. For instance, in reconstructing the Johannine community's

---

21. Kok, "As the Father Has Sent Me," 193.

22. Le Grys, *Preaching to the Nations*, 164.

23. Le Grys, *Preaching to the Nations*, 166.

24. Le Grys, *Preaching to the Nations*, 167.

25. Flemming, *Recovering the Full Mission of God*, 114n.3.

experience of finding more darkness than light among both Jews and gentiles, Raymond Brown said, "By all means Christians must keep trying in various ways to bear a testimony about Christ to the world, but they should not be astounded if they relive in part the Johannine experience [of resistance to the testimony]."[26]

There have been, of course, some significant studies of mission in John, some of which we will note in due course. Teresa Okure's significant study argued that although the Gospel was indeed addressed primarily to believers, its goal was for them to maintain and embody the faith missionally; John is a "Missionsschrift," both encouraging missional faithfulness and attempting to persuade others to believe in Jesus.[27] Mission includes Christlike humble service. But one of the most frequently cited works on John and mission, Andreas Köstenberger's 1998 book *The Missions of Jesus and the Disciples according to the Fourth Gospel*, raises some serious concerns.[28] First of all, we should note the plural "missions" in the title. Köstenberger criticizes what he calls the "incarnational" interpretation of mission in John, which sees Jesus in part as a model of service in the world, arguing that such an interpretation underestimates and even "jeopardizes" the uniqueness of Jesus' own mission in contrast to that of the disciples, which is what his book highlights—the "careful line [that] seems to be drawn between the roles of Jesus and of the disciples."[29] Thus Köstenberger argues for a "representational" model, in which disciples do not *imitate* Jesus but *represent* him. Their sole similarity to Jesus' mission is their relationship to the sender, "one of obedience and utter dependence," like that of the Son to the Father.[30] The disciples' mission, including their "greater works" (14:12) and fruit bearing (ch. 15), is, for Köstenberger, only witnessing to Jesus and gathering people into the church as they offer "the word of 'life in Jesus'" to a sinful world.[31]

To be fair to Köstenberger, in a later co-written book, he does say that mission "proceeds in word and deed" and that the "shape of Jesus' mission

---

26. Brown, *Community of the Beloved Disciple*, 66.

27. Okure, *Johannine Approach*. For the community's missional situation and the Gospel's missional purpose as *Missionsschrift*, see, e.g., 230–35; 264–70. Okure provides a helpful summary of her book on 285–95.

28. Full title: *The Missions of Jesus and the Disciples according to the Fourth Gospel, with Implications for the Fourth Gospel's Purpose and the Mission of the Contemporary Church.*

29. Köstenberger, *Missions of Jesus and the Disciples*; citations from 216, 217.

30. Köstenberger, *Missions of Jesus and the Disciples*, 217.

31. Köstenberger, *Missions of Jesus and the Disciples*, 220. After discussing the greater works of 14:12 (171–75), Köstenberger connects them to the fruit bearing of 15:16 as, in each case, making converts (184–85).

determines the shape of the church's mission."[32] Additionally, in later work he speaks of the disciples not merely representing Jesus, for they actually "re-present" him, such that "Jesus will be present in and through them in his Spirit as they engage in their mission to the world."[33] He even uses language about mission that could rightly be called participatory: "the disciples are taken into the love and unity of the persons of the Godhead as responsible agents and representatives of Jesus the sent Son."[34] Moreover, Köstenberger rightly argues against a sectarian view of John, contending that John is rightly interpreted only if one holds both the Gospel's emphasis on mission and its implicit ethic together.[35]

However, Köstenberger's oft-cited early exegetical work and hermeneutical appropriation of it seem to be a reaction against an evangelical interpretation of Christian mission that is more than evangelism. Furthermore, his more recent discussion of "John's trinitarian mission theology" describes the divine (and the disciples') mission as salvation for eternal life (defined as "communion with Jesus" that begins now), with no obvious ethical implications.[36] In the explicitly hermeneutical section of the earlier *Missions of Jesus and his Disciples*, Köstenberger's primary target is the incarnational-missional theology of the respected evangelical pastor-biblical scholar John Stott.[37] Exegetically, Köstenberger appears to create a huge bifurcation between the first half of the Gospel, focusing on Jesus' unique mission, and the second half of the Gospel, focusing on the disciples' mission (apart from the passion narrative). Although Köstenberger's early work is now somewhat dated, and although many Christians have found other ways to deal with the alleged dichotomy between service (broadly defined) and evangelism, the issues he raises and the solution he offers—somewhat misguided, in my view—are still in need of careful critique. Even in his more recent work,

---

32. Köstenberger and Swain, *Father, Son and Spirit*, 159–62 (quotes from 159, 160). In "Sensitivity to Outsiders," Köstenberger also says, "Believers are to emulate Jesus' example of service and sacrificial love" (181; cf. 183).

33. Köstenberger, "Sensitivity to Outsiders," 173. Köstenberger explicitly follows Brown (*John* 2:1036) in this claim.

34. Köstenberger, *Theology*, 541.

35. See especially his "Sensitivity to Outsiders."

36. Köstenberger, *Theology*, 539–46. For his understanding of the mission and of eternal life, compare 539 and 86.

37. Stott (1921–2011) was a prominent British evangelical known for his insightful preaching and commentary-writing, and for his commitment to mission and theological education, especially in the Majority World.

when Köstenberger speaks of loving "outreach to outsiders,"[38] he limits, or nearly limits, mission to evangelism.[39] This is not at all uncommon.

In this chapter I will argue one significant aspect of my overall thesis—that John is a robustly missional Gospel—by considering John's structure and theme, followed by a look at the signs in the first half of the Gospel. In the following chapters I will consider aspects of the second half of John, where the Gospel's missional spirituality, or missional theosis, appears more explicitly and robustly than it does in the first twelve chapters. Both in this chapter and throughout the book, we will find that mission in John is broader than verbal witness or evangelism. Throughout the main part of the book, I will also make some implicit and explicit claims about the church's mission today in light of that basic claim. At the end of the book, I will discuss some contemporary examples of intense and intensive Christian communities that are also robustly missional in character.

The Structure of the Gospel

For more than a half-century, the Fourth Gospel has been widely understood as comprising a prologue, two "books," and an epilogue. In 1953, C. H. Dodd offered the following outline:[40]

1:1–51	The Proem: Prologue (1:1–18) and Testimony (1:19–51)
2:1—12:50	The Book of Signs
13:1—20:31	The Book of the Passion (The Farewell Discourses and The Passion-narrative)[41]
21:1–25	Postscript

In 1966 Raymond Brown outlined the Gospel as follows:[42]

---

38. Köstenberger, "Sensitivity to Outsiders," 171.

39. While he writes that the "love is extended not only to those in one's community but also to those in the world" ("Sensitivity to Outsiders," 171), he also says that "[at] the heart of John's moral vision is a call to evangelistic mission" (181).

40. Dodd, *Interpretation of the Fourth Gospel*, x, 289–91.

41. Recently, both Richard Hays and Marianne Meye Thompson have picked up on Dodd's phrase "The Book of the Passion," though Thompson does not use it in recounting the Gospel's structure in her commentary. See Hays, *Reading Backwards*, 79, 129n.7; and Thompson, "They Bear Witness to Me," 268. Hays and Thompson would conclude "The Book of the Passion" at 19:42.

42. Brown, *John*, 1: cxxxviii–cxxxix.

1:1–18	The Prologue
1:19—12:50	The Book of Signs
13:1—20:31	The Book of Glory
21:1–25	Epilogue

The major difference between the outlines of Brown and Dodd is Brown's renaming the second major part "The Book of Glory." Brown's outline has become fairly standard, nearly canonical, in fact. It is used, for example, in commentaries by both the Catholic Frank Moloney and the evangelical Protestant Andreas Köstenberger, among others.[43]

This approach, however, is not without its problems. Moody Smith added a couple of significant nuances to the Brown-Dodd sort of structure that he largely followed. Smith labels part one "The Revelation of the Glory before the World" and part two "The Revelation of the Glory before the Community."[44] This sort of approach, which has also attracted others, highlights both the continuity of subject throughout the Gospel (glory) and the shift in audience from the world to the disciples in part two.[45] More significant changes, however, are introduced by Smith's student, Marianne Meye Thompson:[46]

1:1–18	The Introduction to the Gospel and to Jesus
1:19—4:54	Witnesses to Jesus
5:1—12:50	The Life-giving Son of God
13:1—17:26	Jesus and His Disciples
18:1—19:42	The Arrest, Trial, and Crucifixion of Jesus
20:1—21:25	The Resurrection of Jesus

This outline brings out two of the Gospel's important themes: the life-giving person and work of Jesus (5:1—12:50) and the role of witnesses to him (1:19—4:54). In this outline we also see Jesus and his disciples having a

---

43. Moloney, *John*, 23–24; Köstenberger, *John*, 10–11.

44. Smith, *John*, 7–10.

45. See, somewhat similarly, J. Ramsey Michaels (*John*, v–vii, 30–37), who uses the phrase "Jesus' self-revelation" rather than "The Revelation."

46. Thompson, *John*, vii–x. Another of Smith's students, Craig Keener, labels 1:19—6:71 "Witness in Judea, Samaria, and Galilee" and makes other minor changes to the standard outline but does not question its basic approach (Keener, *John* 1:xi–xxiv). Heil (*Gospel of John*, v, 146–66) keeps chapters 20–21 together under the heading "The Risen Jesus Establishes the Worship for Divine Life Eternal."

mission. Furthermore, Thompson keeps chapters 20 and 21 together, which rightly works against a natural tendency to underestimate the significance of something called an "epilogue."[47]

Thompson begins to move further in the direction of recognizing the *missional* focus of the Fourth Gospel that is implied by words like "signs" and "revelation" found in other proposed outlines. She rightly says that this gospel is "the account of Jesus of Nazareth, his works and his words, and their life-giving power."[48] Further, she writes, "Jesus' 'signs' are . . . 'signs' of the Father's indwelling and working through him to bring life."[49] She does not, however, carry this implicit missional focus into the outline of the second half of the Gospel.

There is, of course, more than one way to outline a literary work, especially a rich document with multiple themes. Without negating the appropriate christological emphasis found in most outlines of John, we may need to pay closer attention to the way in which such *christological* themes relate to the *missional* theme: the mission of the Father and the Son and then, by extension, the mission of the Spirit and the disciples.[50]

African New Testament scholar Teresa Okure points out that certain "overtly missionary passages" in John (such as 3:16, 4:31–38, 17:20, and chapter 21) have at times been assigned to the Gospel's "final redactional layers."[51] Whatever the value of trying to discern the redactional history of the Gospel and connect it to the reconstructed history of the reconstructed Johannine community, I proceed on the assumption that some unified structure, purpose, and approach to mission can be discerned within the final form of the text, however it came to be.[52] As Andrew Byers has written,

47. In passing, Richard Hays wonders if chapters 20–21 should be called "the book of the resurrection" (Hays, *Reading Backwards*, 129n.7).

48. Thompson, *John*, 36–37.

49. Thompson, *John*, 68. Cf. Schnelle (*Theology of the New Testament*, 677): the signs "illustrate" ("instantiate" would be better, as Schnelle implies on the same page, describing signs as "divine presence in the world") "*the saving divine presence in the Incarnate One, who as the mediator of creation created life at the beginning (John 1:3), is himself the Life (1:4), and is the giver of life to others*" (emphasis original).

50. A somewhat similar attempt to see the organization of the Gospel is that of John Paul Heil, who sees "worship for divine life eternal" as the Gospel's chief theme. He therefore presents the structure of the Gospel in terms of that theme (*Gospel of John*, v). For instance, the hymnic prologue introduces worship celebrating the gift of divine eternal life (1:1–18); this is followed by disciples and the worship of Jesus (1:19–51); Jesus reveals true worship in the Spirit and the Truth (2:1—4:54); etc. The second half of the Gospel is about Jesus' farewell teaching (chs. 13–17), death (chs. 18–19), and resurrection (chs. 20–21) in relation to this central theme.

51. Okure, *Johannine Approach to Mission*, 34.

52. See, similarly, Skinner, "Love One Another," 25–27. The approach I take to

this sort of approach "focuses not on the community that *produced* John's Gospel, but on the sort of community John's Gospel *seeks to produce*"—and we may add, from the perspective of theological and missional hermeneutics, *to produce both then and now*.[53] Similarly, Andrew Lincoln approaches John's ecclesiology asking, "in the light of its potential contribution to discussions of Christian ecclesiology, how the Johannine writings envisage the relation of Jesus' followers to God, one another, and the world."[54]

A new approach to the structure of the Gospel is therefore possible, one that both looks at the Gospel as a singular whole and takes account of the missional focus of this final form:[55]

---

structure, like that of Skinner, Thompson, and many others today, is to consider the Gospel *as a whole*—to look at the final form of the text. This approach is significant both methodologically and materially when it comes to the subject of mission. If one considers the Gospel's structure primarily as the product of redactional activity, one may come to the conclusion that the various contributors to the task of Gospel-writing represented differing approaches to mission based on the historical circumstances of the contributors and the Johannine community over time. This more literary approach to the Gospel began in earnest with the work of Alan Culpepper, *Anatomy of the Fourth Gospel*.

53. See Byers, *Ecclesiology and Theosis*, 3 (emphasis added). That is, we should focus, not on the world *behind* the text, and not merely on the world *within* the text, but also on the (potential) world *in front of* the text. This is not to deny the validity of the other worlds. As Sandra Schneiders (*Written That You May Believe*, 2–3) describes reading John, it involves entering its three worlds (historical, literary, and spiritual), the third being "the spiritual world of mysterious indwelling of Jesus and his disciples that shaped the spirituality of the early community, comes to expression in the text, and is intended to shape the spirituality of the reader" (3).

54. Lincoln, "Johannine Vision," 100.

55. I have boldfaced several key terms in the outline and underlined the persistent word "mission" and its cognate "commissioning." An early version of this outline was first prepared for the "The Gospel according to John" in the Wesley Study Bible (published in 2009), though the article there is unsigned. A somewhat similar structure for the Gospel, suggesting two main parts, has been proposed independently by Brendan Byrne (*Life Abounding*, vii–viii, 9–11): The Prologue (1:1–18); I. Jesus Reveals His Glory to the World (Israel) (1:19—12:50); II. The "Hour" of Glorification: The Disciples' Future Mission (13:1—21:25). Of particular significance here are two things: first, Byrnes' focus in the second main part of the Gospel on the disciples' mission, as well as its inseparable relationship to the death/resurrection/glorification of Jesus; and second, Byrnes' refusal to relegate chapter 21 to the status of epilogue. Andreas Köstenberger and Scott Swain also independently write about the Gospel's "two-part format" of "presenting the earthly mission of Jesus" and "anticipating the mission of the exalted Jesus" (*Father, Son and Spirit*, 155). Köstenberger himself says that the Gospel has two halves, the first "narrating Jesus' earthly ministry to the Jews," the second "presenting the exalted Jesus' mission to the world through his followers" (*Theology*, 546).

I. Opening: The <u>Mission</u> of God the **Father** and the **Incarnation** of the **Son** (1:1–18)

II. The <u>Mission</u> of the **Father** and the **Son** in Doing **Signs** and Giving **Life** (1:19—12:50)

III. The <u>Mission</u> of the **Son** in **Death** and the Future <u>Mission</u> of the **Spirit-Empowered Disciples** (13:1—19:42)

    A. The <u>Mission</u> Discourse and Prayer of Consecration and <u>Commissioning</u> (13:1—17:26)

    B. The Culmination and Completion of **Jesus'** <u>Mission</u> (18:1—19:42)

IV. The **Resurrection** of the **Son** and the <u>Mission</u> of the **Spirit-Empowered Disciples** (20:1—21:25)

There are several literary and theological features of this outline worth noting.

First, and most obviously, is **the constant focus from beginning to end on mission** (note the underlining). This focus suggests a continuity to the Gospel that is easily missed in conventional four-part outlines that begin with a "prologue" and end with an "epilogue."

Second is **the trinitarian substance of the mission and of the Gospel** expressed in the outline: the embodiment of the *missio Dei* in the Word's incarnation; the Son's mission on behalf of the Father in doing signs and giving life; the Son's imminent death and the promise of his replacement by the Spirit, so that the mission will be continued through the disciples; and the post-resurrection gift of the Spirit by the risen Christ, who commissions and enables the disciples. The *missio Dei* in John truly is the "*missio trinitatis*—the mission of the Trinity"[56]—in which disciples participate.

A third feature of the outline is **the narrative and christological continuity of the mission** indicated by its structure: from preexistence through to exaltation and beyond. But the outline suggests that John's Gospel is not merely a parabola-shaped story with two main parts, Christ's descent and his ascent, corresponding to signs and glory (see further below). Rather, this is a story of Christ's unrelenting mission to and in the world, a mission that is only partially parabola-shaped, for chapter 21 reveals that the risen Christ is not only the *ascended* Christ but also the *present* Christ, guiding and empowering the disciples' mission.

Furthermore, the saving events of Christ's mission that take up the second half of the Gospel—his death and resurrection—are also precisely those

---

56. Harris, *Mission in the Gospels*, xi.

elements that are directly tied to the mission of the disciples, in chapters 13–19 and chapters 20–21, respectively.

A fourth feature of the outline, then, is **the literary and theological rehabilitation of chapter 21**, as Thompson also implies in her outline, by uniting chapter 20 not to chapter 19, but to chapter 21.[57] The Gospel's resurrection appearances and commissioning scenes, which are found in both final chapters, are best understood in tandem. To be sure, the Gospel may *appear* to end for the first time at 20:30–31, and chapter 21 can indeed look like an appendage. However, several important missional aspects of the Gospel as a whole are highlighted in chapter 21. Writes Okure, therefore: "From the Evangelist's approach to mission . . . [chapter 21] forms an integral part of the Gospel narrative."[58]

Moreover, that chapter 21 follows chapter 20—in a sense "re-opening" a closed book after the quasi-conclusion of 20:30–31—suggests something highly important about both the plot and the theological message of John. Often, when the plot of this Gospel is discussed, the focus is either on typical literary aspects of plot (such as action, conflict, and resolution[59]) or on the allegedly parabola-shaped story of Jesus from glory to incarnation and earthly ministry to glory (often known as the Gospel's descent-ascent scheme).[60] Neither of these sorts of approaches is *incorrect*, but each is possibly *incomplete* unless it recognizes the significance of the disciples and their mission for the plot.[61] As I have sometimes told my students, the post-Johannine church is the subject of John 22 (which, of course, does not literally exist). In other words, we should think of John's Gospel as an "open" narrative, one that invites—even demands—that its readers/hearers continue the story.[62] In chapter 21 we are reading much more than an epilogue.

---

57. Raymond Brown is but one of many interpreters who were or are absolutely certain that chapter 21 "is an addition to the Gospel, consisting of a once independent narrative of Jesus' appearance to his disciples" (Brown, *John*, 2:1078). But some would find chapter 21 to be integral to the Gospel. For others who stress the inclusion of chapter 21 in the overall structure of the Gospel, see especially Beverly Gaventa's article "The Archive of Excess" and the earlier essay by Paul Minear, "The Original Functions of John 21." Cf. also Culpepper, "Designs for the Church," 369–71, who concludes that the unity of chapter 21 with the rest of John is "widely held today."

58. Okure, *The Johannine Approach to Mission*, 195. She suggests (194–95) that the "illustrative" function of John 21 accounts for its having "the character of an epilogue."

59. See, e.g., Lincoln, *John*, 11–14. Lincoln refers to the "three most basic categories for plot analysis" as "commission, complication and resolution" (11).

60. E.g., Williamson, *Preaching the Gospel of John*, 165, 221.

61. Similarly, Lincoln, *John*, 13–14, where he recognizes that the Gospel's storyline is not complete even with Jesus' death and resurrection.

62. The notion of an "open" literary work was made popular by Umberto Eco (*The*

The question might then be raised, If there is no epilogue per se, is there also no prologue? Fifthly, then, I have chosen the term *"Opening" over "Prologue"* to indicate that the first eighteen verses do not merely *precede, introduce, summarize,* or even *guide* the narrative but in fact *commence* it. The first eighteen verses are not outside the frame of the book, outside the real text, like a preface, but are an essential part of the Gospel's contents.[63] To the degree that they do function as a "reading guide," so to speak, for the entire Gospel, they do so *from within* the narrative, not outside it. There can be no Gospel narrative for John without the starting point of the Son's eternal, intimate relationship with the Father and the great act of incarnation, which means not only that the Word became human but also that the Father sent the Son—as Jesus says or implies some fifty times in John. The rest of the Gospel is both a continuation and an exegesis of this basic claim about divine love expressed as incarnation, and of its intended result: generating children of God. Summarizing John 1:1–18, Sherri Brown states the mission of God according to John in this way: "The establishment of childhood in God through the Word of God incarnate in Jesus the Christ is the culmination of all God's dealings with the world, the goal of the Creator and creation."[64]

This Gospel of divine childship, or filiation, is also the "Gospel of life" (as we will see below). As such, it begins with the reality that "in him [the Word, Jesus] was life" (1:4). The life-giving mission of the Father through the Son that is narrated in the Gospel begins also with this reality, which actually *precedes* the incarnation, but which came to fullest expression in the incarnation. Once again, the first verses of John's Gospel do not merely survey its contents; they initiate the narrative.

Of course, the Gospel's first eighteen verses do have additional literary, theological, and hermeneutical functions. But if the mission of

---

Open Work), but it has more than one possible interpretation. The one proposed here stresses the need for continuing the story's openness not merely by offering an interpretation but by continuing the mission to which the story bears witness.

63. For a similar claim, arguing against the received view of 1:1–18 as prologue/preface, see Phillips, *Prologue of the Fourth Gospel*, 4–6: "John's Prologue is not a preface to this text [the Gospel], but rather the beginning of it" (6). From a different angle, that of the divisions of the text of John 1 in early manuscripts, translations, commentaries, and lectionaries, Peter Williams ("Not the Prologue of John") argues that there is more literary continuity between the opening verses of chapter 1 and the rest of the chapter (and the Gospel) than is normally assumed. It should be noted that I am not denying that elements of 1:1–18 are picked up throughout the Gospel; they are, as O'Grady's table of themes in 1:1–18 and the rest of the Gospel shows clearly ("The Prologue," 218). I am, rather, saying that these verses do *more* than introduce themes.

64. Brown, "Believing in the Gospel of John," 4. Brown does not, however, use the word "theosis" as this book does.

God—in the Word's incarnation, life-giving ministry, and glorification through death and resurrection—is to draw human beings into that intimate, loving, life-infused relationship, then this relationship is not simply a Johannine *motif*; it is the Johannine *narratival starting point*. We are reading much more than a prologue.[65]

The Theme of the Gospel

We turn next to the question of the Fourth Gospel's theme. This question is not unrelated to the issue of structure and to my proposed emphasis on mission, specifically Jesus' mission of enacting God's life-giving mission as well as the disciples' participating in that mission.

There is certainly more than one significant theme in the riches and depths of John's Gospel. A case can be made for the centrality of love,[66] or of revelation and knowledge.[67] The "signs," the "I AM" claims, the "glory," and the "hour" of Jesus are obvious major christological motifs. The theme of "covenant" may be a less obvious but highly significant theme.[68] And there are images, such as water, that constitute important motifs; some of these appear as binaries, or paired opposites, including light-darkness and belief-unbelief.

There is one theme in John that is often overlooked, and it relates directly to the question of Jesus' mission: the motif of "work," both singular and plural. On two occasions (4:34; 17:4) Jesus identifies the "work" (*ergon*, singular) he has from the Father, while numerous times the word "works" (*erga*, plural) and the verb "to work" (*ergazomai*) are used of Jesus, often in

---

65. Phillips (*Prologue*; e.g., 14–15) suggests, plausibly, that 1:1–18 is a welcoming threshold to the Gospel by virtue of its comprehensibility to people from various "contemporary schools of religious and philosophical thought" (15), a text accessible to outsiders and thus possessing an inherent "evangelistic" function.

66. E.g., Moloney, *Love in the Gospel of John*. On love in the Fourth Gospel, see also van der Watt, "Ethics and Ethos"; van der Watt; "Radical Social Redefinition"; Rabens, "Johannine Perspectives"; Skinner, "Love One Another."

67. According to Craig Keener, the most common theologically significant terms in John are the two verbs for "know" (Keener, *John*, 1:243–47). Keener does not specifically call "knowledge" the main theme, though he hints in this direction by saying it is "a critical theme . . . and an integral part of Johannine polemic" (1:247). He locates it within the broader theme of "revelatory motifs" that include knowledge, vision, and signs, and he stresses that this knowledge is primarily intimate, personal, covenant knowledge of God (1:233–79).

68. See Chennattu, *Johannine Discipleship*; Brown, *God's Promise*; Schneiders, *Jesus Risen in Our Midst*, esp. 99–118; Gorman, *Death of the Messiah*, 43–50.

connection with his "signs." But what is this singular "work" that is manifested in "works"?[69]

I would suggest that in one way or another all of the various Johannine motifs relate to the over-arching theme of Jesus' singular work of bringing *zōē*, "life," which the Gospel also calls "eternal" life (e.g., 17:2–3)[70] and "abundant" life (10:10b), or life "to the full" (NIV, NJB; cf. CEB, "to the fullest"). A vivid rendition of this central theme, and of this verse (John 10:10), appears in the Hawai'i Pidgin translation:

> Da steala guy, he ony come fo steal, kill, an bus up da place. But I wen come so da peopo can come alive inside, an live to da max.[71]

"*Live to da max*": that is certainly an appropriate, if colloquial, précis of John's Gospel.

With respect to the centrality of "life" in John, we can consider it in relation to other themes. Take, for instance, the theme of love. In Frank Moloney's vivid words, Jesus' mission is that we "might be swept into the relationship with God that he has had from all time," an eternal relationship of love.[72] This is the essence, argues Moloney, of "eternal life."[73] Similarly, Jan van der Watt avers that in most instances "the term 'eternal life' may be substituted by 'to be in/receive a state of being which allows participation

---

69. See also the discussion in Carter, *John and Empire*, 277.

70. "Eternal life" appears seventeen times in John, all of which, except two occurrences in 17:2–3, are found in the first half of the Gospel.

71. http://www.pidginbible.org. NRSV: "The thief comes only to steal and kill and destroy. I came that they may have life, and have it abundantly."

72. Moloney, *Love in the Gospel of John*, 56–57. The compelling participatory image of being "swept up" into this divine relationship of love and unity appears throughout Moloney's *Love in the Gospel of John* (see also 4, 22, 23, 34, 103, 122, 123, 182, 203, 208). It reveals Moloney's fundamental participatory understanding of Johannine soteriology and ethics, even though he does not use words like "participate" and "participation." Similarly, according to Bauckham, the inclusion of believers in the love of the Father and the Son is "surely the heart of Johannine soteriology" (*Gospel of Glory*, 40). Hastings also echoes Moloney: "God's first thoughts in reaching out to fallen humanity were to draw them into the fellowship of his triune love and life" (*Missional God*, 271). And Thompson adds, "'Life' and 'salvation' are virtually synonymous in John because salvation is construed as a deliverance from death and participation in the plenitude of God, both in the present life and in the life that follows resurrection" (*John*, 85, commenting on 3:16–17).

73. Moloney, *Love in the Gospel of John*, 61, 62–64. That is, Moloney's work on the theme of love is ultimately about God's love issuing in the sending of Jesus to bring life to the world. This is the fundamental "work," or mission, of the Son, indeed of the Father working *in* the Son. See also, *inter alia*, Nissen, *New Testament and Mission*, 79.

(action and relations) in the divine reality of and with God.'"[74] The succinct phrase "divine life eternal," suggested by John Paul Heil, encapsulates the significance of this theme and its two key dimensions: divine and eternal.[75] "Wherever you are in the Gospel, you are never far from the theme of life," observes Alan Culpepper, adding that God's life-giving mission is rooted in God's love,[76] which is "inescapably missiological."[77]

Consider also the theme of revelation, which was underscored by Rudolf Bultmann.[78] Moloney rightly argues that in John revelation is a *relational* revelation with a corollary *relational* mode of salvation, not a gnostic one.[79] In fact (although Moloney does not use this term), it is a *participatory* mode of salvation, as God wants to "sweep" people into the eternal love of Father and Son, into the very glorious life of God. As noted above, this salvation is also depicted as becoming children of God, admission into God's family. The Opening of the Gospel makes this clear, focusing on the central soteriological claim of 1:12: "But to all who received him, who believed in his name, he gave power to become children of God."[80] Furthermore, this relational, familial, participatory salvation is also *missional*: God (the Father) "has sent the Son so that others may enter the same relationship and continue the mission of Jesus (17:18, 20; 20:21)."[81] God's children naturally want the family to grow as others encounter the revelation, become children of God, and are swept into the divine life.

It turns out, then, that a focus on mission as *revelation* is actually a focus on *love*, which in turn is an acknowledgment of "life"—participation in

---

74. Van der Watt, *Introduction*, 58. Later we will see also that "eternal life" means the life of the age to come experienced in the present.

75. Heil, *The Gospel of John: Worship for Divine Life Eternal*. Heil identifies three concrete dimensions of such worship: confessional (expressed in words and gestures), sacramental, and ethical (1–2).

76. Culpepper, "Creation Ethics," 83.

77. Culpepper, "Creation Ethics," 86–89 (quotation from 87).

78. E.g., Bultmann, *Theology* 2.40–69, esp. 66–69, et passim.

79. Moloney, *Love in the Gospel of John*, 63.

80. Culpepper's chiastic analysis of 1:1–18 ("Pivot of John's Prologue") finds its fulcrum or "pivot" in 1:12b, about becoming children of God; see also Brown, "Believing in the Gospel of John," 8–14.

81. Moloney, *Love in the Gospel of John*, 68. In this context, Moloney also implies that the revelation of God's love is also the manifestation of God's glory. Note: I use "missional" here in the sense of loving outreach beyond the community of disciples, which is what Moloney is primarily noting. The word "missional," however, can and should be understood more broadly, more generally as participating in God's mission to bring all (inclusive of the disciples) fully and deeply into the orb of God's love. See also, e.g., Bauckham, *Gospel of Glory*, 41.

the life of God—as the ultimate missional purpose of God and the "work" of Jesus.[82] Not surprisingly, this basic understanding of God's *missio* as giving life appears frequently elsewhere in Scripture, too.[83] Jesus does not merely *disclose* something, he *delivers* something.[84] That something is life.

We might illustrate this missional purpose of both Jesus and the Gospel in the following way, using and then glossing three of the Gospel's key terms:

LOVE   →   LIGHT   →   LIFE

Motivation   →   Revelation   →   Participation

That is, *in love God has self-revealed in Christ, the world's light, in order to "sweep" (Moloney's phrase) people into the very life of God.*[85] As we have already noted and will argue more fully below, this "participation" should also be understood in John as filiation (becoming children of God), and filiation in turn as deification (becoming like God). But for now we will focus simply on the Johannine term that is the goal of this missional movement: "life," meaning "divine eternal life."

---

82. Van der Watt (*Introduction*, 28) chooses "life" and "mission" as his two examples of key theological themes in the Gospel. Rossé (*Spirituality of Communion*, 18) reminds us that, as the sent one of the Father, Jesus is not merely a revelatory or prophetic agent: "Since the Word is pre-existent, when he is sent he leads others into the inner reality of his own existence with God." Similarly, Schneiders (*Written That You May Believe*, 49) rightly grounds this revelatory work and the divine mission of incorporating people into the divine life in the Gospel's Opening: "John's Gospel begins not with 'In the beginning was God' but with 'In the beginning was the Word.' In other words, God is not a self-enclosed monad, knowing and loving 'himself' from all eternity and only later deciding to let others in on the divine secret. Rather, in the Johannine view, God's very nature is self-communication, self-opening, self-gift."

83. A few examples: Deut 30:15–20; Pss 16:11; 23; 103:1–5; 119:35–42; Prov 4:20–23; Ezekiel 37; Matt 7:13–14; 25:31–46; Mark 8:34–37; 9:43–49; Luke 10:25–37; 15:11–32; Acts 13:42–49; Rom 6:1–11; 8:1–17; Gal 2:15–21; 3:21; Eph 2:1–10; 1 John 1:1–3; Rev 2:1–7; 7:13–17; 22:1–2.

84. Cornelis Bennema summarizes the character of Jesus in John as "The Life-Giving Revealer" (*Encountering Jesus*, 43–60) and calls Jesus the "distributor" of divine life, referencing 4:14, 5:21, 6:33, and 10:10 (45). Occasionally, Bennema may overemphasize the revelatory/teaching/knowledge aspect of Jesus' dynamic, life-giving ministry (e.g., 34, 45).

85. Schneiders (*Written That You May Believe*, 15) writes, "There is no question that the purpose of the Gospel is the mystical union of the disciples with Jesus in God through the Spirit"; it is a union that "will plunge them into the depths of God's very life." Bosch (*Transforming Mission*, 210–16) describes the patristic and Eastern Orthodox missionary paradigm as the revelation of light, originating in love, and issuing in life (specifically theosis)—and rooted in John's Gospel.

In John, the noun *zōē* ("life") occurs thirty-six times, seventeen times qualified by "eternal"; the cognate verb *zaō* ("live") seventeen times; and the related verb *zōopoieō* ("make alive") three times; these are distributed by chapter as follows:

Chapter	*zōē* ("life"); [= with "eternal"]	*zaō* ("live")	*zōopoieō* ("make alive")	Word-family total
1	2			2
2				
3	4 [3]			4
4	2 [2]	5		7
5	7 [2]	1	2	10
6	11 [5]	6	1	18
7		1		1
8	1			1
9				
10	2 [1]			2
11	1	2		3
12	2 [2]			2
13				
14	1	2		3
15				
16				
17	2 [2]			2
18				
19				
20	1			1
21				
Total	36 [17]	17	3	56

Thus, the "life" word-family appears fifty-six times. Fifty of those occurrences are in the first half of the Gospel. Notably, thirty-five of the fifty-six are in chapters 4 through 6, and eighteen are in chapter 6, the Bread of Life chapter, alone.

Of course, recognizing thematic significance is about more than count-ing words; it includes the ways and places the words are employed, the use of related terms from other word-families, the actions that demonstrate and/ or reinforce the significance of the words, and so on. Nonetheless, the data in this table suggest strongly that the Gospel of John is indeed the "Gospel of life," as more than one study of the Gospel's theology has argued.[86] The Gospel's purpose statement in 20:30–31 bears witness to this:

> Now Jesus did many other signs in the presence of his disciples, which are not written in this book. But these are written so that you may come to believe that Jesus is the Messiah, the Son of God, and that (*hina*) through believing you may have life in his name.

That is, in Thompson's words, "John presents Jesus and his works and words to be the life-giving deeds of the one God of Israel for all the world."[87] And in the words of Mira Stare, "life" is "the most important hermeneutical key" to the Gospel: its "frame" and its "'leitmotif.'"[88]

Since most of the occurrences of the "life" word-family are in the Gos-pel's first twelve chapters, which narrate Jesus' ministry prior to his passion, it is quite clear that for John Jesus came into the world to bring life, as Jesus himself says: "I came that (*hina*) they may have life, and have it abundantly" (10:10b). This claim simply summarizes the many ways in which Jesus iden-tifies his mission as giving life, captured especially in "I am" statements such

---

86. See, e.g., the following theologies of John: Beasley-Murray, *Gospel of Life*; Koes-ter, *Word of Life*. See also, e.g., the emphasis on life in the theologically rich commen-tary by Lincoln, *John*, and the more pastoral commentary by Byrne, *Life Abounding*.

87. Thompson, *John*, 23. Tam, in *Apprehension of Jesus*, convincingly contends that this text means that the Gospel is meant to be both "faith-fostering and faith-engender-ing" (summaries on 177–79, 202–4).

88. Stare, "Ethics of Life," 227. This is not to say that alternative readings of the central theme of John are misguided or inappropriate; I take the point of Keon-Sang An seriously that a particular theme "relegated to the periphery in one culture might find a home at the center in another" since "[c]enter and periphery are contextually defined" ("Response to Gorman"). That said, however, I think it is both possible and, in some cases, necessary to claim that certain aspects of a literary work, including a gospel, inherently possess a theme that is central and even, at times, in some sense dominant merely by virtue of statements by the work's author, the presence of specific literary and linguistic elements, etc. For a recent argument for a more traditional understanding of the Gospel's leitmotif and literary structure, focusing on the Son's descent and ascent (combined with going, coming, and being sent), see Humble, *A Divine Round Trip*.

as "I am the bread of life" (6:35, 48), "I am the resurrection and the life" (11:25); and "I am the way, and the truth, and the life" (14:6).[89]

This impression of the centrality of "life" in John is reinforced by the occurrence of purpose clauses (Gk. *hina* clauses) in several key texts, including both 10:10b and 20:31, that explain the nature of Jesus' mission:[90]

- [14]And just as Moses lifted up the serpent in the wilderness, so must the Son of Man be lifted up, [15]that (*hina*) whoever believes in him may have <u>eternal life</u>. [16]For God so loved the world that he gave his only Son, so that (*hina*) everyone who believes in him may <u>not perish</u> but may have <u>eternal life</u>. [17]Indeed, God did <u>not</u> send the Son into the world to (*hina*) <u>condemn</u> the world, but in order that (*hina*) the world might be <u>saved</u> through him. (3:14–17; cf. 5:34; 12:47 for "salvation," there in parallel with "life," in purpose clauses)

- The woman said to him, "Sir, give me this water, so that (*hina*) I may <u>never be thirsty</u> or have to keep coming here to draw water." (4:15)

- "You search the scriptures because you think that in them you have <u>eternal life</u>; and it is they that testify on my behalf. Yet you refuse to come to me to (*hina*) have <u>life</u>." (5:39–40)

- "This is the bread that comes down from heaven, so that (*hina*) one may <u>eat of it and not die</u>." (6:50)

- "The thief comes only to (*hina*) steal and kill and destroy. I came that (*hina*) they may <u>have life, and have it abundantly</u>." (10:10)

- "Father, the hour has come; glorify your Son so that the Son may glorify you, since you have given him authority over all people, to (*hina*) <u>give eternal life</u> to all whom you have given him." (17:1b–2)

- But these are written so that (*hina*) you may <u>come to believe</u> that Jesus is the Messiah, the Son of God, and that (*hina*) through believing you may <u>have life</u> in his name. (20:31)[91]

---

89. Van der Watt (*Introduction*, 12–16) succinctly displays the centrality of (eternal) life to Jesus' public ministry in 1:19—12:50.

90. I have underlined both the (eternal) life phrases and the words/phrases that interpret what John means by "life."

91. It is important that we understand words like "mission," "purpose," and "life" in broad, rather than narrow ways. In John, to have life means participating in the life and mission of the Son, which will include hostility. Thus, as we will see more clearly as we proceed, the purpose of Jesus' coming and of the Gospel is to create a believing, faithful, confessing people—even when opposed by "the world." See especially Beutler, "Faith and Confession." Beutler points to John the Baptist, Nicodemus, the Samaritan woman, the man born blind, Peter, the beloved disciple, Thomas and the

Many people naturally interpret the phrase "eternal life" as a reference to a future, heavenly, everlasting life. But something more is going on in John, as we have already noted: life, in John, means participation in the life and love of God. Yet this basic understanding needs to be further explained. According to Craig Keener, in all but one case (4:50–51) the noun "life," whether or not qualified as "eternal," refers to the Jewish concept of "the life of the age to come," or simply "the life of the age."[92] What is distinctive about John, says Keener, especially in contrast to other Jewish sources, is the Gospel's use of present-tense verbs to indicate that the life of the age-to-come is already present because of Jesus' resurrection.[93] I would simply nuance this claim by emphasizing three things:

- On the one hand, although the "I am" affirmations of Jesus as "life" occur *before* the resurrection in the narrative, these affirmations are made by the evangelist *in light of* Jesus' resurrection; they are part of the Gospel's strategy of what Richard Hays calls "reading backwards" and Marianne Meye Thompson "from back to front."[94]

- On the other hand, however, there is something necessarily ontological about Jesus' being the life; he can convey eternal life even before the resurrection *because he has life in himself and is the source of life by virtue of his sharing in the Godhead* (1:4).[95]

- Therefore, "eternal life" and "divine life" are non-competitive; indeed, they are fundamentally synonymous.

In other words, while it is true, *chronologically*, that the resurrection guarantees that Jesus is able to offer abundant, eschatological life in the present, it

---

other disciples, Mary Magdalene, Joseph of Arimathea, and the crypto-Christians as examples of courageous confession.

92. Keener, *John*, 1:329. Thompson's long, helpful excursus on the subject (*John*, 87–91) is more nuanced, but she agrees that the Jewish notion of eternal life is partly behind the Johannine vision of life; most important, she argues, is that (eternal) life is both present and future. Carter (*John and Empire*, 204–34) contrasts the promises of eternal Rome and its supposed golden age with John's future-yet-present eternal life.

93. Keener, *John*, 1:330; so also, e.g., Beasley-Murray, *Gospel of Life*, 3–4, who contrasts John with the Old Testament, the Synoptics, and other early Jewish literature. Of course, both say that life in John also has a future dimension.

94. Hays, *Reading Backwards*; Thompson, *John*, 9, 269, 270, 283, 345, 365.

95. Similarly, Beasley-Murray, *Gospel of Life*, 4. As Keener (*John*, 1:385) also notes, Judaism associates both Wisdom and Torah with life, and John associates Jesus with the embodiment of Wisdom and Torah. This association would also be part of the reason for the Gospel's affirmations of Jesus as the life.

is also true, *theologically*, that Jesus himself, qua Jesus—qua Son of God—is able to offer abundant, eschatological, divine life in the present.

All of this raises the question of what this abundant, eternal, divine life looks like. What is its content? To answer that question, we must turn more carefully to the contexts of the Gospel's focus on life. John 10:10b, as a concise statement of the Gospel's theme, is an appropriate entrée into this topic.

"Abundant Life" in its Johannine and canonical contexts

It will be instructive, and in fact critical to our understanding of Jesus' mission of bringing life, to look at John 10:10b—"I came that they may have life, and have it abundantly"—in its Johannine and canonical contexts.[96] This sentence is part of the Good Shepherd discourse (10:1–21), and we read it well only when we read it intertextually as well as culturally.[97]

What is this "abundant life"? Marianne Meye Thompson ably summarizes it in John as a comprehensive reality:

> It looks back toward creation; it anticipates the blessings of the new life of the resurrection, especially the blessing of being in the divine presence; and it lies at the intersection of past and future, while in the present it offers communion with the living God.[98]

Three specific points about this abundant life in the context of John 10 need to be made, the third of which will lead us to the text's chief intertext.

First, when Jesus identifies himself as the Good Shepherd (10:11–18), he focuses on his death and resurrection—mentioned five times (10:10–11, 15b, 17–18) and twice (10:17–18), respectively—as an essential part of offering abundant life. Throughout the Gospel, the life-giving mission of Jesus is not separated from his death and resurrection. Christian theology and Christian mission, therefore, must also always keep them together.

---

96. In this section I draw on my article "The Spirit, the Prophets, and the End of the 'Johannine Jesus.'"

97. In John 10, Jesus claims to be both the gate and the shepherd. When he identifies himself as the gate, he may be reflecting the cultural practice of shepherds lying in front of the opening to the sheepfold (10:7–10). (On the entire Good Shepherd discourse, see Skinner, "The Good Shepherd.") But he is probably also alluding to Ezekiel's images of a protective watchman at the city walls and an open gate for access to the temple. See Peterson, *John's Use of Ezekiel*, 141–42, referring to Ezek 3:17; 33:6–7; 43–48. That is, Jesus is the way into God's pasture of salvation, security, and presence—God's gift of abundant life.

98. Thompson, *John*, 91.

Second, the very notion of a life-giving mission suggests that there is a need for transformation, either from minimal to abundant life, or even from death to life. Paradoxically, it is Jesus' death "for the sheep" (10:15) that is the source of such life. Death is undone by means of death, neglect by means of intimate, self-donating compassion. Jesus' life-giving ministry can be considered a mission of reversing the death-dealing actions of evil shepherds.[99]

Third, as the shepherd theme continues after the Good Shepherd discourse in 10:22–39, at the Festival of Dedication (Hanukkah), Jesus tells us that his "works" testify to his being the life-giving shepherd who is one with his Father (10:25–30). Together with his earlier claims about being the Good Shepherd, these words point us to Ezekiel 34. Gary Manning notes that John 10 and the LXX of Ezekiel 34 "share three phrases, eleven key words, five close synonyms, and four weaker synonyms."[100]

In the prophetic oracle we find in Ezekiel 34, there are two figures who are assigned the role of (good) shepherd: the Lord God and the Lord's Davidic servant. In John 10, Jesus is taking on the identity of the *human*, Davidic, messianic shepherd (Ezek 34:23–24, underlined text below; cf. 37:24), but also sharing in the missional identity of the *divine* shepherd: "I myself will be the shepherd of my sheep . . . , says the Lord God. . . . You are my sheep, the sheep of my pasture and I am your God" (*italicized text*; many references throughout the passage below).[101] The life that the Lord/ the messianic prince will inaugurate (**boldfaced type**; again, many references below) is worthy of note.

> [11]For thus says the Lord God: *I myself will search for my sheep, and will seek them out.* [12]As shepherds seek out their flocks when they are among their scattered sheep, so *I will seek out my sheep.* **I will rescue them** from all the places to which they have been scattered on a day of clouds and thick darkness. [13]*I will* **bring**

99. Carter, *John and Empire*, 138, speaks of "rolling back imperial damage," referring to the effects of Jesus' ministry and the Gospel's purpose (cf. 277–78). Although Carter specifically has the Empire's injustices in mind, John's understanding of death and life is no doubt bigger than that specific concern—he is certainly referring to religious leaders—without excluding concern about the Empire.

100. Manning, *Echoes of a Prophet*, 113.

101. See also John 5:36 for this identifying function of Jesus' works. Manning (*Echoes of a Prophet*, 114–19) notes that Jesus' relationship with his sheep in John 10 parallels that of both God and the Davidic figure in Ezekiel 34. This helps (according to Manning) explain the humanity and divinity of Jesus in John, including the notion of his unity with the Father. Manning also notes (114–15) that the phrase "my sheep" occurs only in Ezekiel 34 and Jeremiah 23 in the Old Testament, echoed by Jesus in John 10.

them out from the peoples and **gather them** from the countries, and will **bring them into their own land**; and **I will feed them** *on the mountains of Israel*, by the watercourses, and in all the inhabited parts of the land. ¹⁴*I will feed them with good pasture*, and the mountain heights of Israel shall be their pasture; there *they shall lie down in good grazing land*, and *they shall feed on rich pasture* on the mountains of Israel. ¹⁵*I myself will be the shepherd of my sheep, and I will make them lie down, says the Lord God.* ¹⁶*I will seek the lost, and I will bring back the strayed, and I will bind up the injured, and I will strengthen the weak*, but the fat and the strong I will destroy. *I will feed them with justice. . . .* ²³I will set up over them one shepherd, my servant David, and he shall feed them: he shall feed them and be their shepherd. ²⁴And I, the Lord, will be their God, and my servant David shall be prince among them; I, the Lord, have spoken. ²⁵**I will make with them a covenant of peace and banish wild animals from the land, so that they may live in the wild and sleep in the woods securely.** ²⁶I will make them and the region around my hill **a blessing**; and **I will send down the showers** in their season; they shall be **showers of blessing.** ²⁷The **trees of the field shall yield their fruit**, and the **earth shall yield its increase**. They shall be **secure** on their soil; and **they shall know that I am the Lord**, when I **break the bars of their yoke**, and **save them from the hands of those who enslaved them.** ²⁸**They shall no more be plunder** for the nations, **nor shall the animals of the land devour them**; they shall **live in safety**, and **no one shall make them afraid**. ²⁹I will provide for them a **splendid vegetation** so that they shall **no more be consumed with hunger** in the land, and **no longer suffer the insults of the nations.** ³⁰**They shall know that I, the Lord their God, am with them, and that they, the house of Israel, are my people**, says the Lord God. ³¹*You are my sheep, the sheep of my pasture and I am your God*, says the Lord God.

The text from Ezekiel to which Jesus refers should help us understand not only the Christology of John 10, but also its soteriology: its understanding of abundant life. What is the life that God will bring to the people? By any account, Ezekiel 34 is a word-picture of "abundant life," as the boldfaced words demonstrate:

- being rescued and found;
- having good pasture and grazing;
- having injuries treated;

- being strengthened;

- tasting justice;

- being secure and at peace;

- having a plentiful crop and no longer being hungry;

- being liberated from slavery;

- no longer being afraid;

- experiencing deliverance from insults; and, last but far from least,

- being in intimate covenant relationship with God.[102]

This is what Jesus in John has in mind when he speaks of life in abundance. As Richard Bauckham notes, "Eternal life in John is much more than the goods of earthly, mortal life, but it is *certainly not less than them*. It surpasses them *by including them, not leaving them behind*."[103] John, then, is the original "prosperity" gospel—highly physical and material as well as spiritual and relational.[104] But, as we will see in the next chapter, because it is life that comes via Jesus' death, it is a Gospel of *cruciform* prosperity.[105]

---

102. See also Carter, *John and Empire*, 217–18, who sees Ezekiel 34 and hence John 10 as depictions of the blessings of divine sovereignty, though he perhaps underestimates the context of Ezekiel and overestimates the context of imperial Rome.

103. Bauckham, *Gospel of Glory*, 71 (emphasis added). He continues, "eternal life is the healing and transfiguration of life in all the ways that mortal life falls short of life in its fullness."

104. Carter (*John and Empire*, 215–27) argues that for John eternal life is somatic, material, political, and societal. (Unfortunately, he does not explicitly include spiritual/covenantal per se.) We do not have to follow Carter all the way in finding John as the antithesis of Rome's version of eternal life to agree with him that future eschatological blessings have now appeared in and through Jesus. In "The Spirit, the Prophets, and the End of the 'Johannine Jesus,'" I demonstrate that John also portrays Jesus in the language of Isa 61:1–3. It is critical, however, that we not reduce Ezekiel's (or John's) vision of abundant life to the purely material or "somatic," eliminating the spiritual/covenantal (i.e., relations with God). This has been the mistake made regarding mission by some heirs of the "Social Gospel" (Bosch, *Transforming Mission*, 347).

105. I therefore quite agree with Scott Sunquist's basic definition of mission as "*our participating with Jesus Christ in his suffering love for the greater glory of God to be revealed*" (*Understanding Christian Mission*, 172). I would simply add that Irenaeus rightly said that the glory of God is humanity fully alive; John shares this sort of view, for he records Jesus praying, "The glory that you [Father] have given me I have given them, so that they may be one, as we are one" (17:22). Moreover, glory is given to God by the disciples' bearing fruit (15:8), which is a missional activity of embodying the cruciform love of Jesus (chapter 13) by abiding in him (chapter 15)—cruciform missional theosis. See further in subsequent chapters.

John is also the original "pro-life" gospel, but it has a comprehensive rather than a narrow pro-life message.[106] It is pro-life because it derives from the source of creation, the one in whom was life (1:4) and who became incarnate to bring that life, in its fullness, to the world. Or, in the language that is more common in the Synoptics, Jesus in John is speaking of, and inaugurating, the prophetically promised reign of God. When the disciples of Jesus (then or now) offer salvation through and in Jesus, therefore, they "do not simply offer a 'spiritual' salvation—forgiveness of sins or experience of God," writes Geoffrey Harris. Why? Because "the incarnate Christ"—that is, the Good Shepherd, the good king—"is the one who sweats and agonizes with the little ones of the earth, who bleeds for those who are victims of corruption and the brutal misuse of power. Those who follow such a Christ in the world are in solidarity with those he most obviously came to help."[107] The Gospel does not offer a narrow version of abundant life as either material *or* spiritual. It offers eschatological life, which is the divine life, and vice versa. Thus Warren Carter is right to say that eternal life, in the sense of the life of the age to come experienced already to a degree in the present, "participates in the very life of God."[108] It is "divine life eternal," to reiterate Heil's phrase.

This comprehensive understanding of "life" in John will have much to say to all of us who wish to read this gospel in our particular contexts as a word about the mission of God in Jesus by the Spirit and through the church today. *This* Gospel, like *the* gospel, is holistic. To begin to consider some of the implications of reading John in the way we have been exploring, we turn finally in this chapter to the depiction of Jesus as the one bringing us the holistic divine life eternal through the gifts of new birth and the Spirit, and through the doing of signs.

The Gifts of New Birth and the Spirit: Becoming Children of God

As we will see, the bulk of the Fourth Gospel's explicit discussion of missional participation in the life and life-giving mission of God, or missional theosis, appears in the second half of the Gospel. But there are also strong intimations of this topic in the first half of the Gospel in two major ways.

106. For a similar view, stressing the sanctity of life in Jewish tradition and in John, see Culpepper, "Creation Ethics," esp. 81–83, 89–90.

107. Harris, *Mission in the Gospels*, 228–29.

108. Carter, *John and Empire*, 215. Many others make a similar point, but it is striking that Carter does so in the context of reading John as a counter-imperial text.

First, we have the theme of the gifts of new birth and the Spirit, such that those who are brought into relationship with Jesus receive the Spirit and become children of God, both of which imply participation in the divine life and sharing in the divine "DNA." Such sharing in God's life and such family resemblance imply participation in God's activity, or mission. Second, this implication is strengthened and made slightly more explicit in Jesus' signs (and their connected discourses) that focus on the Gospel's theme of Jesus' bringing God's life to the world. We begin with the gifts of new birth and the Spirit.

Becoming Children of God

Interpreters of the Gospel's Opening (1:1–18, the so-called Prologue) have often been torn as they consider the "main point" of these critical verses: is it Christology or soteriology? That is, is the Opening primarily about Christ or his benefits for humans? The answer is "Yes." It is about both, and they should not be separated.

John 1:1–18 is a story of participation, specifically of God's participation in the world by means of the incarnation of the Word (1:14): "The Word became flesh and blood, and moved into the neighborhood."[109] As the "self-exegesis of God,"[110] the Word makes God known as only God's unique/only Son—who is in intimate relation with God and is in fact God (while remaining a distinct "person" in relationship to his Father)—can do.[111] Yet this revelation-by-participation is not merely a revelation of knowledge *about* God but a gracious invitation to join this intimate divine family: "He came to what was his own, and his own people did not accept him. But to all who received him, who believed in his name, he gave power to become children of God, who were born, not of blood or of the will of the flesh or of the will of man, but of God" (1:11–13). Indeed, as noted earlier, Culpepper's influential structural analysis of 1:1–18 sees the reference to becoming God's children as the "pivot" of the passage.[112] Furthermore, we have already seen that this passage has often been understood, since the patristic era, as a text about theosis: God/Christ becoming like us so that we could become like God/Christ. Becoming children of God is a participatory real-

109. The rendering of 1:14 in *The Message*.

110. So Schnelle, *Theology of the New Testament*, 674; cf. Rossé's phrase: "Jesus, Exegete of God" (*Spirituality of Communion*, 11).

111. "From the beginning, this Word is intrinsic to the identity of God" (Thompson, *John*, 25).

112. Culpepper, "Pivot of John's Prologue."

ity—beginning to share in the sonship of the Father's Son. Godlikeness will be Christlikeness, and vice versa.[113]

In antiquity it was often assumed, and sometimes explicitly taught, that children of God would or should become like their father—that is, for children of God, like God. For the writers of the New Testament, this assumption could be found implicitly in Scripture by joining together the covenantal motifs of being God's children and being called to Godlike holiness.[114] Such an assumption could also be found in certain early Jewish texts, including some of the Dead Sea Scrolls.[115] Infamously, 1QS 1.9–10 calls on the children of light to imitate God by loving the children of light and hating the children of darkness.[116]

Although John 1:1–18 does not make an explicit call for the children of God to become like God, it is likely that such a call was understood, implicitly, to exist. For one thing, other uses of the phrase "children of" in John suggest that the children described resemble their father: children of the devil side with their lying, murderous father (8:44), while children of Abraham do what Abraham did (8:39).[117] For another, the entire first epistle of John is predicated on this ancient assumption and articulated, of course, in Johannine language.[118] Both the Gospel and 1 John suggest that being God's children, for John, means acting in a Godlike way, which includes acting missionally like God the Father. And, as we will see momentarily, the gift of the Spirit makes such family resemblance possible for disciples in at least one concrete dimension of mission.

Commenting on John in its ancient context, Jan van der Watt notes that ancients "believed that a person's character and personality were given" by means of the father's "seed," meaning that those "born of (the seed of) God are not only given the ability to partake in the divine reality of God, but are also born with the divine characteristics in them, much like those that an ordinary baby received from his father through birth." This, says van der Watt, is the essence of salvation in John.[119] The contemporary image for theosis suggested above—possessing and exhibiting the divine DNA—is in line with this ancient anthropology.

---

113. That is, theosis is Christosis, and Christosis is theosis. Cf. 12:36: "While you have the light, believe in the light, so that you may become children of light."

114. See, e.g., Vellanickal, *Divine Sonship*, 18, 27.

115. On the Scrolls, see Vellanickal, *Divine Sonship*, 29–43, esp. 35–37.

116. We will return to this in chapter 6 on enemy-love.

117. See Vellanickal, *Divine Sonship*, 93–94.

118. See esp. 1 John 3:1–10; 4:7–21; 5:1–5, 18–21.

119. Van der Watt, *Introduction*, 55. Van der Watt rightly adds that believers do not "become divine or become gods" but do "carry the characteristics of God in them."

The topic of new birth mentioned in 1:11–13 is famously developed in John 3, where we find John's quintessential dialogue and the Gospel in miniature. In this chapter, three especially critical elements of the new birth—the birth from above (anōthen),[120] meaning from God, and thus the birth that produces children of God—emerge.[121] First, the new birth is the work of the Spirit (3:3–10). Second, the new birth is required for entrance into the kingdom of God (3:3, 5) and for reception of "eternal life" and salvation (3:15–17). And third, the new birth involves a response to the Son's participation in the human condition in both incarnation (narrated as his descent, being sent, and coming into the world) and crucifixion (3:13–21).[122] In addition, there is a clear, if not precisely articulated, connection between this response of "com[ing] to the light" and deeds (3:19–21). This connection at least suggests that belief and deeds are inseparably linked;[123] indeed, belief is not merely a matter of giving assent to Jesus but of pledging allegiance to him.[124] One of the primary "signs" of being God's children is doing deeds "in God" (3:21), that is, participating in the divine life such that God is the source of the power to do, including to do "like God." That is certainly the case with the unique Son, too, whose deeds are wrought by the Father (14:10).[125]

The gift of the Spirit

Between these two passages about new birth from above (1:11–13; ch. 3) comes an important summary statement about Jesus' mission: he has come as the one who "baptizes with the Holy Spirit," in the words of John the Baptist's

120. The Greek adverb anōthen has both meanings: "anew" and "from above." This double entendre is coupled with another one in pneuma, meaning both "wind" and "Spirit."

121. I am treating John 3:1–21 as a coherent literary unit that manifests an integration of the themes of new birth and healing/salvation/eternal life.

122. Although Jesus' death is not explicitly named in 3:13–21, the reference to Jesus' being lifted up there (3:14) is repeated in 12:32–34 and explained explicitly as signifying the sort of death he would die.

123. On the link between belief and action in John, see Brown, "Believing in the Gospel of John."

124. On belief as pledging allegiance, see Bennema, Mimesis, 27, 83, 104n.70, 124, 139, 147, 155, 162. Bennema specifically links the new birth to an initial pledging of allegiance (155).

125. It should also be noted that John 3 describes the new birth as the activity of the divine triad of Father, Son, and Spirit as people become children of God by virtue of the person and work of the Spirit and their faith in the person and work of the Son. John 3 is thus implicitly trinitarian.

testimony (1:33). The word "baptism" connotes participation in the fullest sense: it is an image of being completely immersed in a reality outside the self that (or "who") transforms the self. The importance of this mission statement for John has been generally underestimated. It serves as a bridge between the two passages about birth from God, suggesting that becoming God's children (1:11–13), baptism with the Spirit (1:33), and new birth/birth from above (ch. 3) are various ways of articulating the same fundamental reality: entering into the family of God in order to participate in the divine life by taking on the family resemblance and sharing in the family mission.

The last part of this claim is not explicitly stated in John's witness to Jesus' mission. But the context suggests that mission is precisely what baptism in the Spirit will entail. In the immediate context (1:29–34), the narrative explicitly tells us that Jesus himself is endued with the Spirit, who descended and remained on him (1:32), and implicitly tells us that this Spirit was the power that enabled Jesus to carry out his mission of being "the Lamb of God who takes away the sin of the world" (1:29; cf. 1:36). It will therefore be no surprise that, after his death and resurrection, Jesus gives the disciples the Spirit, by breathing into them, and tells them that their mission will involve the forgiveness of sins (20:21–23).[126] In other words, as we will see more fully in considering chapter 20, the disciples as children of God will be Spirit-empowered participants in Jesus' Spirit-empowered mission, a mission that is ultimately, for John, the mission of God. In other words, to be God's children is to be born from above by, and baptized with, the same Spirit that enabled Jesus to do God's work. Hence to be God's children is, in part, to do God's work—to join the family trade because of sharing in the family's life and DNA. This implicit missional call—even missional theosis (participation)—becomes fully explicit in John 13–17, but there are additional intimations even in the first half of the Gospel.

Among these intimations is an additional explicit reference to the gift of the Spirit. In John 7, which situates Jesus at the festival of Tabernacles, or Booths, we read this:

> [37]On the last day of the festival, the great day, while Jesus was standing there, he cried out, "Let anyone who is thirsty come to me, [38]and let the one who believes in me drink. As the scripture has said, "Out of ['that one's'; *autou* = 'his'] heart [*koilias*; 'belly'] shall flow rivers of living water.'" [39]Now he said this

126. Commenting on the Spirit's remaining on Jesus, Thompson (*John*, 47) says that Jesus "*has* the Spirit, and he has it uniquely and permanently; hence, he subsequently confers it on others as one breathes out one's own breath (3:34; 7:37–39; 20:22)." To receive this Spirit is, implicitly, to receive the very life of Jesus, which life includes his mission of giving life.

about the Spirit, which believers in him were to receive; for
as yet there was no Spirit, because Jesus was not yet glorified.
(John 7:37–39; NRSV alt)

Although many translations interpret the possessive pronoun *autou* ("his")
in v. 38 as a reference to the believer—"Out of the believer's heart shall flow
rivers of living water" (NRSV)—"his heart/belly" much more likely refers to
Jesus as the source or "conduit" of the gift of the Spirit to believers, as elsewhere in the Gospel, including (it will be argued in ch. 5) 19:30, 34.[127] In
either interpretation, however, there is once again deeply participatory imagery at play here—a gift that flows from within, either from within Jesus to the
disciples or from within the disciples outwards, into the world. In either case,
the disciples' mission is implied. The glorified Jesus will baptize and infuse
them with the Spirit, such that the Spirit will both surround and indwell the
disciples. Having received the Spirit, the disciples will also be conduits of the
divine life as it flows through (or, less likely, from) them. The gift of the Spirit
will be life-giving both for the disciples and also for others.

Indeed, since the theme of "life" is so central to this Gospel, it is not
surprising that Jesus would at least hint that the disciples—who will later be
given the Spirit and sent into the world—will participate in his life-giving,
Spirit-empowered mission, which is itself narrated in various ways throughout the first half of the Gospel, as we will see momentarily.

Another of the intimations of missional theosis in chapters 1 to 12
is one additional reference to a kind of rebirth, a rebirth that is also implicitly missional. In 12:36, while summarizing his message and mission—
which will culminate in his drawing all people to himself as he is lifted up
(12:32)—Jesus, the light of the world, tells the listening crowd, "While you
have the light, believe in the light, so that you may become children [lit.
"sons"; *huioi*] of light." As the light of the world (1:9; 3:19–21; 8:12; 9:5;
12:46), Jesus seeks to bring children into the divine light that he incarnates.
"[T]o become 'sons of Light' means to share in the life of the sonship of
Christ."[128] This participatory aspect of being children of the light, together
with the operative theology of "family resemblance" that we see throughout
the Fourth Gospel, suggests—as it does, for instance, also in the Dead Sea
Scrolls—that children of the light take on the characteristics of the light that
is their "parent."[129] This ethical/missional implication is spelled out explicitly

127. For the much more common latter interpretation (Jesus), see, e.g., Brown, *John*
1:321–23; Lincoln, *John*, 254–57; Keener, *John* 1:728–30. For the former interpretation
(the believer), see references in Keener, *John* 1:728.

128. Vellanickal, *Divine Sonship*, 158.

129. As we will see in chapter 6 on enemy-love, the children of the light in John

in 1 John,[130] but it is present implicitly also in the Gospel itself, symbolized in the witness of the man born blind and healed by Jesus: "'I do not know whether he [Jesus] is a sinner [as 'the Jews' charge]. One thing I do know, that though I was blind, now I see'" (9:25). To believe in the light is to bear witness to the light and, as well, to become like the light, for it is those who abide in Jesus and bear much fruit who become his disciples (15:8)—that is, they become children of the light, which means also children of God.

Life, light, love: these words, as we have seen, summarize the mission of God and of his Son in John; they also recapitulate, at least by way of implication and anticipation, the status and the mission of the disciples, of those who believe in Jesus. That is, the first half of the Gospel implies that the disciples both receive and pass on the divine life, light, and love. That will become explicit in the second half of the Gospel, but it is apparent also in the way Jesus' mission of doing signs and giving life is narrated in the first half of the Gospel.[131]

Jesus' Life-Giving Signs and Missional Discipleship in the First Half of the Gospel

"Jesus is the protagonist in the Johannine narrative and dominates every account in the Gospel."[132] The first major section of the Gospel consists primarily of Jesus' signs and discourses, the latter entailing both dialogues and monologues. These twelve chapters narrate and explain Jesus' ministry of bringing God's love and life to humanity, a work that will not be fully completed until the cross and resurrection, but which nonetheless really does occur during Jesus' earthly ministry. In these chapters, the mission of the Son *is* the mission of the Father, for the Son is sent by the Father and acts on the Father's behalf as his agent. But Jesus' role is more complicated and

---

and in the Scrolls are radically different in how the parent-light shapes their ethical practices, specifically toward enemies.

130. See esp. 1 John 1:5–7; 2:8–10. See also "You [pl.] are the light of the world" (Matt 5:14), which, in context, is derivative of being in relationship to Jesus and which also has an inherently missional sense.

131. In terms of word count for these three key terms, "life" and "light" dominate the first half of the Gospel, in which "love" appears only a half-dozen times. The situation is reversed in the second half, where "life" appears a half-dozen times, "light" occurs not at all, and "love" dominates. As C. H. Dodd noted (*Interpretation*, 399), however, "The evangelist does not intend for a moment to abandon the belief that Christ brings life and light, or even to subordinate that belief. His intention is to emphasize the truth that the final reality [i.e., the *telos*] of life and light is given in *agapē*."

132. Bennema, *Encountering Jesus*, 43.

nuanced than that. Because of the intimacy of the Father-Son relationship (1:14, 18), which is ultimately one of mutual indwelling (10:38; 14:10–11; 17:21), the Father acts *in* the Son:

> Do you not believe that I am in the Father and the Father is in me? The words that I say to you I do not speak on my own; but the Father who dwells in me does his works. (14:10)

This text from part two of the Gospel (to which we will return) interprets what happens in part one. In the words of Murray Rae, "Jesus is not merely a deputy in the Father's stead—though he is sent by the Father—but the one in whom the Father is at work."[133]

We consider now the significance of the signs, which are integral to part one of the Gospel (1:19 through chapter 12), and then, more briefly, the call to missional discipleship in the same chapters.

The significance of the signs

Signs are indeed pervasive in the first half of John.[134] A frequent characterization of the signs in John is that they point to something, or someone, beyond themselves. Raymond Brown said that in John faith means "see[ing] *through* the signs *to* their significance."[135] Craig Koester, in *Symbolism in the Fourth Gospel*, says, "The term *signs* (*semeia*) is appropriate for these miracles, since a sign is not an end in itself but a visible indication of something else."[136]

Yet the Gospel itself never says, and does not imply, this understanding of the signs. As just noted, the signs are also termed "works" because they are instantiations of the *singular*, life-giving work of God in Jesus, the *missio Dei*.[137] To be sure, the signs point to Jesus' identity as the Son and Messiah, the bringer of God's abundant life (e.g., 10:25; 20:31). They are also, as Robert Kysar says, "provocateurs of faith"[138]—specifically faith in Jesus. But these functions of pointing *to* Jesus and provoking faith in him do not point *away from* the event that is termed a "sign" or "work."

---

133. Rae, "Testimony of Works," 295.

134. We find the word *sēmeion* in 2:11, 18, 23; 3:2; 4:48, 54; 6:2, 14, 26, 30; 7:31; 9:16; 10:41; 11:47; 12:18, 37; and 20:30.

135. Brown, *John*, 1:cxxxix (emphasis added).

136. Koester, *Symbolism*, 79.

137. For the plural, see 5:20, 36; 7:3; 9:3–4; 10:25, 32, 37; 14:10–11; 15:24; for the singular, 4:34; 17:4.

138. Kysar, *John: The Maverick Gospel*, 93–113.

This common understanding of the Johannine signs is actually, if unintentionally, a kind of "supercessionist" reading of them: the deeds are replaced by Jesus, and the physical reality of feeding people or healing a blind man is replaced by faith in this Jesus. This sort of reading is ultimately—though, again, inadvertently—also a dualistic or Platonizing approach to the signs. Jesus' bodily act of healing or raising from the dead, for example, becomes comparable to a human body: it is of no consequence but merely houses (i.e., points to) an inner soul of "spiritual" existence, which is what really matters.[139]

This "supercessionist," Platonic interpretation of the signs in John can have profound negative consequences for Christian theology and mission. For one thing, it minimizes, or even nullifies, the significance of physical, bodily ministry, as if this were inferior to the "real" ministry of telling people about Jesus. This is quite ironic, since the Jesus to whom the disciples are called to bear witness is precisely the one who healed the royal official's son and opened the eyes of the blind man. For another, therefore, and perhaps more importantly, this sort of account of the signs gets its Christology and soteriology wrong. It implies that Jesus did not come to bring eternal life in the sense of the life of the age to come, beginning now, but only in the sense of a *disembodied* future existence preceded by an *embodied* existence in which the body has little if any spiritual significance. In such a reading, *Ezekiel 34, which we discussed in some detail above, has vanished from sight.*

Furthermore, this approach to the signs implies that Jesus (and/or John as his interpreter) was not serious about his ministries of healing and feeding, but only used them as ploys for a message about something altogether different—a theological and missional bait and switch, so to speak. *The end result, even if unintended, is a gnostic Jesus offering a gnostic salvation to potential gnostic believers who will engage in a gnostic mission.* They certainly will not do "greater works" (14:12).

The signs in John do not point to something or someone beyond themselves that *minimizes* or *negates* them. Rather, they point to Jesus, the Father's Son, as their divine source and the source of abundant life; they ought to elicit faith in him, not faith in some other figure, or some generic faith. Thus, the evangelist does not point *beyond* the sign-making Jesus to

---

139. For a view similar to the one articulated here, see Thompson's excursus on signs (*John*, 65–68, esp. 67): "the signs are revelations of Jesus' identity precisely in the material realm as material deeds" (67). Although I am not using the term "supercessionist" here in the common way of referring to the notion of the church replacing Israel, the reading of the signs offered here may have implications for a way of reading John that does not negate the foundation (Israel) while affirming the structure that organically grows out of it, namely the entity called Jesus-and-his-disciples.

some other Jesus or to something else, but he points us *through* the signs precisely *to* the sign-making Jesus. In reading John 6, for instance, we do not need to choose between the Jesus who feeds the crowd and the Jesus who feeds the soul, whether spiritually or sacramentally; he is *one and the same Jesus*.[140] The signs are polyvalent, as Koester rightly points out,[141] and John indicates various aspects of that polyvalence. But John never deletes the literal meaning of the polyvalent signs for a completely allegorical one, any more than Jesus discards the Scriptures themselves because they point to him (5:39). The Scriptures matter; the signs matter.

To be sure, "signs faith" (faith in direct response to a sign, without its necessarily leading to discipleship) is ultimately inadequate in the Fourth Gospel. But it is inadequate because it stops at the sign, the experience of abundant life, and fails to proceed to the source—not because the sign itself is deficient. The deficiency is in the beneficiary, not in the sign.

A Johannine sign is not like a voting booth—choose this Jesus or that Jesus. It is more like a lovely musical concert to which the composer has invited, free of charge, a group of people who do not know her personally. Some enjoy the gift of the music without ever acknowledging or wanting to know the giver; others receive both the gift and the giver. So it is with the Johannine signs (and, indeed, with Christian mission). In fact, the Gospel's most profound theology of life is found at this intersection of gift and giver: to receive abundant and eternal life, to experience the life of the age to come, is to know God the Father and the Son intimately (17:3), to participate in the abundant and eternal life of God the giver: Father, Son, and Spirit.

So what are the missional implications for this interpretation of the signs? Harold Attridge, writing about the implicit ethics in John, perceptively suggests that some of the "concrete actions" expected of disciples

> might be embedded within Jesus' "signs," which become not only the basis or content of Christological faith but pointers to what is expected of disciples. Jesus gives drink to the thirsty, on many levels, at Cana and in Samaria; Jesus feeds the hungry on the Galilean lakeshore; Jesus heals those who are lame or blind

140. Eating and drinking Jesus' flesh and blood has at least two meanings: (1) a spiritual, or perhaps sapiential, sense that focuses on taking in Jesus and his death with a participatory faith and (2) a sacramental sense, referring to taking in Jesus and his death via the eucharistic elements.

141. Koester, *Symbolism*, 81–82. One could say about the signs something similar to what Koester says about the symbolic function of various individuals and groups in the Gospel: "Each person and group has its own characteristics, and their representative roles do not diminish their uniqueness but actually develop their most distinctive traits" (45).

in Jerusalem; his disciples should try to do all these things as well. Jesus raises up one who is asleep in death; his disciples should, in some probably metaphorical [I (MJG) would say "analogous"] sense, do the same thing.[142]

That is, the divinely empowered "works" of Jesus will become the divinely empowered, analogous "greater works" of the disciples (14:10–12), all of which will, or should, point to Jesus. These Johannine works are not unlike what the Christian tradition calls the corporate works of mercy, such as those enumerated in Matthew 25.[143]

The significance of the discourses

Much of what Jesus says in his various monologues and dialogues in chapters 1–12 can be classified theologically as Christology. There is more, however, to these discourses than Christology. Jesus is about the business of calling and making disciples—people who not only follow him, but also bear witness to him, to the divine light, life, and love that he brings. In the words of Stanley Skreslet, John presents numerous examples of people making disciples by "sharing Christ with friends."[144]

We see this clearly in the "chain of witness" in chapter 1, with its pattern of invitation-response-invitation summarized in the words "Come and see" (1:39, 46; cf. 4:29). And beginning in chapter 3, we find the individuals whom Jesus encounters, and with whom he dialogues, as representative also of his mission as "Savior of the world" (4:42), to quote those to whom the Samaritan woman has borne witness as a new disciple.[145] The narratives about and conversations with Nicodemus the Jew, the Samaritan woman, and the almost certainly gentile (or gentile-sympathizing) "royal official"

142. In Attridge, Carter, and van der Watt, "Quaesttiones disputatae," 485. This text was originally part of a presentation at the 2015 meeting of SNTS (Studiorum Novi Testamenti Societas) in Amsterdam. (Note: the original oral presentation called the signs "polyvalent pointers.") My insertion of "analogous" is meant to suggest (adding to Attridge's point) that the disciples' resurrecting activity could be both "spiritual" and "literal" or physical. Acts of raising the dead are not unknown in the worldwide Christian experience.

143. So also, Attridge, "Quaesttiones disputatae," 485. Similarly, Carter, *John and Empire*, 277–78. "Just as Jesus' healings and feedings rolled back imperial damage, so also do the healing actions of Jesus-believers," which include but are not limited to "miracles."

144. Skreslet, *Picturing Christian Witness*, 79–117, esp. 88–98. Skreslet focuses on John 1, 9 (the man born blind), and especially 4 (the Samaritan woman).

145. There have been a number of important studies on the missional nature of John 4. See, for example, Okure, *Johannine Approach to Mission*.

(*basilikos*) of chapters 3–4 indicate Jesus' highly contextualized, particularized-but-universal mission.[146] The implication for disciples then and now is clear: an analogous universal, but highly particularized and contextualized approach to mission. In the words of missiologist Scott Sunquist, we need the "three-legged stool of sacred Scripture, the Great Tradition, and the local context" for a sound missiology.[147]

Something significant about this mission is indicated in chapter 4, where we find a mini-mission-discourse sandwiched, Markan-style, into the story of the Samaritan woman (4:31–38). The chain of witness reappears here in a new form that will place its mark on the Gospel as a whole:[148] the Father has sent the Son who sends the disciples:

> [34]Jesus said to them, "My <u>food is to do the will of him who sent me and to complete his work</u>. [35]Do you not say, "Four months more, then comes the harvest"? But I tell you, look around you, and see how the fields are ripe for harvesting. [36]The reaper is already receiving wages and is gathering fruit for eternal life, so that sower and reaper may rejoice together. [37]For here the saying holds true, "One sows and another reaps." [38]<u>I sent you</u> to **reap that for which you did not labor. Others have labored, and you have entered into their labor.**"

This mini-mission-discourse is somewhat puzzling since, in the Johannine narrative, the disciples have not yet been sent by Jesus and will not be formally sent until after the resurrection. The narrator's assumption, then, must be that simply to *be* Jesus' disciple is to be sent.

The disciples do not, however, work as independent contractors, taking their own initiative, but as participants in, and beneficiaries of, the work of others (v. 38).[149] Despite the plural pronouns in v. 38, the sense here is most

146. See further discussion in chapter 6. It is possible to speak of the "stages" of Jesus' mission in John, from a Jewish mission to a Samaritan mission to a gentile mission; see, e.g., Harris, *Mission in the Gospels*, 159–72, who looks at both the narrative and, in conversation with the work of Raymond Brown, possible connections between the narrative and the historical developments in the Johannine community. Canonically, as various interpreters have suggested, one might also correlate the flow of John's Gospel in the early chapters with the missional program set out in Acts: "[Y]ou will be my witnesses in Jerusalem, in all Judea and Samaria, and to the ends of the earth" (Acts 1:8b).

147. Sunquist, *Understanding Christian Mission*, 170.

148. Bennema repeatedly refers to various "mimetic chains" throughout the Gospel (*Mimesis*, 38, 52, 74, 79–81, 106, 114, 137, 142, 163, 167–68, 194, 200).

149. In the reception history of John (see Edwards, *John*, 59), these laborers have been interpreted in various ways, including the Old Testament prophets (so Augustine, *Homily* 15.32; Chrysostom, *Homily* 34.2); John the Baptist and his followers; Jesus' own disciples (assuming the discourse is directed at later disciples); the writer's

likely that Jesus is the chief "other laborer." Disciples are reapers, harvesting the crop that has been sown by Jesus, who in turn has also been doing someone else's work—that of his sending Father (v. 34). It is likely, then, that the plural pronouns in v. 38 refer to the Father and the Son as the laborers—and perhaps even implicitly to the Spirit as well.[150] In any case, the disciples are sent to participate in, bring to fruition, and eventually celebrate the mission that is fundamentally not theirs.

The missional implications for the church are significant. Three things stand out:

- First, *discipleship* is inherently *missional*; it involves being sent.[151]

- Second, Christian mission is *derivative*, an extension of the Son's work on behalf of the Father.

- And third, Christian mission is *participatory*; it is entering into "their labor"—the activity of the divine persons.

It is especially important to stress this third point: participation. A number of studies of the disciples' mission according to John have argued or implied that it is characterized by, and limited to, "witness" or "testimony."[152] "Witness" is of course an important Johannine theme, as we have seen in considering the testimony of the man born blind, but it should be clear from texts such as 13:35 ("By this everyone will know that you are my disciples, if you have love for one another") that witness is more than verbal; it includes activity—ecclesial practices. Our consideration of the second half of the Gospel will further challenge the sort of interpretation of John that limits Christian mission to verbal witness. Furthermore, "participatory" is probably a more comprehensive theological descriptor for understanding mission in John than a term like "incarnational."[153]

---

contemporaries; and the Samaritan woman.

150. Similarly, Nissen, *New Testament and Mission*, 80; Lincoln, *John*, 180; and Bennema, *Mimesis*, 52. Michaels (*John*, 267) thinks "others" is intentionally indefinite but include "Moses and the prophets, John, Jesus, the woman, and even the Samaritans themselves."

151. See especially Köstenberger, *The Missions of Jesus and the Disciples*, 176–98. See also Sunquist, *Understanding Christian Mission*, 218, commenting on John 20: "if we are called *to* Jesus Christ, we are sent *by* Jesus Christ."

152. See, e.g., Köstenberger, *The Missions of Jesus and the Disciples*.

153. This is not, however, to disparage the notion of incarnational ministry or mission, as some have done. Participation, in fact, depends theologically on the priority of divine participation in human life, including especially the incarnation. For a contemporary exposition of incarnational ministry/mission, see *Incarnational Ministry* and *Incarnational Mission* by Wells.

The mini-mission-discourse in chapter 4 will be supplemented by a major mission discourse and commissioning prayer in chapters 13–17.[154] There we will especially find the requisite participatory spirituality for participatory mission hinted at in this mini-discourse.

Conclusion: Jesus' Signs, His Death, and the Gift of Life

Our explorations thus far lead to a conclusion articulated well by Andreas Köstenberger: "Positing a sectarian mindset behind John's Gospel . . . represents a fundamental misunderstanding of the ethos underlying it."[155] We have seen that the Gospel's structure, theme, signs, and call to discipleship are evidence of a missional gospel and a missional Jesus offering abundant life and calling disciples who will share in that mission. It is important, however, to close this chapter by returning to the intimate connection between this gift of abundant life and the death of Jesus. The narrative of that saving death will of course take place in the second half of the Gospel; it is, paradoxically, the exaltation/coronation of Jesus and the completion of his mission: "It is finished" (19:30). But we have indications already in the first half of the Gospel that the abundant life that Jesus comes to bring will come in its fullest form through his own death. We see this in chapter 3, which connects being born anew and from above with belief in the dying, healing, saving Son sent to the world by God. We see it also in chapter 6, in which life from and in Jesus is paired with consuming his flesh and blood, another connection between life and (his) death. We see it as well in chapter 10, the discourse about the Good Shepherd who lays down his life for the sheep, and for their abundant life. And we see it in chapter 12, the conclusion to the first half of the Gospel, when Jesus speaks of his death both as his glorification and as the means of drawing all people to himself—and thus into eternal life as children of the light (esp. 12:23–25, 32–36, 50).

What are we to make of all this? Do Jesus' works (signs) bring life, or does his ultimate work, his death, do so? For John this is a false either-or. We have indications already in the first half of the Gospel, especially in chapters 3, 6, and 12, that the abundant life that Jesus comes to bring will come in its fullest form through his own death. The death of Jesus does not cancel out his signs; nor do the signs of life render his death unnecessary. Moreover, the "I am" statements that accompany and interpret some of the signs (and

154. Teresa Okure (*The Johannine Approach to Mission*, 194–95) argues that chapters 13–17 are an expansion of 4:31–38.

155. Köstenberger, "Sensitivity to Outsiders," 192.

are found as well in the second half of the Gospel) are "images [that] direct attention to the cross, the distinctive lens through which all [Johannine] symbols should be viewed."[156]

Although John does not expound the "mechanics" of Jesus' death at length, it is clear, as in the rest of the New Testament, that abundant life comes, paradoxically, through death. John, not to mention Paul and others, understands Jesus' death as the ultimate act of love; the signs too are manifestations of love, for it is God's love that motivated the sending of Jesus and that was manifested in his various works. So also the church sent by this Jesus will be driven by God's love, manifesting it, and thus God's abundant life, in numerous analogous ways as disciples are baptized and empowered by the Spirit. And a central aspect of the church's (the disciples') being sent will be sharing in the death-like but life-giving ministry of Jesus: "Those who love their life lose it, and those who hate their life in this world will keep it for eternal life. Whoever serves me must follow me, and where I am, there will my servant be also" (12:25–26a). This is a clear Johannine echo of similar words in the Synoptics, as well as the Synoptic invitation to take up one's cross, and a marked foreshadowing of what is about to happen in chapter 13.[157] The servants of the Servant will share in his servanthood (13:13–17), as we will see in the next chapter.

A survey of Jesus' mission in the first half of the Gospel and of the brief commissioning of the disciples in John 4 leads, then, to the following major conclusions.

First, John is a missional Gospel in structure, theme, and contents, bearing witness to a missional Jesus who has come to bring the love, light, and abundant life of God into the world.

Second, a primary aspect of Jesus' mission is to be the agent of spiritual rebirth that creates an extended family of God, disciples of the Sent One from the Father who are swept up into the love and life of God. The privilege of being God's children, the vocation of being Jesus' disciples, the reality of new birth by the Spirit: this is all inherently missional. The mission is both derivative and participatory, and it is also *cruciform*; that is, it participates in the paradoxically life-giving death of Jesus. These themes will play out more fully in the second half of the Gospel.

~

156. Nissen, *New Testament and Mission*, 86. To "symbols" we should add "signs."

157. E.g., Matt 10:39 and Luke 17:33; cf. Luke 14:26; 16:13; Mark 8:34–35 par.; 9:33–37 par.; 10:42–45.

As we go forward in the remaining chapters, we do so with these first two chapters as the foundation. To repeat the principal thesis, which is hinted at throughout the first half of the Gospel and which will explode in the second half:

> *Johannine spirituality fundamentally consists in the mutual in-dwelling of the Triune God (Father, Son, and Spirit) and Jesus' disciples such that disciples participate in the divine love and life, and therefore in the life-giving mission of God, thereby both demonstrating their likeness to God as God's children and becoming more and more like God as they become like his Son by the work of the Spirit.*

We will call this "missional theosis," meaning missional transformative participation, or participatory missional sanctification. In sum: "abide and go." Which leads us to the next chapter, and to John's Mission Discourse.

3

Abide and Go

Missional Theosis in John 13–16

In this chapter we consider a significant dimension of the portion of the Fourth Gospel normally called the Farewell Discourse—what we have labeled John's Mission Discourse. We will focus especially on chapters 13 and 15.[1] But before turning our attention to these two chapters, we will first briefly consider one important cluster of texts, both from the Mission Discourse and in related texts elsewhere, that figure significantly in the theology of John's Gospel and in the overall framework of this book's approach to John.

The Theological Starting Point(s) of Participation

As we begin to speak of a participatory missional spirituality in John, whether or not we use the word theosis, we should begin theologically with two prior realities articulated in John: first, participation, or mutual indwelling, within (the Triune) God; and, second, God's participation with humanity, culminating in the incarnation.

---

1. Some scholars do not consider chapter 13, or at least most of chapter 13, to be part of the Farewell Discourse. For our purposes, it is indeed part of the entire unit of chapters 13–17 with the longer designation, from the outline in chapter 2, "The Mission Discourse and Prayer of Consecration and Commissioning."

Participation within the divine life

The most fundamental theological starting point for the reality of human participation in the life of God is the reality of participation, of mutual indwelling, within God, particularly between the Father and the Son. The technical term for this is perichoresis. (In John, the Spirit is implicitly included in this divine life of mutual indwelling, but because the focus is on the Father-Son relationship and its consequences for believers, the explicit texts generally highlight that relationship.)[2] Mutual indwelling is "spatial terminology [that] is used to describe relational reality."[3] Several texts make this divine mutual indwelling especially clear:

> But if I [Jesus] do them ["the works of my Father"], even though you do not believe me, believe the works, so that you may know and understand that <u>the Father is in me and I am in the Father.</u>" (10:38)

> [10]Do you not believe that <u>I am in the Father and the Father is in me</u>? The words that I say to you I do not speak on my own; but <u>the Father who dwells in me</u> does his works. [11]Believe me that <u>I am in the Father and the Father is in me</u>; but if you do not, then believe me because of the works themselves. (14:10–11)[4]

> On that day [when I come to you] you will know that <u>I am in my Father, and you in me, and I in you.</u> (14:20)

> [21][I ask] <u>that they may all be one.</u> As <u>you, Father, are in me and I am in you, may they also be in us</u>, **so that the world may believe that you have sent me**. [22]The glory that you have given me I have given them, <u>so that they may be one, as we are one,</u> [23]<u>I in them and you in me, that they may become completely one,</u>

---

2. For example, if the Son will come to/into the disciples (14:18, 28), and the Father and the Son will both come to/into the disciples (14:23), and the Spirit will be sent/come into the disciples (14:16, 26; 16:7), then some sort of mutual indwelling of these three figures ("persons") is implied. The joint activity of the Father sending, and the Spirit being sent, in the Son's name (e.g., 14:26; 15:26) also implies a similar interrelationship. The opposite position (the exclusion of the Spirit from the divine perichoresis), but the inclusion of the *disciples* in that divine coinherence, is argued by Crump in "Re-examining the Johannine Trinity: Perichoresis or Deification?" For Crump, the "trinity" is the Father, the Son, and the disciples. This proposal has a certain narrative and theological appeal, but it ultimately under-values the role of the Spirit in relation to the Father and the Son indicated by the verses cited in this note.

3. Gifford, *Perichoretic Salvation*, 2.

4. "The Son is the permanent and eternal 'home' of the Father, as the Father is the eternal home of the Son" (Leithart, *Traces of the Trinity*, 139).

**so that the world may know that you have sent me and have
loved them even as you have loved me.** (17:21–23)

That is, in John, "perichoresis is not a sideshow";[5] it is at the very core of the
Gospel's good news. In addition to being spatial language that functions to
describe a relational reality, the Johannine language of perichoresis is likely
grounded in the metaphor of Jesus and the community of the disciples both
being the dwelling place—the temple—of God.[6] In these perichoretic texts,
from both halves of the Gospel, we see four main things:

- First, there is a divine mutual indwelling, or perichoresis, which is
  demonstrated to us through Jesus' missional activity, which is in fact
  God's missional activity. Theologically, this indicates the coherence of
  the immanent and the economic Trinity: God *does* as God *is*.

- Second, we may therefore speak of (the incarnate, human) Jesus' own
  "spirituality"—his relationship with the Father and the Spirit that
  enables his mission. The mission (seen in the works) of Jesus is the
  mission of his Father, and the energy for that mission, the power for
  those works, is Jesus' unity with the Father, his mutual indwelling with
  the Father. Similarly, although the Spirit is not specifically mentioned
  in the texts quoted above, we know from the very beginning of the
  Gospel that "the Spirit descend[ed] from heaven like a dove, and it
  remained on him" (1:32–33).[7] The key word here is "remained"—the
  same verb often translated "abide" (*menō*). That is, we can assume that
  John wants us to know that Jesus' mission was the result of his union
  with and abiding in the love and power of the Father and the Spirit.

- Third, believers are invited into this divine intimate, missional life. In
  John 17, Jesus "prays that the disciples will be brought into the perichoretic fellowship of the Father and the Son."[8]

- And fourth, the ultimate purpose of believers' participation in God's
  own unity and mutual indwelling is missional: to demonstrate the

---

5. Leithart, *Traces of the Trinity*, 136.

6. See esp. Coloe, *God Dwells with Us*, 159–60. Somewhat similarly, Talbert ("The
Fourth Gospel's Soteriology") finds the sources of mutual indwelling language in both
Scripture (the covenantal language of divine presence/indwelling) and classical Greek
(dwelling in God), each referring primarily to divine empowerment. Thus, mutual indwelling is not only about intimacy, but also about faithful functioning.

7. For more on Jesus and the Spirit, see my "The Spirit, the Prophets, and the End
of the 'Johannine Jesus'" and the works noted there.

8. Leithart, *Traces of the Trinity*, 137. In John 17, "the mutual penetration of the
Father and Son extends in an ecclesiological direction" (140).

reality of God's love for the world in Jesus (see boldfaced text in 17:21–23). The church's perichoretic unity with God and within its fellowship "is integral to the church's mission," for if "the church is not a place where the members 'dwell within' one another's loves, the world will not believe that the Son 'dwells within' and 'came forth from' the Father."[9]

Thus, we have a missional, mutually indwelling God who is forming a unified, missional people who will be in a mutually indwelling relationship with that God. This is the fundamental missional theology and spirituality of the Fourth Gospel, and the two aspects (theology and spirituality) are inseparable in John. Accordingly, for John, there is also no spirituality without mission, and no mission without spirituality; that is, *there is no participation in God without mission, and no mission without participation in God*. If we use the language of theosis, then we must say that theosis is inherently missional.

Divine participation in human life

Second, we must also consider God's participation with, in, and for humanity. As the Opening of the Gospel tells us (1:1–18), this divine participation in human life began with the very creation of human life (1:3), continued in the life of Israel (represented by Moses and the gift of Torah; 1:16–17), and reached its climax in the incarnation (1:14), which is the gift of the Word's fullness and of abundant divine grace (1:16), the living exegesis of God the Father (1:18). This divine participation also includes the mysterious presence of the Logos in human history as "the light of all people" (1:4, 9–10):[10]

> [3]All things came into being through him, and without him not one thing came into being. What has come into being [4]in him was life, and the life was the light of all people. . . . [9]The true light, which enlightens everyone, was coming into the world. [10]He was in the world, and the world came into being through him; yet the world did not know him. . . . [14]And the Word became flesh and lived among us, and we have seen his glory, the glory as of a father's only son, full of grace and truth. . . . [16]From his fullness we have all received, grace upon

9. Leithart, *Traces of the Trinity*, 140.

10. After a long study of *logos* in 1:1–18, Peter Phillips concludes that the Gospel does not have a *logos* doctrine, but only Christology; using the multivalent word *logos* is "just a way of getting as many readers as possible into the story . . . a clever ruse to grab the reader's attention" in order to focus not on *logos* but on Jesus (*The Prologue*, 141).

grace. [17]The law indeed was given through Moses; grace and truth came through Jesus Christ. [18]No one has ever seen God. It is God the only Son, who is close to the Father's heart, who has made him known. (1:3–4, 9–10, 14, 16–18)

So too, when Jesus tells us that there will be a mutual indwelling of God and believers, he insists that the Triune God takes the initiative:

[16]And I will ask the Father, and he will give you another Advocate, to be with you forever. [17]This is the Spirit of truth, whom the world cannot receive, because it neither sees him nor knows him. You know him, because he abides with you, and he will be in you. [18]I will not leave you orphaned; I am coming to you. . . . [20]On that day you will know that I am in my Father, and you in me, and I in you." . . . [23]Jesus answered him, "Those who love me will keep my word, and my Father will love them, and we will come to them and make our home with them. . . . [26][T]he Advocate, the Holy Spirit, whom the Father will send in my name . . . . (14:16–18, 20, 23, 26)

"When the Advocate comes, whom I will send to you from the Father, the Spirit of truth who comes from the Father, he will testify on my behalf." (15:26)

Many scholars have rightly suggested that this sort of language implies that the community of disciples constitutes a temple, whether as a replacement of, fulfillment of, or parallel to the Jewish temple (and/or people) or as an alternative to the pagan temples, such as the famous temple of Artemis in Ephesus, where John may have been written (and where it was at least read and heard).[11] But as we will see with the image of the vine in chapter 15, the Johannine temple imagery is inseparable from the Gospel's missional emphasis. This divine temple is a holy community of God's presence, but it is a temple that both draws people into itself and is sent into the world that, according to 3:16, God loves (more on this below).

With this two-dimensional theological framework of divine priority and divine initiative in indwelling/participation in mind, we turn to the so-called Farewell Discourse, the Johannine Mission Discourse. After some introductory remarks, we will concentrate especially on John 13 and 15.

---

11. The first, more common interpretation (Jesus as replacement and fulfillment of the Second Temple, continued in the Johannine community) is made at length by Coloe, *Dwelling in the Household of God*; the second (alternative to the temple of Artemis) by Carter, *John and Empire*, esp. 257–64.

The Johannine Mission Discourse

The Gospel's second major section, 13:1—19:42, narrates Jesus' saving, loving death and the preparation of his disciples to continue his salvific, loving mission in the Spirit's power and with the Father's blessing. Chapters 13 through 17 record Jesus' final meal and words with his disciples— his "Farewell Discourse," sometimes called his "testament" or "farewell speech" of consolation and instruction to his soon-to-be survivors. This sort of speech generally included such elements as prediction of death, consolation, provision for a successor, admonition and even commissioning, prediction of future opposition, and a final blessing or prayer—and these are all present in John 13–17.[12] However, although speaking of these chapters as the "Farewell Discourse(s)" or a "testament" tells us something about the form and one aspect of the *rhetorical* function of these chapters, such generic labels reveal very little about their *theological* content and only part of their function.[13]

There is, then, more than one legitimate way to look at the overall theology and rhetorical function of these rich chapters. We could, as with the question of the Gospel's theme discussed in chapter 1, focus here on love,[14] or

---

12. Some interpreters would say "Farewell Discourses" (plural), but that issue is largely irrelevant for our concerns. For the literary parallels of "farewell speeches" in biblical and post-biblical literature, see, e.g., Brown, *John* 2:597–601; Kurz, *Farewell Addresses*; Segovia, *Farewell of the World*, 5–20; Talbert, *Reading John*, 207–9; Moloney, *John*, 377–78. Segovia, who focuses on John's artistry and rhetoric, considers only chapters 13–16 as the farewell discourse, which "leads up to the climactic prayer of John 17" (Segovia, *Farewell of the Word*, 288). He considers the discourse to be an "extended commentary" (291, 299, 300) on 13:31–32, which concerns Jesus' glorification. While not at all ignoring mission, Segovia finds the basic purpose of the discourse to be "a sustained exercise in the teaching and consolation of the disciples" (291).

13. Calling these chapters the Farewell Discourse(s), or, similarly, a "testament," is probably too limiting with respect to genre, let alone rhetorical and theological function—which is of course related to genre. George Parsenios (*Departure and Consolation*) finds generic resonances with Greek tragedy, consolation literature, and the literary symposium—a "generic polyphony" that is "no ordinary testament" (152). Among other differences from ordinary testaments, Parsenios argues persuasively, John 13–17 functions not merely to provide a successor, as such discourses generally did, but to tell the disciples that the absent Jesus will in fact be with them after his death in two ways—by the presence of the Paraclete, who is more than a mere successor to Jesus (77–109), and by his words that are to be remembered and kept (111–49). Parsenios cleverly refers to the latter form of presence as "And the *Flesh* became *Words*" (111).

14. Moloney, *Love in the Gospel of John*, 99–133.

on the new covenant,[15] or on the notion of dwelling in God's household.[16] We could consider the focus on peace, suggested by Willard Swartley, interwoven with four themes: the love command, Jesus' departure, the promise of the Spirit, and preparation for living in a hostile world.[17] Warren Carter interprets these chapters as a treatment of the "sacred identity of John's Jesus-believers." He focuses on five dimensions of the disciples' "identity and lifestyle" as "an act of imperial negotiation," of "[d]istance and distinctiveness, much more than accommodation."[18] And Cornelis Bennema rightly draws attention to the significance of mimesis (imitation) in these chapters.[19]

Similarly to Carter and Bennema, but more generally, Rekha Chennattu is also on to something significant, calling chapters 13–17 "discipleship discourses" that focus on community, intimacy, love, covenant-keeping, and sharing in the divine mission enacted in Jesus, with similar obligations and risks. According to Chennattu, John 20–21 actualizes the promissory teaching given in chapters 13–17.[20] If that is the case, and I think it is, then the term "Mission Discourse" is even more appropriate. John Ashton argued, in fact, that the genre of John 13–17 is a mixture of the "testament" form and the "commission" form.[21] Whatever the merits of this generic proposal, Ashton's point stands: John 13–17 is at least as much a text of commissioning as it is a text of consolation. Moreover, Ashton suggests, the discourse that Jesus will give to his disciples combines into one the two commissions

---

15. Chennattu, *Johannine Discipleship as a Covenant Relationship*. See also Schneiders, *Jesus Risen in our Midst*, esp. 99–118; Gorman, *Death of the Messiah*, 43–50.

16. Coloe, *God Dwells with Us*; Coloe, *Dwelling in the Household of God*.

17. Swartley, *Covenant of Peace*, 302.

18. Carter, *John and Empire*, 256–88 (here, 257). The five areas of focus are the disciples as sacred household or temple; their faithfulness, loving service, and greater works; and their being a community of friends. Carter does not ignore mission outside the community (276–78); neither, however, does he stress it.

19. Overview in Bennema, *Mimesis*, 58–62.

20. Chennattu, *Johannine Discipleship*. For a summary of her claim, see 176–79.

21. Ashton, *Understanding the Fourth Gospel*, 341, 418–53. Ashton (418) limits the discourse to chapters 14–17. He points to several examples of testament-plus-commission texts in the Old Testament (1 Kgs 2:1–9; Deut 31; Josh 1:1–9; Hag 2:4–5) as well as *The Testament of Moses*. The most important feature of the commission form (432) is the injunction to do something, often to complete the task of the speaker who is facing death (e.g., Deut 31:23). Other features include encouragement and a promise of divine aid (443). Despite his focus on the commission form, however, Ashton does not recognize the breadth of the commission itself, focusing almost exclusively on the injunction to intra-communal love (431–34), with only a brief mention of 14:12 "(greater works";445) and some attention to the community's Spirit-inspired "prophetic and teaching functions" (452). Moreover, for Ashton the commission form, in combination with the testament form, functions primarily to bring consolation (453).

of Deuteronomy 31, one from YHWH and one from Moses.[22] Even more in line with the thesis being developed here, John Stube argues that while John 13–17 is definitely a farewell speech, its most important function, through actions and words, is "to prepare and move the disciples in their calling, their vocation, their mission" after Jesus' departure. What is that mission? It is "continuing Jesus' mission to the world."[23]

Similarly, but in more depth, Teresa Okure finds John 13–17 to be "Jesus' Commentary on the Missionary Task."[24] For her, these chapters constitute an exposition of the Johannine approach to mission parallel to 4:31–38 (what we have termed the "mini" mission discourse).[25] Its central themes, according to Okure, are humility (slave-like service) in the exercise of mission, the universal scope of the mission, fellowship in mission in spite of the world's hatred, and dependence on Jesus.[26] John 21, for Okure, is the demonstration of this Johannine understanding, parallel to 4:28–30, 39–42.[27]

Okure rightly claims that, in addition to looking ahead to John 20–21, John 13–17—as the Johannine mission discourse—also summons us to look back to the first half of the Gospel.[28] In chapters 1–12 we learn from various narratives something of what it means, concretely, to become or be a disciple of Jesus and to participate in his mission in specific contexts. For example, disciples (or potential disciples):

- hear (e.g., 1:37; 4:42; 5:24–25, 28; 6:45; 8:38, 47; 10:3, 27);

---

22. Ashton, *Understanding the Fourth Gospel*, 431. Ashton is referring specifically to Jesus' words of comfort and exalted claims in 14:1–10, but the point is germane to the interpretation of all of John 13–17.

23. Stube, *Graeco-Roman Rhetorical Reading*, 2, 211; cf. his summary of the book (211–21). Stube (5–34) notes that many interpreters of John 13–17 have overlooked the mission focus of these chapters.

24. Okure, *Johannine Approach*, 196–219.

25. Okure, *Johannine Approach*, 192–96.

26. Okure, *Johannine Approach*, 211–13.

27. Okure, *Johannine Approach*, 192–96. Cf. the position of Chennattu noted above.

28. I am indebted to Marianne Meye Thompson, in a response to one of my Payton Lectures at Fuller Seminary in April 2016, for stressing the importance of using Johannine language and Johannine ways of depicting discipleship, especially in John 1–12, when we speak of Johannine missional spirituality. She also rightly emphasizes the continuity between discipleship in the first half of the Gospel and in the second half. I am also indebted to Professor Thompson for starting the helpful list of disciples' activities in chapters 1–12. Our conversation about participation is certainly enriched and "thickened" by considering the "faith and struggles" (Thompson's words) of Jesus' first disciples.

- see (e.g., 1:39, 45, 50–51; 3:3, 11, 32, 36; 4:29, 45, 48; 6:40; 7:3; 9:7, 15, 25, 37, 39; 11:40, 45; 12:21, 45);[29]

- perceive/contemplate/understand (e.g., 2:23; 4:19; 6:2, 19, 40, 62; 7:3; 10:38, 41–42; 12:16, 40);[30]

- know (e.g., 4:42; 6:69; 7:17; 8:19, 32; 10:4, 14; 10:38);

- remember (e.g., 2:17, 22; 12:16);

- believe (e.g., 1:7, 12; 2:11, 23; 3:15–16, 18, 36; 4:39, 4:41–42, 53; 5:24, 38, 46–47; 6:29, 35, 40, 47, 69; 7:31; 8:31; 9:38; 11:25–27; 12:36)—the verb *pisteuō* ("believe, have faith, be faithful," etc.) occurs ninety-eight times in John, and while some of these are followed by the content of faith ("believe that"), many suggest more than intellectual conviction or even emotional attachment, but active commitment and loyalty;[31]

- follow (e.g., 1:37, 43; 6:2; 8:12; 10:4, 27; 12:26);

- abide/remain (Gk. *menō*—see further below);[32] and

- bear witness/testify (e.g., 1:15, 34; 3:11; 4:39; 12:17; see also below).[33]

It is these last two items, the verb "abide" and the notion of "witness," that especially connect the first half of the Gospel to the second half with respect to the theme of missional discipleship. The connections suggest that

29. This semantic field overlaps to some degree with "perceive/contemplate/understand" noted next.

30. One of the main verbs for this semantic field is *theōreō*, sometimes translated "see." David Rensberger argues that contemplation in John is what we would label "participatory": it is "active rather than passive," for the believer "not only perceives the deeds of God that Jesus does but enters into them as well" ("Spirituality and Christology," 183).

31. See, e.g., Brown, *John* 1:512–13. Carter (*John and Empire*, 264–73) understands the verb as indicating, in part, a contrast between loyalty to Jesus and loyalty to the emperor: "fundamentally incompatible loyalties and lived commitments" (272).

32. The verb *menō* appears forty times in John: twenty-three times in chapters 1–12, three times in chapter 14, eleven times in chapter 15, once in chapter 19, and twice in chapter 21. For discussion, see Brown's appendix in *John* 1:510–12. Its overall significance to the Johannine literature and spirituality is further demonstrated by its twenty-four occurrences in 1 John, as Brown notes.

33. These are, for the most part, commonly recognized activities of the characters/believers in John. See, e.g., Tam, *Apprehension of Jesus* for most of this list. Tam finds a four-stage apprehension of Jesus in the plot of John, from initial encounters (chs. 1–4), which are generally positive; to subsequent encounters (chs. 5–12), which are generally hostile; to deepening encounters (chs. 13–17), which are deeply relational, even emotional, involving Father, Son, and Paraclete; and finally the climactic encounters (chs. 18–21). The telling of these encounters is meant to enable the Gospel's audience to apprehend Jesus well and follow him.

we must keep these two halves of the Gospel together when we think about participation and mission.

Regarding the disciples' abiding, in chapters 1–12, the Greek verb *menō* ("abide," "remain," "continue") is associated with humans in significant ways on several occasions that anticipate the abiding that dominates John 15, discussed later in this chapter (translations of *menō* are underlined):

- In 1:39, two disciples "<u>remained</u> with him [Jesus] that day"; the literal abiding is an example of Johannine double entendre and prefigures a less literal but more significant abiding.

- In 5:38, Jesus testifies against those who do not believe in him that they "do not have his [the Father's] word <u>abiding</u> in" them, a natural corollary to not believing in and therefore not abiding in the Son. Similarly, in 9:41 Jesus tells the disbelieving, spiritually blind Pharisees, "If you were blind, you would not have sin. But now that you say, 'We see,' your sin <u>remains</u>."

- On the other hand, says Jesus in 6:56, "[t]hose who eat my flesh and drink my blood <u>abide</u> in me, and I in them." Whether this mutual abiding is interpreted in terms of Eucharist or belief/loyalty—or both—it signifies the opposite of unbelief and hints at the importance of, and perhaps also the means of, the intimate mutual indwelling of Jesus and disciples that we find in chapter 15.

- In 8:31, Jesus says to those who have believed in him, "If you <u>continue</u> in my word, you are truly my disciples."

- Finally, Jesus describes his mission as "com[ing] as light into the world, so that everyone who believes in me should not <u>remain</u> in the darkness" (12:46), which implies moving into the light—that is, coming to and remaining in Jesus the light.

In light of these texts and John 15, Andrew Brower Latz highlights the role of "abiding" throughout the Gospel, arguing that it is John's preferred and primary way to characterize discipleship.[34]

Regarding the disciples' witness, the first half of the Gospel provides real-life vignettes of bearing witness—for instance, the Samaritan woman (ch. 4) and the man born blind (ch. 9)—that prevent us from turning the lofty spirituality of "mutual indwelling" and "theosis," together with the witness-bearing work of the Spirit, that we will find in John 13–17 into existentially vacuous experiences, or into a spirituality that lacks real-world missional activity. There are already inherent checks against this misguided

---

34. Brower Latz, "A Short Note toward a Theology of Abiding," 161.

direction in chapters 13–17 (not least the nitty-gritty-ness of the foot wash-ing scene), but chapters 1–12 further anchor discipleship in the richly de-picted Johannine characters.[35]

Another way to state this is to say that coming to the earthly Jesus, loyally following him, remaining with him, and bearing witness to him, on the one hand (as narrated in chapters 1–12), and abiding in the crucified and resurrected Christ, being indwelt by the Triune God, and being taught by the Spirit who recalls Jesus and empowers faithfulness in witness, on the other hand (as anticipated in John 13–17), *are not two different realities but two different ways of describing one reality.* Nevertheless, although John portrays (some of) the figures in chapters 1–12 as paradigms of faithful wit-ness, hermeneutically speaking, in many ways readers today are more like the missional Johannine community anticipated in John 13–17 (with Jesus physically absent) than they are like the disciples depicted in John 1–12. Nevertheless, both halves of the Gospel speak to the nature of participatory mission; it is at once this-worldly and spiritual.

A "Mission-Only" Discourse?

We have suggested that John 13–17 looks both back at and ahead to partici-patory missional themes in other sections of the Gospel. But do these chap-ters merit the title "Mission Discourse"? As we have seen, some interpreters have noted the missional concerns of the Farewell Discourse but have not gone so far as to call it the *Mission* Discourse. Is this terminology too nar-row? For instance, what about the words of reassurance that are so typical of farewell discourses before a death? And what about the focus on internal unity and love? Are these subjects "missional"?

Those who argue that there is more to John 13–17 than mission have a legitimate point, especially if mission is understood narrowly as evange-listic activity or even outreach more generally. But the counter-argument, in defense of a wholly missional interpretation of these chapters, is twofold. Accordingly, we will briefly consider two questions.

First, what is the *purpose* of the reassurance and instruction Jesus of-fers in this discourse? Some interpreters would agree with Udo Schnelle, who implies that the life of communal love and harmony Jesus enjoins is

---

35. On the characters throughout the Gospel, and their function of depicting vari-ous kinds of responses to Jesus, see Bennema, *Encountering Jesus.* Not every character in the first half of the Gospel is a model of discipleship and mission (e.g., Nicodemus in ch. 3 and, perhaps, the man at the pool in 5:1–16—see Bennema, *Encountering Jesus*, 185–200), but many are.

primarily a form of survival: "to safeguard [the community's] endangered identity," that is, the disciples' communion with the Father and the Son.[36] This rather common sectarian interpretation does not, however, do justice to the evidence. My proposal is that the greater end of Jesus' words of reassurance and his call for unity is participation in the dangerous mission of God by the power of the Spirit during the period of Jesus' "absence."[37]

Second, should the word "mission" be confined to evangelism or even outreach? Many people naturally understand mission as outreach, and many interpreters of mission in John see it only as verbal witness, or evangelism. But if the mission of the Father and the Son, according to John, is to give abundant life to the world, then the formation of a joy-filled, love-filled, hope-filled, life-filled, unified community is *part of that divine mission*.[38] To be sure, once again, there is a still greater end involved here; the existence of such a community is not the climax of the story, for it is intended to participate in God's mission of bringing love, light, and life to the whole world. Yet there can be no continuation of the mission apart from the existence of such a community. Thus, the existence and growth of the community of disciples is both part of the *divine* mission and part of the *community's* mission. Without a healthy community, external mission endeavors are, in a profound sense, self-contradictory activities.

Such an understanding of mission does not, however, allow the community to remain focused on itself and become a kind of sectarian entity, a "holy huddle," to use once again the colloquial term. Rather, this sense of mission understands the *missio Dei* to be "formational" as well as "missionary," or (better yet) centripetal (spiraling inward) as well as centrifugal (spiraling outward). Thus, part of the mission of the church is to attend to

36. Schnelle, *Theology of the New Testament*, 709. Similarly, Rensberger, "Spirituality and Christology," 178–79. Rensberger is right to stress that abiding in Jesus means a profound relationship, not merely tenacity in the face of danger, but he over-emphasizes the necessity of the community's maintaining its distance from the mainstream without connecting that different existence to mission.

37. I put absence in quotes because, according to chapters 14–16, Jesus is both coming/returning and present, and in chapters 20–21, the exalted, "absent" Jesus remains, in some sense, present. As noted above, George Parsenios (*Departure and Consolation*, 143) argues that a primary function of the "farewell discourses" is to assure the disciples that Jesus will be present with them after his death by means of both the Paraclete and his words. Parsenios refers to the discourse(s) as a "banquet of words"—like an ancient literary symposium (post-dinner conversation)—that "invites Jesus' later disciples into *his* presence, drawing them into the feast of words that Jesus shared with his original followers."

38. For this sort of understanding of mission, see Barram, *Mission and Moral Reflection*. His point in reference to the Pauline letters—that mission includes community formation—applies here as well.

itself even as it attends to the world. The community's own mission is inevitably, and inextricably, both centripetal and centrifugal, internally and externally oriented, each dimension of mission leading to the other in an unending back-and-forth, a missional circle comparable to a hermeneutical circle or spiral.[39]

All of that said, the *primary focus* of the Farewell Discourse is mission in the centrifugal, or outward, sense, and it is in that sense that most people use the term. I propose, therefore, similarly to Chennattu, that *the focus of the Farewell Discourse and, in fact, of the disciples' being the community of the new covenant, is the disciples' centrifugal (externally oriented) mission after Jesus' departure.* Similar is the suggestion of Teresa Okure, who notes the close parallels, sometimes nearly verbatim, between the mission discourses in Matthew 10 and Luke 9 and 10, on the one hand, and the Johannine Farewell (Mission) Discourse, on the other:[40]

---

39. See also Gorman, *Becoming the Gospel*, 18–20. For a classic statement of this dynamic, see Karl Barth, *CD* IV/3.2, 833, cited in Flett, *The Witness of God*, 286. Willard Swartley, writing about care for persons with disabilities but implying a more general perspective, speaks of "God's two hands," or "God's two arms of love: the internal soul of the church and its external witness, both flowing from the same divine compassion" (*Health, Healing and the Church's Mission*, 164).

40. I have constructed this table in large measure from Okure's list of parallels (*The Johannine Approach to Mission*, 196n.11). She implies that the list of parallels is not exhaustive. Okure (196) wonders whether John 13–17 "might not be the Johannine version of the Synoptic missionary charge" in Matthew 10 and Luke 9–10 (196), referring specifically to all of Matthew 10 and to Luke 9:1–6; 10:1–24. The parallels certainly suggest, at the very least, an overlap in concerns. Together with other dimensions of the Farewell Discourse, this overlap becomes part of a compelling case for the primacy of mission in John 13–17. Okure's interpretation (196) of the proximity of the Farewell/Mission Discourse to Jesus' death is that the evangelist "again underlines his position that Jesus alone does and completes the Father's work (17:4)," but that is not the only significance of the literary proximity. It is also the case that the mission of the disciples is to share intimately in the shape of Jesus' own mission, i.e., they will participate in the kind of foot washing (cruciform) activity that is an icon of his death and hence of his mission. The Synoptic Gospels agree with this, as the passion predictions followed by calls to discipleship (taking up one's cross, serving, etc.) make especially clear (Mark 8:31—9:1 par; 9:30–37 par; 10:32–45 par.).

John	Matthew and Luke
Very truly, I tell you, servants are not greater than their master, nor are messengers greater than the one who sent them. (13:16) Remember the word that I said to you, "Servants are not greater than their master." If they persecuted me, they will persecute you; if they kept my word, they will keep yours also. (15:20)	A disciple is not above the teacher, nor a slave above the master; it is enough for the disciple to be like the teacher, and the slave like the master. If they have called the master of the house Beelzebul, how much more will they malign those of his household! (Matt 10:24–25; cf. Luke 6:40)
Very truly, I tell you, whoever receives one whom I send receives me; and whoever receives me receives him who sent me. (13:20; cf. 12:44)	Whoever welcomes you welcomes me, and whoever welcomes me welcomes the one who sent me. (Matt 10:40; cf. Matt 18:5; Mark 9:37; Luke 9:48) Whoever listens to you listens to me (Luke 10:16a)
If the world hates you, be aware that it hated me before it hated you. (15:18) But they will do all these things to you on account of my name, because they do not know him who sent me. (15:21; cf. 1 John 3:13)	[Y]ou will be hated by all because of my name. But the one who endures to the end will be saved. (Matt 10:22; cf. Matt 24:9b; Luke 21:17)
Whoever hates me hates my Father also. (15:23; cf. 5:23)	[W]hoever rejects you rejects me, and whoever rejects me rejects the one who sent me. (Luke 10:16b-c)
They will put you out of the synagogues. Indeed, an hour is coming when those who kill you will think that by doing so they are offering worship to God. (16:2)	Beware of them, for they will hand you over to councils and flog you in their synagogues . . . . (Matt 10:17; cf. Matt 24:9a; Mark 13:9; Luke 21:12, 16) Brother will betray brother to death, and a father his child, and children will rise against parents and have them put to death . . . . (Matt 10:21; cf. Mark 13:12; Luke 21:16)
When the Advocate comes, whom I will send to you from the Father, the Spirit of truth who comes from the Father, he will testify on my behalf. You also are to testify because you have been with me from the beginning. (15:26–27; cf. John 14:26)	When they hand you over, do not worry about how you are to speak or what you are to say; for what you are to say will be given to you at that time; for it is not you who speak, but the Spirit of your Father speaking through you. (Matt 10:19–20; cf. Mark 13:11; Luke 12:11–12; 21:13)

The evidence, then, is quite strong that John 13–17 is rightly considered to be the Mission Discourse. Not only is the centrifugal, outward aspect of mission related to its centripetal counterpart, but the disciples' centrifugal mission is directly related to Jesus' own mission, especially his giving life by dying. This paradoxical mission of life through death is symbolized in the foot washing that begins the second half of the Gospel. In fact, the Farewell Discourse—the Mission Discourse—constitutes an extended commentary on the foot washing. It, and the commentary on it, explain what Jesus' disciples are to do once he is gone. They will wash feet, both internally (as everyone notes) and—as we will see—externally (which interpreters frequently overlook).

The Hour and the Mission: Overview

Throughout the first half of the Gospel, "the hour" has not yet come—until it is announced as present in the final, climactic scene at the end of chapter 12 (12:23, 27). As we move into the second half of John's story, the notice of the hour's arrival (13:1) commences a time of danger for Jesus and for his disciples, both now and in the future. There is need for consolation and assurance. But much more, of course, is going on. The hour indicates the christological and soteriological focus of the Gospel for the next seven chapters. Jesus' impending death is, at root, both the manifestation of love (13:1) for "his own" (a phrase that needs unpacking) and a battle between God and Satan (13:2).[41]

Jesus will love his own "to the end" (13:1; *eis telos*). This phrase is a double entendre that means both "to the finish" and "to the uttermost"; it anticipates Jesus' final words from the cross: "It is finished" (19:30; *Tetelestai*), or "Mission accomplished!" This love is Christ's undying and, quite literally, dying love. As we will see more fully in chapter 6, it is divine enemy-love for a hostile world (however we interpret "his own"), including betrayers and deniers like Judas and Peter. As the manifestation of divine love, even divine enemy-love, Jesus' death is also both the impetus and the paradigm for the disciples' centripetal and centrifugal mission in the world.[42] Moreover, if in Jesus' death God's *love* is revealed, then in Jesus' death *God* is revealed.[43]

41. We will see below why the reference to loving "his own" does not exclude the world. On the battle with Satan, see also 13:27; cf. 12:31; 14:30; 16:11.

42. Cf. Nissen, *New Testament and Mission*, 79: "the Father's sending of the Son serves both as the *model* and [as] the *ground* for the Son's sending of the disciples."

43. Moloney (*Love in the Gospel of John*, 108), concurs: in Jesus' death, "God is made manifest."

Thus, for the disciples to participate missionally in Jesus' loving death is, paradoxically, to participate in God's life.

We turn now to examine and justify these sorts of claims by looking especially at John 13 and 15. These two chapters each highlight the commandment to love one another, which has sometimes been interpreted as sectarian, exclusive, and non-missional (i.e., in the sense of non-centrifugal). In addition to Meeks and Sanders, quoted early in the previous chapter, we could add Robert Gundry, who wrote, "Just as Jesus the Word spoke God's word to the world, then, so Jesus' disciples are to do. But they are not to love the unbelieving world any more than Jesus did. . . . It is enough to love one another and dangerous to love worldlings."[44] A careful reading of John 13 and 15 will challenge such an assessment.

John 13

Foot washing was a regular necessity in ancient cultures, where roads and streets were generally dusty and/or dirty from garbage and even excrement.[45] Offering water for guests to wash their feet was a sign of hospitality, and if a homeowner had slaves, offering a slave's foot washing services would also be a hospitable act. But stooping that low—both physically and metaphorically—was not normal for the host or for anyone with significant status; it was at, or perhaps even beneath, the level of slaves' work.[46] That Jesus the "Teacher and Lord" washed his disciples' feet was an act "unparalleled in ancient literature" and "unrivalled in antiquity."[47] On the other hand, having one's feet washed could also be a way to prepare to encounter the living God.[48] Both dynamics are at work here: the living Lord is being encountered in a completely unexpected and unprecedented way.

---

44. Gundry, *Jesus the Word*, 61.

45. For a thorough discussion, see Thomas, *Footwashing*; for a brief overview, see Keener, *John*, 2:903–4. Biblical texts referring to this act of hospitality include Gen 18:4; 19:2; 24:32; 43:24; Exod 30:19; Judg 19:21; 1 Sam 25:41; Luke 7:44; 1 Tim 5:10.

46. Mary Coloe ("Welcome into the Household of God," drawing on Thomas, *Footwashing*, ch. 3) notes that in the Jewish/scriptural context, servants only provided the basin and guests washed their own feet, while slaves did the actual washing in the Greco-Roman context. For the original disciples and for some audiences, therefore, "Jesus' actions subvert the social order even more than is usually thought" (Skinner, "Virtue in the New Testament," 308n.31).

47. Thomas, *Footwashing*, 53, 84, 114.

48. Brown, *God's Promise* (57) points to Exod 30:17–21, which concerns priestly preparation for their ministry.

Although Jesus may have intended his disciples literally to wash feet,[49] his washing of the disciples' feet is above all a "living parable," or an icon, of both the saving and the ethical and missional significance of his death. Sandra Schneiders calls it a "prophetic action," by which she means it is "divinely inspired, revelatory in content, proleptic in structure, symbolic in form, and pedagogical in intent."[50] At the same time, since Jesus is the "unique self-exegesis" of God, or "der Exeget Gottes"—so Udo Schnelle[51]—then *Jesus* in motion is *God* in motion; the act of foot washing tells us something profound, not only about the self-giving love of Jesus, but also about the gratuitous, hospitable, kenotic love of God. Here we enter "'the heart'" of this gospel, where we find "the extraordinary revelation of God—'God at our feet,'" in the words of Brendan Byrne.[52] This is a counter-intuitive, countercultural God, who is in stark contrast to normal conceptualities of deity, not least in the imperial world of the first or twenty-first century. And this God's people will resemble the God they worship.[53]

Much could be said about this profoundly moving, theologically significant text, which reads like a living commentary on the Christ-poem in Philippians 2.[54] We will focus on its participatory and missional dimensions.

---

49. So Thomas, *Footwashing*. For other proponents of this view and their reasons, see Bennema, *Mimesis*, 92n.38. Bennema argues that "the Johannine concept of mimesis is primarily about faithful expression rather than exact replication, although the latter may be a valid articulation of the former" (93). Many Christian traditions occasionally practice a ritual of foot washing (especially on Holy/Maundy Thursday), and some do so regularly. A few traditions consider foot washing to be an ordinance or sacrament.

50. Schneiders, *Written That You May Believe*, 167 (including n.21).

51. Schnelle, *Theology of the New Testament*, 674; *Das Evangelium*, 43.

52. Byrne, *Life Abounding*, 228.

53. On this, see Carter, *John and Empire*, 273–78, with emphasis on the human (ethical) side.

54. For an interpretation of the properly theological sense of Phil 2:6–11, see my *Inhabiting the Cruciform God*, 9–39. The connection between John 13 and Philippians 2 was noticed already by the church fathers, starting at least in the early third century with Origen. For a sample of writers making the connection, see citations in Elowsky, *John 11–21*, 83 (Leo the Great, Origen), 84 (Cyril of Alexandria), 86 (Severian of Gabala), 87 (Origen, Theophilus of Alexandria, and Augustine). Many of the fathers also note the great theological irony in the fact that the one who, clothed in light, made both the waters and our feet of clay now stoops to wash those feet, clothed in a towel.

The participatory character of the foot washing

The brief narrative of the foot washing itself is followed by two interpretations of it. In the first (13:6–11), Jesus says to Peter, "Unless I wash you, you have no share (*meros*) with me" (13:8). The word "share" is key; being cleansed by Jesus is more than an act of purification; it is also an event of *transformative participation* in his death.[55] At first, this participation is as beneficiary. Jesus, on the Father's behalf, lovingly offers the life-giving cleansing that the foot washing represents, as an icon and parable of the cross. In this sense, the participation in the foot washing, and hence in Jesus' death, is what we might call "non-reciprocal"—we do not contribute to our own cleansing or to the significance of the cross. This is a participation that is characterized by "unequal mutuality," a participation of receptivity.[56] Nonetheless, the beneficiary is not merely a passive recipient of Jesus' love and life but inevitably becomes benefactor—"imitator," in traditional moral terms.[57] "Foot washing is an invitation to the disciples to become participants with Jesus in his 'hour'"[58]—both metaphorically and, for some, literally. Recipients are not to be containers but conduits.

In John 13:15, Jesus claims, "For I have given you an example: that you also should do (*poiēte*) as I have done (*epoiēsa*) to you."[59] This classic text of Johannine "ethics" is normally understood as a summons to imitation, which in fact it is—at one level. We find in the context the explicit language of obligation (v. 14), imitation of an example (*hypodeigma*; v. 15),[60] concrete action

---

55. Brown (*John*, 2:548), among others, translates this as "you will have no heritage with me." He sees it as an allusion to the promise to Israel of a heritage of the land (Num 18:20; Deut 12:12; 14:27) that later became understood as eschatological reward (2:564–65). Although there is clearly an eschatological dimension to the disciples' sharing in Jesus in John 13–17 and elsewhere, that dimension does not seem prominent here. The present tense of the verb "have" (which Brown acknowledges—2:552) should therefore not be given a (distant) future sense. The disciples' future sharing is imminent, just like Jesus' death. For a reading closer to the one offered here, see, e.g., Lincoln, *John*, 368–69; Moloney, *John*, 375.

56. I owe this important point and the terms "non-reciprocal" and "unequal mutuality" to Marianne Meye Thompson in her response to a lecture at Fuller Seminary in April 2016. We might also use the term "asymmetrical."

57. For a participatory interpretation, see also Moloney, *Love in the Gospel of John*, 106, who refers as well to Barrett, *John*, 441.

58. Coloe, "Welcome into the Household of God," 409.

59. The Greek verbs actually appear here out of sequence because most translations alter the order of the Greek clauses.

60. See Culpepper, "The Johannine Hypodeigma"; the term was used in Hellenistic circles for an exemplary death.

(vv. 14, 17), and the promise of divine favor (v. 17), as well as the implicit language of obedience and servant activity. The verse is about *doing*.

But for Jesus in John, such activity requires more than obedience to, or imitation of, a person external to the disciple(s), even if the "more" that is required is not explicitly named here. The key is in the simple verb "do" (*poieō* in all its forms), which, not surprisingly, occurs frequently in John's Gospel, and four times here in 13:12–17. Later in the Mission Discourse we learn from Jesus two important things about "doing." First, the disciples' works will both mimic and exceed those of Jesus: "Very truly, I tell you, the one who believes in me will also do (*poiēsei*) the works that I do (*poiō*) and, in fact, will do (*poiēsei*) greater works than these, because I am going to the Father" (14:12). Second, the disciples will be unable to do anything—including the imitation of Jesus as their servant-example—apart from Jesus, and specifically apart from their mutual indwelling with him:

> ³You have already been cleansed by the word that I have spoken to you. ⁴Abide in me as I abide in you. <u>Just as the branch cannot bear fruit by itself unless it abides in the vine, neither can you unless you abide in me.</u> ⁵I am the vine, you are the branches. Those who abide in me and I in them bear much fruit, because <u>apart from me you can do (*poiein*) nothing</u>. . . . ⁷If you abide in me, and my words abide in you, ask for whatever you wish, and it will be done for you. ⁸My Father is glorified by this, that you bear much fruit and become my disciples. (John 15:3–5, 7–8)

We will consider chapter 15 in more detail later, but for now we note that we find the disciples' activity, or mission, expressed in the metaphor of bearing fruit, grounded thoroughly in a spirituality of indwelling—indeed a spirituality of *mutual* indwelling or abiding. The impossibility of "doing" apart from mutual indwelling could hardly be voiced more strongly or clearly: "apart from me you can do (*poiein*) nothing" (v. 5).[61] (It should be noted that the corollary of this claim is that those who *abide* will *do*.) The imitation Jesus requires in chapter 13 is, implicitly, made a function of the mutual indwelling described in chapter 15. This is because "[t]he believer is united to Jesus, and Jesus to the believer, so that the latter is given a new identity, that proper to the reality of Jesus as Son. The mutual indwelling formula says that the *two* become *one* without ceasing to be *two*."[62] Thus the *doing* is actually *participating*.

---

61. This truth is reinforced by the word in 15:7 about the granting of prayer requests (which spring from dependence) as "that which will happen (*genēsetai*) to you" (NRSV "will be done for you").

62. Rossé, *Spirituality of Communion*, 51.

Moreover, the words "cleansed" (*katharoi*) in 15:3 and "disciples" (*mathētai*) in 15:8 connect chapter 15 back to chapter 13 more directly, where "cleansed" (*katharos* or *katharoi*) occurs three times in 13:10–11 and "disciples" (*mathētōn*) in 13:5. The vine-and-branches metaphor of chapter 15 works off the play-on-words expressed by the word-group *kath*-, which can mean either "prune" or "cleanse." Jesus pronounces the disciples to be those who have been cleansed (13:10–11) and pruned (15:2–3) by his word, which in chapter 15 seems to indicate the initial and ongoing formation (and reformation) of disciples as branches of Christ-the-vine on a mission: to bear fruit. The verbs "cleansing" and "pruning" each indicate a reality of participation and transformation for action. Disciples are those who exist in a relationship of mutual indwelling with Christ in order to *do* something. That something has already been spelled out, at least in part, by chapter 13's commandment to imitate Jesus in servant-love.

Thus, we should not see the foot-washing scene simply as a symbolic call to self-giving, to sacrificial love—though it is that. It also "serves to draw the disciples into Jesus' coming glorification [on the cross] as an *incorporating act*,"[63] as Mark Matson puts it. It is more like a sacrament, an invitation to *participate* in Jesus' death, both as beneficiaries and as benefactors. And if Jesus' death is the missional manifestation of God's love for the world (3:16), then to participate in Jesus' death is to participate in God's love, and in so doing to be transformed into that love—to take on the divine DNA. And what an odd set of genes the disciples receive from this God: "a contestive alternative to imperial practices"[64]—and to all notions of God and of participating in God (including theosis) as self-aggrandizing power. David Rensberger rightly refers to the foot washing as Jesus' act of "downward mobility," in continuity with his incarnation,[65] but he also rightly adds that the "climactic deed of God that Jesus performs is the *most Godlike* of all acts, the giving of life, which he does by means of his own death" (symbolized in the foot washing), revealing the counterintuitive glory of God.[66] Participation in this counterintuitive divine glory is theosis—but it is *cruciform* theosis. Indeed, it is cruciform *missional* theosis.

---

63. Matson, "To Serve as Slave," 130 (emphasis added).

64. Carter, *John and Empire*, 273.

65. Rensberger, "Spirituality and Christology," 182–83.

66. Rensberger, "Spirituality and Christology," 183 (emphasis added). See also, e.g., Bauckham, *Gospel of Glory*, 73–74.

The missional scope of the foot washing

We turn now from the *character* of the foot washing to its *scope*. Jesus' foot washing is often thought to be community-oriented and not at all outwardly directed—that is, not "missionary" in nature.[67] The phrase "Having loved his own who were in the world (*tous idious tous en tō kosmō*)" in 13:1 is often interpreted in an exclusive way as a reference to Jesus' disciples who are "in the world" (17:11). This view could reinforce the "sectarian" interpretation of the Gospel. Some have even suggested that God loved the world, but Jesus only loved his own disciples.[68] But—apart from the theological absurdity of that sentiment for John (and I trust for us!)[69]—the echo of 1:10–11 in 13:1 should at least give us pause about this exclusive interpretation:

> He was in the world (*en tō kosmō*), and the world (*ho kosmos*) came into being through him; yet the world (*ho kosmos*) did not know him. (1:10)

> He came to what was his own (*ta idia*), and his own people (*hoi idioi*) did not accept him. (1:11)

> Having loved his own who were in the world (*tous idious tous en tō kosmō*), he loved them to the end. (13:1) [70]

That Jesus washes the feet of Peter and of Judas, whom Jesus knows will betray him (13:10–11, 18–19, 21–26), implies that this reconsideration of the exclusive interpretation is appropriate.[71]

The second interpretation of the foot washing (13:12–20) directly challenges the exclusive interpretation. The second interpretation, like the first (see 13:6), begins with a question, this time from Jesus: "Do you know what I have done to you?" It suggests that the full meaning of the act is not self-evident, inviting both the original and subsequent audiences to pay

67. For instance, the Scripture index to Stanley Skreslet's fine book *Picturing Christian Witness*, on images of mission in the New Testament, unfortunately has no references to John 13. Cf. Lee (*Hallowed in Truth and Love*, 153): "this is not a text about mission but about relations within the community of faith."

68. E.g., Gundry, *Jesus the Word*, 58–59.

69. If, throughout the Gospel, Jesus is the Father's sent one doing the works of his Father-Sender, he must certainly be engaged in loving the world that God loves.

70. In his *Commentary of the Gospel of John* 9, Cyril of Alexandria interprets Jesus' love for his own as his love for (all of) humanity rather than concern for angels, connecting this text to Heb 2:16 (citation in Elowsky, *John 11–21*, 84).

71. Bennema (*Mimesis*, 121–23) argues for a wide scope for the recipients of foot washing/love because Jesus washed the feet of Judas, already identified in the Gospel as an outsider, and because the disciples' love is "centrifugal" and salvific as an extension of the divine love. On Judas and Peter, see also chapter 6 below.

careful attention. On the surface, Jesus' explanation looks like an admonition merely to intra-community imitation of his service: "Wash one another's feet" (13:14). In fact, however, the scope is much wider. The structure, movement, and content of 13:14–20 support this interpretation.

In vv. 14–15, Jesus twice offers himself as an example and issues a parallel imperative:

> [14]Therefore, since I, the Lord (*kyrios*) and Teacher, have washed your feet, you also ought to wash one another's (*allēlōn*) feet. [15] For I have given you an example (*hypodeigma*): that you also should do (*poiēte*) as I have done (*epoiēsa*) to you. (13:14–15; my trans.)[72]

Although the first imperative (v. 14) is internally focused (*allēlōn* = "one another"), when its substance is repeated in v. 15, the reference to "one another" disappears and a much more general "do as I have done" appears. Although one might interpret this as synonymous parallelism without any change in focus or scope, v. 16 suggests otherwise:

> Amen, amen, I tell you, no slave (*doulos*) is greater than his or her master (*kyriou*), nor is a sent one (*apostolos*) greater than the one who sent (*pempsantos*) that person. (13:16; my trans.)

This verse consists of two sayings, which we may call the *doulos*-proverb (v. 16a) and the *apostolos*-proverb (v. 16b). The images are of slave and of messenger, or agent. The first one (v. 16a) corresponds nicely with v. 14, reinforcing the image of Jesus as the disciples' Lord.[73] The second aphorism (v. 16b), however, shifts the cultural reference to that of sender and sent one.[74] It demonstrates that the disciples "are more than just followers." Together the two images suggest that the disciples relate to Jesus both as their Lord and as their Sender, and they have similar but not synonymous responsibilities corresponding to the two relationships. Although the word *apostolos* appears only here in John, it is clear that in this Gospel

72. I have used my own translation of 13:14–16, especially to maintain the singular sense of both sender and sent one in the gnomic saying of v. 16, where the NRSV has pluralized the singular nouns: "I tell you, servants are not greater than their master, nor are messengers greater than the one who sent them."

73. This text is not so much a *prescription* as it is a *description* of relationships: "Jesus takes a slave role toward his disciples as a reflection of his own relationship with God, and . . . as a result the disciples should be prepared to take that same role with respect to one another as a reflection of their own inclusion 'in Christ'" (Matson, "To Serve as Slave," 126).

74. The verbs *apostellō* (twenty-eight times), related to *apostolos*, and *pempō* (thirty-two times) are basically synonymous in John.

the disciples are apostles of Jesus the Apostle—sent ones of the Sent One (see especially 17:18; 20:21).[75]

If the *doulos-*, or slave-, proverb in v. 16a echoes and corresponds to v. 14, then it is highly likely that the *apostolos-*, or emissary-, proverb in v. 16b corresponds to the more generic v. 15. The disciples, after all, do not need to be "sent" anywhere in order to wash one another's feet. The *apostolos-*proverb implies an imperative of metaphorical foot washing in the disciples' role of being *sent ones*: washing the feet of the world in the name of Jesus. That is, *the call to foot washing is also directed outside the community of disciples.*[76] The disciples have two imperatives, one internal and one external, that are also in a profound sense a single mandate: Jesus-like foot washing, that is, cruciform service; indeed, cruciform participation.[77]

We can set out this reading of vv. 14–16 in the form of a table (my translation):

Verse	Jesus' example	Disciples' imperative	Verse	Jesus-disciples relationship as rationale for the imperative
14	Therefore, since I, the Lord and Teacher, have washed your feet	you also ought to wash one another's feet	16a	no slave (*doulos*) is greater than his or her master (*kyriou*)
15	For I have given you an example	that you also should do as I have done to you	16b	nor is a sent one (*apostolos*) greater than the one who sent (*pempsantos*) that person

This interpretation is validated by several additional aspects of the passage, but especially by the presence of v. 20, which echoes the second proverb of v. 16 and is decidedly centrifugal, that is, outward-oriented:

75. Stube, *Graeco-Roman Rhetorical Reading*, 90. Stube cites halakhic evidence that the Jewish principle of agency included the provision that "an agent can appoint an agent." In this case, that is, Jesus the Sent One (implicitly the *Apostolos*) sends others (each of whom is *apostolos*).

76. The presence of "for" (*gar*) in v. 15 suggests that vv. 14 and 15 are closely connected. It does not, however, mean that they refer to precisely the same activity, intra-communal foot washing. Rather, the intra-communal foot washing of v. 14 is grounded in the more generic apostolic mandate of v. 15.

77. It is critical both to note the two forms of service and to keep them united as manifestations of one essential practice and one exemplar, Jesus.

> "[W]hoever receives one whom I send (*pempsō*) receives (*lambanei*) me; and whoever receives (*ho lambanōn*) me receives (*lambanei*) him who sent (*ton pempsanta*) me." (13:20)

This is a Synoptic-like saying found in the Matthean mission discourse. "Whoever welcomes you welcomes me, and whoever welcomes me welcomes the one who sent me," says Jesus (Matt 10:40).[78] John 13:20, like Matt 10:40 and similar texts, offers us a concise statement of the chain of sending (Father → Son → disciples) found in 4:34–38 and the corollary chain of reception (disciples → Son → Father),[79] both aspects of the notion of agency, that will appear several times later in the Gospel. Moreover, another Matthean missional text parallels the first proverb in v. 16: "A disciple is not above the teacher, nor a slave above the master" (Matt 10:24; cf. Luke 6:40). That is, this is not only a chain of *sending* but a chain of *similarity*.[80]

Indeed, the increasingly explicit and emphatic missional tone of 13:15–20, as the passage moves toward its climax in v. 20, suggests that the ultimate emphasis of the foot washing image is not internal but external. This is not to underestimate the value of internal loving service, but to set it in its proper context, as 13:31–35 does explicitly:

> [34]I give you a new commandment, that you love one another. Just as I have loved you, you also should love one another. [35]By this everyone (*pantes*, "all") will know that you are my disciples, if you have love for one another.

The preeminent commandment given to Jesus' disciples is mutual, cruciform love. Since this intra-community love is actually a participation in the divine love shared between the Father and the Son (15:9–10; 17:26), it is inherently missional. "As the community formed by the distinctive love of Jesus, from now on they [the disciples] must become the sign of God's liberation and salvation in the world."[81] A hidden assumption in 13:35 is that the community of mutually loving disciples will also be a community of hospitality, a community of gathering others into its presence.[82] Otherwise, no one would be able to witness the disciples' intra-community love. Because the intra-divine (i.e., intra-trinitarian) love for the world is precisely

78. See also Matt 18:5; Mark 9:37; Luke 9:48; 10:16; John 12:44.

79. The chain of sending is found, though less succinctly, in 4:34–38 (as noted in ch. 2), in 12:44, and perhaps implicitly in 9:4.

80. Cf. the related text in 15:20, which promises that this will include similarity in mistreatment.

81. Spohn, *Go and Do Likewise*, 52.

82. One of the most significant marks of what is known as the "new monasticism" is hospitality. See, e.g., Wilson-Hartgrove, *Strangers at My Door*.

the love that has brought the community of disciples into being, that same shared, participatory love within the community will, eventually, spill over into the greater world. But even before it does so, it can *already* be characterized as missional love simply by virtue of its participation in the divine love. And that is communal theosis.

Yet spill it will. The disciples' love is witness-bearing; it is *missional* communal theosis. It is how "everyone"—literally "all" (*pantes*)—will come to know that the disciples are disciples of Jesus (13:35; cf. 17:21–23). This could sound like a rather minimalist goal, conveying knowledge of identity. But far more is at stake. The disciples' mutual love is necessary for an effective witness that ultimately points not to themselves, but to Jesus the Son and to God the Father, that is, to the One whose own love is the means and mode of the world's salvation (cf. 17:20–26). The goal is for others to enter the eternal life that consists, not in knowing facts, but in knowing the Father and the Son (17:3).

Implicitly, then, love for "one another" is not meant to *exclude* love of others but to *overflow to* others and even to be deliberately directed at others outside the community; otherwise the communal life and love of the disciples would not bear witness to the Gospel's central claim that God loves the *world* and wants *all* to be drawn into that love. Thus, the disciples' foot washing is a *centripetal* activity that becomes *centrifugal* as they exist as a hospitable community of cruciform love and as they naturally move out from their community as cruciform apostles and witnesses. "Very truly, I tell you, the one who believes in me will also do (*poiēsei*) the works that I do (*poiō*) and, in fact, will do (*poiēsei*) greater works than these, because I am going to the Father" (14:12; cf. the verbs in 13:15, noted above).[83]

To summarize this examination of chapter 13: the disciples' foot washing is not merely an act of imitation but one of participation, and it is not merely internal but also external in scope. Foot washing is missional theosis, and specifically both *cruciform* and *communal* missional theosis, part of the process of becoming more like Jesus the Sent One and therefore more like the Sending Father, who *is* love and who *practices* love.[84]

Christian mission, then, is both centripetal and centrifugal. It means "abide and go": abide in the community, and go into the world. This is a seamless garment of participation in a love that sweeps us into the life of God, who loves the world—and does so through disciples of Jesus, who

83. For another argument for the centrifugal character of centripetal love in John, see Bennema, *Mimesis*, 120–23, though his claims find centrifugal love to be more implicit than explicit.

84. For this theme in Paul, see my "Paul's Corporate, Cruciform, Missional Theosis in Second Corinthians" and, more generally, my *Becoming the Gospel*.

are sent into that world just as the Son was sent. Cornelis Bennema argues appropriately that the result for disciples (then or now) is not mindless cloning but creative re-articulation.[85] This means "a tangible love act that corresponds to the original but need not be identical to it."[86] Where disciples imaginatively but faithfully wash feet in Jesus' name, the Son, the Father, and the Spirit are present and active.[87]

John 15

The teaching of Jesus presented in John 15, with its "allegorical parable" of the vine, is grounded in similar Old Testament images of God's people as God's vine.[88] This parable of "the true vine" (Jesus) and its branches is "both christocentric and ecclesiocentric."[89] As the chapter progresses, Richard Hays observes, "the focus of attention shifts from Jesus as the true Vine to the role of the *disciples*," and we find "the language of *missio*."[90] The parable provides for John the heart of Christian spirituality and the basis of Christian mission: communion with Jesus, a mutual indwelling (15:4). Spirituality and mission are not only related; they are inseparable: the verb "abide" or "remain" (Gk. *menein*) appears *eleven* times in 15:1–16, and the verbal phrase "bear fruit" (*karpon pherein*) occurs *eight* times.[91]

85. Bennema, *Mimesis*, 91–105. "John presents mimesis as a cognitive and creative process that is concerned with both the interpretation of the original act and the formulation of a corresponding mimetic act" (194, summarizing his earlier argument). At the same time, says Bennema, there is enough similarity between the original act and the imitation that "mimesis involves cloning *and* creative articulation" (105).

86. Bennema, *Mimesis*, 111.

87. William Spohn (*Go and Do Likewise*, 52) claims that John 13 is not about washing feet every Sunday; rather, "Jesus tells Christians to use their imaginations, to think analogically." (Nonetheless, both Spohn [cf. 52–54] and I support the practice of literal foot washing.) Spohn refers to this analogical thinking as "spotting the rhyme" (54–55, 63, 152), the similarities between Jesus' context and ours that provoke appropriate imaginative, faithful action.

88. "Allegorical parable" is Raymond Brown's term for the more technical term *mashal* (*John* 2:660, 668–69). Among the Old Testament references, see esp. Ps 80:8–16; Isa 5:1–7; 27:2–6; Jer 2:21; 5:10; 6:9; 8:13; 12:10–11; Ezek 15; 17:5–10 (cf. 17:23); 19:10–14; Hos 10:1; 14:7. Manning (*Echoes of a Prophet*, 139–41) shows the thematic parallels between these texts, especially those from Ezekiel, and John 15. For a helpful study of relevant biblical and Second Temple texts, as well as John 15 itself, see Munene, *Communal Holiness*.

89. Manning, *Echoes of a Prophet*, 147.

90. Hays, *Echoes*, 337.

91. The word "fruit" appears one additional time, associated with the verb *menein* (15:16). Before chapter 15 the verb *menein* has already appeared twenty-six times in

We will once again describe this dynamic missional spirituality not only as missional theosis but also, more simply yet paradoxically, as "abide and go"—or, colloquially, "stay put and get going." Chapter 15 thus has much in common with chapter 13.

But neither spirituality nor mission can be separated from consequences—both positive and negative. There will be fruit, but there will also be opposition (15:18 through 16:3 or 4a). Thus the sense of chapter 15 continues into chapter 16, with warnings about being thrown out of synagogues and even martyrdom, making the promise of hatred and persecution in 15:18–25 specific.[92] Thus, Frank Moloney titles 15:1—16:3 "To Abide, to Love, and to be Hated."[93]

The chief questions that normally arise in considering this text are What does "abide" mean? and What does "bear fruit" mean?"

Abiding and bearing fruit in brief

Part of what Jesus says in chapter 15 is as follows:

> [4]Abide in me as I abide in you. Just as the branch cannot bear fruit by itself unless it abides in the vine, neither can you unless you abide in me. [5]I am the vine, you are the branches. Those who abide in me and I in them bear much fruit, because apart from me you can do (*poiein*) nothing. . . . [7]If you abide in me, and my words abide in you, ask for whatever you wish, and it will be done for you. [8]My Father is glorified by this, that you bear much fruit and become my disciples (*mathētai*). [9]As the Father has loved me, so I have loved you; abide in my love. [10]If you keep my commandments, you will abide in my love, just as I have kept my Father's commandments and abide in his love. (John 15:4–5, 7–10)

John (out of forty total occurrences), most significantly for our purposes in 6:56 (of eating and drinking Jesus' flesh and blood) and 14:10, 17, 25 (of the "dwelling" of Father, Spirit, and Son), along with the cognate verb *monē* in 14:2 (many dwelling places in the Father's house) and 14:23 (the Father and Son making their dwelling with those who love and obey Jesus). On *menein* and on the vine imagery, see the perceptive work of Lee, *Flesh and Glory*, though she does not appear to perceive the missional character of the image. (For example, John 15:16 is absent from the book's Scripture index.)

92. Whatever precise historical situation these verses reflect, they are consonant in spirit with the Synoptics and with the experience of many of the early churches narrated in the rest of the New Testament.

93. Moloney, *John*, 416–18. The three sections correspond to 15:1–11, 15:12–17, and 15:18–16:3.

Abiding in Jesus—remaining in union with the crucified and resurrected Messiah—is here presented as the *modus vivendi*, or *modus operandi*, of believers, a relationship of mutual indwelling, or reciprocal residence, not unlike that found in Paul.[94] Although this relationship is personal and individual, for each "branch" must abide and bear fruit (e.g., vv. 2, parts of 4–5, 15), it is not private. The majority of the pronouns and verbs referring to the branches in John 15 are plural: "All of you, together, must abide in me and bear fruit."

At the very least, "abide" means maintaining an intimate, permanent, covenantal relationship with Jesus (15:4–7), as part of the community of disciples (which make up Jesus the vine). This includes remaining attuned to Jesus' words and love (15:7, 9–10).[95] Munene and Kanagaraj rightly stress that this relationship is both "vertical" and "horizontal."[96] The word-family "abide" or "dwell" connotes being in the presence of God in the intimacy of the divine household and within the pre-existing, eternal mutual indwelling of the Father and Son by means of the Spirit.[97] Kanagaraj suggests that this "mysticism" of abiding in Jesus is a polemic against Jewish Merkabah ("chariot") mysticism: the goal of Merkabah mysticism's heavenly trips to the divine throne—union with God—is actually accomplished here on earth by abiding in Jesus.[98] Furthermore, the kingly glory of God to which such mysticism aspires is, for John, found in Christ crucified. The result, argues Kanagaraj, is a "cross-mysticism"—what we have termed (communal) cruciform theosis.[99]

94. The term *modus vivendi* comes from Caragounis, "'Abide in Me,'" 263. There have been various hypotheses about the origin of this spirituality of mutual indwelling. Kanagaraj (*Mysticism*, 271–72) offers the reminder that the themes of God and/or Wisdom indwelling and being indwelt by the people of God have scriptural roots.

95. On abiding as intimacy as well as obedience, see Rabens, "Johannine Perspectives."

96. Munene, *Communal Holiness*, 102; see also 87–88, 108–9, 121, 123–25; Kanagaraj, "Mysticism," 264–81, esp. 264.

97. See, e.g., Coloe, *Dwelling in the Household of God*, esp. 145–66. Caragounis ("'Abide in Me,'" 263) rightly notes that this relationship is possible only by the Paraclete, even if the Paraclete is not specifically mentioned here.

98. Kanagaraj, "Mysticism."

99. Kanagaraj, "Mysticism," 184–310. It is unfortunate that Kanagaraj claims that John has no room for deification (e.g., 311), when he rightly argues that "the revelation of God's character is very much bound with Jesus' death on the cross" (310). That is, by implication, John advocates a *cruciform* deification that obtains by abiding in Jesus and thus in the Father. Munene, on the other hand, does not hesitate to use the word theosis as the result of mutual indwelling (*Communal Holiness*, 208). Munene also implicitly sees theosis as missional. He finds missional hospitality to the world in John generally and John 15 in particular (e.g., *Communal Holiness*, 86–87, 99–100, 179–86, 214–16),

"Abiding" is also a relationship of profound dependence: "Apart from me you can do *nothing*" (15:5; emphasis added).[100] Concretely, this abiding is effected and nurtured by obedience: keeping Jesus' word (14:21–24), allowing his words to abide within (15:7). "To be a disciple abiding in the love of Jesus means to 'do' something."[101] Abiding in Jesus is further sustained by consuming Jesus' flesh and blood—whether that is interpreted sacramentally or non-sacramentally: "Those who eat my flesh and drink my blood abide in me, and I in them" (6:56).[102] In either case, the words of Richard Bauckham capture the participatory character of this "consuming": "actual participation in Jesus' own life, made available through his death" and thereby, since Jesus lives "out of the eternal divine life of his Father [6:57]," becoming "alive with this same divine life."[103] The language of eating Jesus' flesh and drinking his blood represents believing, not only in Jesus as the incarnate one, but also in Jesus as the crucified one.

Exegetical arguments about "bearing fruit" abound. Does it refer to mutual love among the disciples, to Christian virtue, to winning converts (see 4:36)[104]—or to all of these? Or to something different? Lesslie Newbigin stated that it is "simply the life of Jesus being made visible in the midst of the life of the world."[105] Nuancing this sort of interpretation, we might consider John 15 as Jesus' exposition of the claims made in 14:12–14:

---

as disciples "are to live out the mutual love of the Trinity to which they have been invited" (184).

100. Brown (*John* 1:510–12) has a helpful appendix on *menein* in John and 1 John. For a survey of commentary treatments of the theme and an essay on its importance, see Brower Latz, "A Short Note toward a Theology of Abiding."

101. Moloney, *John*, 421.

102. A non-sacramental reading—sometimes called a spiritual, figurative, metaphorical, or christological interpretation—of this text generally understands eating and drinking as a metaphor for faith in the sense of a total embrace of Jesus and of his humanity and/or his death—an incarnation- and cross-mysticism, so to speak. It implies allegiance to, intimacy with, and participation in Jesus. These implications are also aspects of a sacramental (eucharistic) reading. There are variations on these two major approaches to the passage, including some that find both eucharistic and non-eucharistic dimensions of the passage, often with one being primary and the other secondary. Consult the commentaries for the discussion.

103. Bauckham, *Gospel of Glory*, 102–3. Bauckham sees eucharistic language here being used in non-eucharistic ways to signify (participatory) belief in Jesus as the crucified one as well as the incarnate one.

104. Stube (*Graeco-Roman Rhetorical Reading*, 137–70) has made a strong case for 15:1—16:15 being about "A Mission of Love," with fruit being converts, in light of 4:36 and 12:24 (see esp. 141). As will become clear, I see converts more as the fruit of the fruit—(part of) the result of continuing the works of Jesus.

105. Newbigin, *The Light has Come*, 197.

> [12]Very truly, I tell you, the one who believes in me will also do the works that I do and, in fact, will do greater works than these, because I am going to the Father. [13]I will do whatever you ask in my name, so that the Father may be glorified in the Son. [14]If in my name you ask me for anything, I will do it. (14:12–14; NRSV alt.)

From this perspective, the "fruit" of chapter 15 is the ongoing missional presence and activity of Jesus—his works—in his disciples. This will of course mean that chapter 15 is a sort of continuation of, or perhaps commentary on, chapter 13, where the fundamental "work" of Jesus—self-giving, life-giving love for the salvation of others—is portrayed.

John 14:12–14 makes three essential claims:

1. believers will do greater works than Jesus;

2. they will do so by asking Jesus to do things appropriate to his name, or identity, that glorify God; and

3. it is Jesus who will actually do the doing.

This is missional participation, or missional theosis.[106] The "greater" works cannot possibly be "better" works than those of the Son, for if they are done in his name, if they are participatory acts, they will correlate with his own person and work. Thus, they will be analogous to the life-giving signs of Jesus' earthly ministry.[107] Moreover, who can outdo the Son of the Father? Indeed, in some sense the works will be "lesser," for (as Harold Attridge has implicitly reminded us[108]) disciples will not normally raise the dead—or even multiply loaves. It is probably best, with Thompson and most interpreters, to understand "greater" as greater *in scope*, more expansive.[109]

It is implied in John 14 that somehow Jesus will not do these works from a distance, but in the disciples' presence, even though he is leaving. How? He will come to the disciples (14:18, 28), which means also that the Father and Son will both come and make their home with them (14:23, using the noun *monēn*, related to the verb *menein* that populates chapter 15). This,

106. Bennema's insightful notion of mimesis via relational empowering in John 15 (*Mimesis*, 171–77) is perceptive but may, however, underestimate the *participatory* emphasis here.

107. So also Carter, *John and Empire*, 277–78. "The emphasis is on continuity with his revelatory, life-giving work" (277), which is in turn "often at odds with imperial ways" and therefore "difficult and dangerous" (278).

108. In Attridge, Carter, and van der Watt, "Quaestiones disputatae: Are John's Ethics Apolitical?" 485.

109. Thompson (*John*, 312n.70) points to BDAG's (Danker, *Lexicon*) lexical interpretation (1a) of *megas* ("great"; cf. *meizona*, "greater" in 14:12): "of any extension in space in all directions."

in turn, also means the sending and coming of the Spirit (14:26). It is difficult to resist a trinitarian conclusion, a trinitarian missional spirituality.

John 15 elaborates on this trinitarian missional spirituality with the image of the vine. To "abide" or "remain" in the vine is necessary to bear fruit—to do the greater works, to participate in, and perpetuate, the mission of Jesus. This can hardly mean staying put physically and simply loving one's fellow disciples, even though such love is the centripetal *starting place* for centrifugal mission. Thus, a critical word in chapter 15 is "go," or "depart" (*hypagēte*)—"go and bear fruit":

> You did not choose me but I chose you. And I appointed you to
> go [depart] and bear fruit, fruit that will last, so that the Father
> will give you whatever you ask him in my name. (John 15:6)

In the words of Richard Hays: "The charge to go and bear fruit . . . is the language of *mission*."[110] The sent ones of the Sent One will point people to him and his Father, not only with words, but also with Spirit-empowered deeds. To participate in the divine love embodied on the cross is to participate in the drawing of all people to the one lifted up on the cross: "'And I, when I am lifted up from the earth, will draw all people to myself'" (12:32). If that is love, and love's purpose, then sharing in that love will be a natural and inseparable witness to both the Love and the Lover.

The images of abiding and departing to bear fruit combined: the mobile, creeping vine

Having proposed brief answers to the separate questions about the meaning of "abide" and "bear fruit," we may now return to the vine image to tease out somewhat more fully the combining of these two verbal images in the one metaphor of the vine.

We find a creative and significant paradoxical tension within the text between the main verb, "abide," on the one hand, and the verbs "do" (*poiein*; v. 4) and especially "go," or "depart" (*hypagēte*; v. 16), on the other. "Abiding" has to do with resting, staying put; it connotes, or could connote, spiritual ease or even apathy. A vine and its branches can certainly bear fruit by staying put. The verbs "do" and "depart," however, have to do with acting and moving. Although healthy vines and branches naturally grow and bear fruit, they do not naturally move from place to place. The disciples, however, have been appointed to go, to depart (15:16). They constitute, in other words, a *mobile* vine, a community of centripetally oriented love that shares that love

110. Hays, *Echoes*, 337.

centrifugally as they move out from themselves, all the while abiding in the vine, the very source of their life, love, and power to do.

Perhaps the image of a "creeping vine" might capture the missional dimension of vine-ness here, though I suspect that what Jesus in John has in mind is still more peripatetic. Richard Hays contends that the hope of John 3:16, expressing God's saving love for a rebellious world and enacted in the disciples' mission, "is precisely the hope foreshadowed" in Ps 80:11 (LXX 79:11) "It [God's vine] sent out its branches to the sea, and its shoots to the River."[111] The disciples comprise, in other words, a vine on the move, a *Spirit-driven* vine, a community of internally oriented love that shares that love externally as they move out from themselves, all the while abiding in the vine, the very source of their life, love, and power to do.

In John 15, then, we have perhaps *the most potent symbiosis of spirituality and mission in the New Testament.* This chapter, rooted in chapters 13–14 and further developed in the rest of chapter 16 through the end of chapter 17, is the quintessence of a participatory missiology. As Jesus "departs" for his Father at the conclusion of his mission, so also he tells the disciples, using the same verb (*hypagein*[112]), to "depart" (15:16) and begin their mission— paradoxically by abiding in the absent-but-present Jesus, the vine.[113] It is in the Christ-empowered missional activity of bearing fruit that God is glorified, according to 15:8, which is why Augustine connected that verse to Matt 5:16—"In the same way, let your light shine before others, so that they may see your good works and give glory to your Father in heaven."[114]

John 15, then, expresses a robust theology and spirituality of abiding in Jesus, not as a private and vacuous mysticism, not even as a sectarian love-feast, but as a communal mysticism that is, paradoxically, this-worldly and missional—and transformational, both for those engaging in and those benefiting from the missional activity.[115] It is precisely centrifugal, outward-oriented, because it is shaped by Jesus' own words and deeds of love. "Abide in me" (15:4) means "let my words abide in you" (cf. 15:7) and "abide in my love" (15:9), which means keeping Jesus' commandments

---

111. Hays, *Echoes*, 339–40.

112. The verb is used of or about Jesus' imminent departure in, e.g., 7:33; 8:14, 21–22; 13:3, 33, 36; 14:4–5, 28; 16:5, 10, 17.

113. "In the Fourth Gospel the idea of death as a final journey has been transformed into that of *the return from a mission*" (Ashton, *Understanding the Fourth Gospel*, 426).

114. Augustine, *Tractates on the Gospel of John* 82.1, cited in Elowsky, *John 11–21*, 170. Augustine also stresses the role of grace in the performance of these good works, citing Eph 2:10.

115. For further explorations of this paradox elsewhere in the New Testament, see Gorman, "This-Worldliness," 151–70.

(15:10). And Jesus' chief commandment to his disciples in this Gospel is, of course, "love one another as I have loved you" (15:12–17, echoing 13:34–35). It is commandment-keepers who experience the mutual indwelling of themselves and God (Father, Son, and Spirit), which means a reciprocity of love (14:15–24). Ultimately, this is participation not only in Jesus, but also in the Father's life and love.[116]

Two aspects of the vine metaphor are overlooked by most interpreters. First, in a certain way, *Jesus is not the vine apart from the disciples.* This is not in any way to detract from the person or role of Jesus, but it is to think through the metaphor: there is no such thing as a fruit-bearing vine without branches. In that sense, the vine, Jesus, *depends* on the branches, the disciples—us. To be related to Christ is to be part of someone who exists in this world only by including within his identity a community of people related to him, to one another (the other branches), and to the world in which the community exists and to which it offers its fruit. This does not mean that the branches have caused the vine to exist or give it life; precisely the opposite is clearly the case.[117] And the fruit that is produced is always due to the vine, the source of the branches' life and thus of their bounty. *But the vine metaphor does mean that Jesus has chosen to convey his life to the world by means of the branches.*

Second, however, and simultaneously, *Jesus is distinct from and greater than the disciples.* He is the chooser, the sender (15:16); the disciples are the chosen, the sent. Participation in Christ does not blur the distinction between him and his disciples. Their participatory role does not make them, or their deeds, messianic. The disciples always remain other than Christ, and their activity must always point to Christ. If we are tempted to *minimize* the inherent value of Jesus' signs and consider them only as pointers to Jesus and to faith, we may be tempted to *maximize* the inherent value of our own works and eventually neglect their character as pointers

---

116. Stube (*Graeco-Roman Rhetorical Reading*, 146) suggests that 15:9–11 implies *imitatio Dei*, but it is more Johannine to express this as *participatio*, not simply *imitatio*.

117. I am grateful to Marianne Meye Thompson for insisting on this point in response to the original text of this paragraph. Similarly, Augustine stresses what Thompson calls, in reference to John 13 (see note above), the non-reciprocal character of the relationship between Jesus and the disciples: "They are not in him in the same kind of way that he is in them. . . . For the relation of the branches to the vine is such that they contribute nothing to the vine but derive their own means of life from it, while that of the vine to the branches is such that it supplies their vital nourishment and receives nothing from them. And so their having Christ abiding in them and abiding themselves in Christ are in both respects advantageous not to Christ but to the disciples" (*Tractates on the Gospel of John* 81.1, cited in Elowsky, *John 11–21*, 166). My claim does not ultimately conflict with this insistence on Christ alone as the source of the disciples' life, and not vice versa.

to Jesus and to faith. We may also be tempted to separate the *experience* of abundant life from the *source* of abundant life. We might refer to this as the "YMCA effect"—the transformation of Christian mission into something that has no connection to the Christian faith or to following Jesus. When this happens, missional fruit does not "last" (15:16) in the form of new and faithful disciples of Jesus, but it languishes.[118]

Jesus interprets this missional spirituality, when lived properly, in a way that might surprise us:

> My Father is glorified by this, that you bear much fruit and become (*genēsthe*) my disciples. (15:8)

The end of this verse should not be softened, indeed misconstrued, by being translated "prove to be" my disciples or something similar.[119] Matthew Vellanickal was largely right to say that 15:8 implies growth of the reborn children of God into disciples by "being incorporated into the divine and filial life of Jesus," which "produces fruits and results in discipleship."[120] This is Christosis, or theosis. (But Vellanickal—like many others—seems to limit this fruit primarily, if not exclusively, to "brotherly love."[121]) For it is by simultaneously abiding in the vine *and going forth* to bear fruit that, paradoxically, disciples become disciples. Indeed, it is in and through this God-glorifying missional activity that discipleship is possible, and thus that theosis occurs. That is, *mission is a primary mode of theosis.*[122]

It is actually in bearing fruit, then, that disciples become disciples. It is for this that they were chosen by Jesus (15:16). Jesus' words in 15:12–17

118. If bearing fruit is understood as missional activity, then the fruit that lasts includes the new disciples who are drawn to Jesus through the loving works of current disciples. This is parallel to the works and words of Jesus' earthly ministry, which were similarly intended to have the "lasting" effect of eliciting faith and hence new disciples.

119. So CEB, NASB, NET, NIV, RSV. Augustine apparently agrees with the interpretation offered here (*Tractates on the Gospel of John* 82.1, cited in Elowsky, ed., *John 11–21*, 170). The NRSV and NAB rightly maintain the meaning "become."

120. Vellanickal, *The Divine Sonship of Christians*, 291.

121. Vellanickal, *The Divine Sonship of Christians*, 295–316. Vellanickal does say that "though actually realized in the Christian Community," this love "is virtually and dynamically oriented to the whole mankind through Christ" (300). This is an indirect missional thrust.

122. Vellanickal (*The Divine Sonship of Christians*, 316) actually says something rather similar: "a life of love is a sort of existential definition of 'being born of God,'" and "'love' is a participation of the life of God," so "love becomes not only an expression of one's divine sonship and knowledge of God, but also *a means of growing in the life of divine sonship*" (emphasis added). I use the words "a primary mode" so that it is clear that there are other dimensions of the spiritual life that contribute to theosis. For John, however, these would be ultimately inseparable from mission.

about the communal, "centripetal" love the disciples are to share for one another as his friends—a self-giving, Jesus-like love that will go even to the point of death (15:13)—must not be ripped out of its missional context: "I appointed you to go and bear fruit, fruit that will last" (15:16). Ultimately, this centripetal love for friends and centrifugal love for the world cannot be separated because they were inseparably joined in the mission of Jesus, both in his life and in his death. Disciples who both abide and go (to bear fruit) are being changed from one degree of fecundity to another, to paraphrase Paul (2 Cor 3:18)—and hence into the image of Jesus, who is the image, the exegesis, of God. Of course, this transformation, this theosis, does not fully take place in this life; even John's highly realized eschatology—the gift of divine life from Christ by the Spirit can be experienced now—has an eschatological "reserve."[123]

The non-sectarian vine

Our examination of chapter 15 demonstrates clearly that the Johannine community, and the one the Gospel seeks to produce, is not sectarian. Later texts in John, especially the commissioning texts of 17:18 and 20:21, make the point that John is not sectarian even more sharply and succinctly. But it is highly significant that in this chapter, which (like chapter 13) highlights intra-community love and can thus provide fodder for those who wish to accuse John of sectarianism, this intra-community or centripetal love is *ultimately centrifugal*. Johannine vine-ecclesiology is characterized by mission, reflecting a community that may *appear* to have certain sect-like features but is fundamentally characterized by conformity to Christ, both in internal, communal holiness and in external mission. This means that John's theology of mission is ironic, for it means "a distancing from the world verging on the absolute, *and* a deep unity with the world, also verging on the absolute."[124]

This engagement with the world is dangerous. The movement from vv. 12–17, which are literally full of love, to v. 18 and following, which are literally full of hate, is dramatic. "Love one another" (15:17) becomes "if the world hates you" (15:18):

> [17]I am giving you these commands so that you may love one an-
> other.[18] If the world hates you, be aware that it hated me before
> it hated you. . . . [23]Whoever hates me hates my Father also. [24]If I

123. I am indebted to Marianne Meye Thompson for the language of reserve and for stressing this point.

124. Dokka, "Irony and Sectarianism," 106.

had not done among them the works that no one else did, they
would not have sin. But now they have seen and hated both me
and my Father. (15:17–18, 23–24)

In the shift from 15:17 to 15:18 there is a clear echo of John 3:16 in the
words "love" and "world." The *literary* movement from love to hate only
makes sense existentially if it follows from a *missional* movement—that is,
only if the loving disciples have obeyed Jesus and gone out into the world to
bear fruit, participating in the love of God that sent the Son into the world.
(In fact, the disciples themselves were at one point technically part of that
world that God loved but that did not love God in return.)

Without this passage, claims Brendan Byrne, the community "might
simply float in the air, so to speak, removed from all contact with its sur-
roundings in a way that would deny the central truth of the gospel: that
the Word became flesh in the world."[125] Now, however, as the disciples
participate in the *missio Dei*, they experience the reality of the world's rejection, hatred, and persecution, which is what both the Son and the Father
have known (15:18—16:4a; cf. 1:11). "'The world' is a mission field," writes
Geoffrey Harris, "but it is also a minefield" for the disciples, the covenant
community.[126] The chain of mission, Father → Son → disciples, has an exact parallel in the chain of hatred, as 15:18, 21, and 23–24 especially stress:
Father → Son → disciples.

To summarize chapter 15: abide and go. Love one another, but also go
and bear fruit, even in the face of opposition. Once again, as with chapter
13, loving in the way of Jesus may lead to the cross: "the world that rejects
Jesus is conquered and saved by him through its very rejection of him."[127]
Something similar is true with respect to the disciples.

Conclusion

In this chapter we have considered the theological starting points of missional participation in John's Gospel, the nature of the discourse in chapters
13–17, and the specific content of the missional spirituality of chapters 13
and 15. We have seen that participation is first of all to be predicated of God,
both in terms of the relationships among Father, Son, and Spirit and in terms
of the initiative of incarnation. As for the disciples, throughout chapters 13
to 17 they are being prepared and commissioned for Spirit-enabled mission,

---

125. Byrne, *Life Abounding*, 260.
126. Harris, *Mission in the Gospels*, 175.
127. Bauckham, *Gospel of Glory*, 129.

both centripetal and centrifugal, when Jesus departs. One overlooked key word in chapter 13 and one in chapter 15—"sent one" (*apostolos*) in 13:16 and "go [depart]" in 15:16—unlock, in context, the fully missional character of those chapters and the fully missional identity of the disciples. We have characterized this mission as participating in the mission of Jesus and in that way becoming his disciples. Hence the language of missional theosis, in fact, *communal* missional theosis.

Yet we have also repeatedly seen that the language of "missional theosis" does not tell the full story, for this participation in the mission of Jesus is inherently difficult and dangerous, for the mission is a mission of self-giving, life-giving love for a hostile world. Thus, this communal missional theosis is *cruciform*. It is this characterization of the world and of missional theosis that we must carry into our reading of John 17, in which Jesus prays for the unity that the disciples must embody as a critical dimension of this missional theosis. Moreover, as we will find explicitly in John 17, we find implicitly throughout the Mission Discourse, including John 13 and 15: Its "narratives, discourses, and prayer . . . address both the *reader in the narrative* and the *reader of the narrative*."[128] To read—or, better, to receive—John theotically and missionally is to be drawn into the missional life of the Triune God to whom the Gospel bears witness. John 17, to which we now turn, makes this point with new words and images.

---

128. Moloney, "The Function of John 13–17," 282.

4

As the Father Has Sent Me (I)

Missional Theosis in John 17

We have looked in some depth at the presence of missional theosis, or missional transformative participation in the divine life, in John 13–16, focusing on chapters 13 and 15. We turn now to the conclusion of those chapters, the Johannine Mission Discourse, in chapter 17, and then in the next chapter to the Gospel's two final chapters, John 20–21. What binds these two sections of John together, and thus this chapter to the next, is especially the well-known parallel texts of 17:18 and 20:21:

> "As you have sent me into the world, so I have sent them into the world." (17:18)

> Jesus said to them again, "Peace be with you. As the Father has sent me, so I send you." (20:21)

The first of these texts appears in Jesus' direct address *to his Father* as he commissions his disciples by way of a prayer just *before* his arrest, trial, and crucifixion. The indirect audience, so to speak, consists of the disciples, those present in the narrative context and those who will hear or read Jesus' words later. The similar text in 20:21 is Jesus' direct address *to the disciples* just *after* his crucifixion, resurrection, and (probably) ascension. The *implicit* commission by prayer of the about-to-be-glorified Jesus in chapter 17 will become the *explicit* commission of the glorified Jesus in chapter 20.

John 17: Jesus' Prayer of Consecration and Commissioning

In John 17, "a veritable collage of Johannine themes,"[1] we find what is often called Jesus' "high priestly prayer" at the conclusion of the Mission Discourse. It has also sometimes been labeled Jesus' "last will and testament" for his disciples.[2] Prayers often conclude ancient farewell discourses, as in the song of Moses in Deuteronomy 32 or his blessing in chapter 33.[3] The prayer Jesus offers is clearly a departing prayer that simultaneously focuses on communion (even perichoresis), consecration, and commissioning. Since it is speech to Jesus' Father rather than to his disciples, it is not technically part of the Mission Discourse, and yet at the same time it is the culmination of the discourse, a kind of rhetorical *peroratio* (finale) that the disciples will hear and, one assumes, be moved by. In the outline of the Gospel in chapter 2, we called it "the Prayer of Consecration and Commissioning." It is "an 'apostolic prayer,' a missionary one" in which "John's entire missionary concern is summed up."[4] It has a hybrid character, being as much didactic and declarative as it is intercessory.[5]

In terms of the Gospel narrative, chapter 17 is also the last of the lengthy discourses in John, and in many ways it not only brings together many of the themes of the Gospel but also serves, like the Opening of the Gospel (1:1–18), as a kind of hermeneutical key to the Gospel's message as a whole: Jesus has come to bring God's life, and to enlist others in the task of sharing that life with the world. This prayer "indicates that the commissioning of the disciples [in 20:21] by the risen Jesus is not simply an afterthought or addition to the storyline."[6] It especially catches up some of the key themes of the previous four chapters—participation in the sense of mutual indwelling, sentness, and mimesis, or imitation.[7] That is, it highlights the symbiosis of spirituality and mission we find in the Mission Discourse per se, and thus

---

1. Kysar, *John's Story of Jesus*, 73.

2. Käsemann, *The Testament of Jesus*.

3. Thompson (*John*, 348n.168) points to Deuteronomy 32, Lincoln (*John*, 432) to Deuteronomy 33.

4. Legrand, *Unity and Plurality*, 141.

5. It is didactic, indeed revelatory, according to Moloney ("To Make God Known"); declarative, according to Thompson (*John*, 346). Moloney stresses that this revelation reveals that the mission of Jesus and of the disciples is itself revelatory: to make God known (see, e.g., "To Make God Known," 310–12).

6. Lincoln, "Johannine Vision," 101.

7. Moloney speaks of "an ongoing 'relecture' of 13:31–38 into 15:1—16:3, climaxing in 17:1–26" ("To Make God Known," 311n.71).

also the significance of the disciples' relationship to the Father, Son, and (implicitly) Spirit; to one another; and to the world.[8] It is, fundamentally, a deeply spiritual and deeply missional prayer.[9]

Andrew Lincoln refers to the prayer in this chapter as "the Lord's Prayer transposed into a Johannine key," arguing that it functions, like the Lord's Prayer in Matthew (especially) and Luke, as "a summary of what Jesus stood for" and as a model for the disciples' prayer (for John, "in Jesus' name").[10] If we take Lincoln's point as largely correct, we must stress the prayer's missional character (as in fact Lincoln does[11]), as we ought also to do with respect to the Lord's Prayer in Matthew and Luke. Indeed, John's prayer may help us read the Lord's Prayer in those gospels more carefully as the missional prayer that it clearly is: "Your kingdom come."

The structure of John 17 is relatively straightforward, but highly significant:[12]

17:1–5	Jesus Prays for Himself and the Conclusion of His Mission
17:6–19	Jesus Prays for his Immediate Disciples and Their Mission
17:20–26	Jesus Prays for His Future Disciples and Their Mission

8. Bennema (*Mimesis*, 126), despite his fondness for "mimesis" language, finds in chapter 17 a "'relational ontology,'" a "quasi-literal union between the believer and God" that is about a "dynamic, transformative communion or relationship, which affects both the believers' identity and behaviour, both their being and doing in the world."

9. Although the word "Spirit" is absent from John 17, thematically speaking with respect to the Gospel as a whole, the Spirit is present because of the language of the presence of Father, Son, and Spirit in and among the disciples in John 14 and 16. The Spirit is also implicitly present by virtue of the connection between 17:18 and 20:21–22. Moreover, theologically speaking, for many from at least Augustine on, the Spirit is implicitly present here because the third person of the Triune God, the Spirit, is in fact the love of God—the mutual love between Father and Son. Those who love truly, love with and in the love of God, i.e., by means of and within God's Spirit. For a recent argument in this vein, see Mark C. Gorman, "On the Love of God."

10. Lincoln, *John*, 432–33.

11. See esp. Lincoln, *John*, 440–41.

12. Some major interpreters (e.g., Brown, *John* 1:749–51; Moloney, "To Make God Known," 289–91; *John*, 459; Lincoln, *John*, 434) extend the first section to 17:8, but it makes more sense to see the shift in parts of the prayer, not when praying for "them" is mentioned in v. 9, but when the referent of "them" is identified in v. 6—"those whom you gave me from the world."

The movement of the chapter suggests an intimate similarity and connection between the mission of Jesus and that of his current and subsequent followers.[13] But it also suggests an intimacy between all disciples, present and future, on the one hand, and the Son and the Father, on the other. The disciples are being drawn into the intimate Father-Son relationship, into the life of God, such that they do not merely imitate, but actually participate in, the divine unity, mission, and glory.[14] They share in the missional love and life of God. That is the essence of a "missional spirituality," and specifically of missional theosis.

The point of view of John 17 has sometimes been called "retrospective,"[15] as if it were written from a post-death-and-resurrection perspective, since Jesus makes claims that are not quite true in the Gospel's narrative sequence (finished work, absence from the disciples, etc.). Another approach is to see these statements as examples of the "futuristic" use of the present tense. While either of these interpretations may be correct, it is more significant rhetorically and theologically to note that what Jesus is doing is passing the baton: inviting the disciples, in the presence of the Father, into the intimacy and mission of the relationship they share. The theology here is a powerful claim that there is only one God but that "Jesus in his relationship as Son to the Father is intrinsic to this one God's identity."[16] The point is spiritual as well as theological: to be involved in the life and mission of *Jesus* is to be involved in the life and mission of *God*.

We turn now to the three sections of the prayer.

Jesus Prays for Himself and the Conclusion of His Mission (17:1–5)

Jesus' prayer to his Father reflects the fact that he has arrived at the culminating point in his mission, the "hour" (17:1) that had not arrived for so long (2:4; 7:30; 8:20; 12:23, 27) but that was finally announced as present in the introduction to the Mission Discourse at the start of the foot washing

13. Thompson notes "the striking parallels between his [Jesus'] status, mission, and purpose" and that of the disciples (*John*, 346). See also, e.g., Moloney, "To Make God Known," 310–12.

14. John 17, writes Lincoln (*John*, 433–34), is the Gospel's "most extensive reflection on what is entailed in the intimate union between the Son and the Father, which was experienced in this world yet transcends its categories of time and space. What is just as striking . . . is that the community of Jesus' followers is also envisaged as being able to share in this same intimate union while it carries on its mission in the world."

15. E.g., Thompson, *John*, 346–47.

16. Lincoln, *John*, 435.

scene (13:1). That hour is, of course, his death and the exaltation associated with it. Accordingly, Jesus asks that this hour be a time of glorification, too, which suggests both that the cross will be a moment of glory and honor and also that the glorification will continue after the cross in the events of Jesus' resurrection and return to his pre-existent glory (17:5; cf. 1:14; 17:24). It is this glory that Jesus shares with his disciples, both now (17:22) and in the future (17:24). Oddly enough—but not surprisingly in light of the preceding chapters—this present glory is cruciform.[17]

Jesus' mission, as summarized in these five verses, is clear: "to give eternal life to all whom you [the Father] have given him," which means to "know you, the only true God, and Jesus Christ whom you have sent" (17:2–3). Thus "eternal" life—the divine life that is simultaneously the life of the eschatological age (see the discussion of "life" in John in chapter 2)—begins in the present for those who have come to know God in Jesus. In fact, the close association here between eternal life and glory suggests that (a) having eternal life, (b) knowing God, and (c) experiencing, through Christ, the glory of God are three different ways of saying the same thing.

Marianne Meye Thompson, therefore, rightly interprets 17:3 in light of the Eastern tradition:

> Eternal life is knowing "the only true God" and the one sent by him, Jesus Christ. John does not write that knowing God leads to eternal life, as if it were the reward for faith, but that knowing God, to be in communion with God, *is* life, because God is the source of all life (cf. Col 3:4). Such a formulation lends itself to a view of salvation as participation in the divine life typical especially of the Eastern Church. Thus Clement of Alexandria expounds, "To know [the Father] is eternal life, through participation in the power of the incorrupt One. And to be incorruptible is to participate in divinity."[18]

17. See, similarly, Thompson, *John*, 350–51: "Even though that glory cannot always be seen or discerned by human eyes, especially when it appears in unexpected ways—including in the death of this man on a Roman cross—there is never a time when Jesus does not manifest the glory of God, because it is intrinsic to his identity. Yet there is a peculiar hiddenness to the manifestation of his glory: the light shining in the darkness is visible only to faith."

18. Thompson, *John*, 349, citing in n.169 Clement, *Strom.* 5.10. She continues in n.169: "The Lord 'has given a share of his own divinity' (Origen, *Comm. Jo.* 172–73) to believers, who through faith are 'partakers of the divine nature' (Cyril of Alexandria 1874, 106). The first-century Alexandrian Jewish exegete Philo, who certainly influenced the entire Alexandrian school of interpretation, asserted that 'eternal life [*zōē aiōnios*] is to find refuge with the one who is [*to ōn*]' (*Fug.* 78). But Dodd (1953, 163) also points out the genuine parallel to John 17:3 in the Septuagint—which Philo used extensively—of Hos 6:2–3: 'We shall rise from the dead [*anastēsometha*] and shall live

Glory, then, the divine radiance that marks God off as God, is both something that Jesus has by nature from before time (cf. 1:14) and something that he shares with human beings, who participate in this divine glory, not by nature, but by grace.[19] This, then, is the language of theosis (though Thompson does not use the word)—right at the start of the Commissioning Prayer. Hidden from view, but implicit in the passage, is the notion of the Spirit, or Paraclete, as the presence of God and the agent of human participation in the life and mission of God, as we will see in chapters 19 and 20. Paradoxically, this revelation of the divine glory, and thus also participation in that glory by the work of the Spirit, occurs most fully at the cross.[20]

Although Jesus has not yet died, he claims to have completed this God-given mission (17:4, using *teleiōsas*; cf. 19:30, "It is finished!" using *tetelestai*). This, in turn, has brought glory to God (17:4), perhaps at least in part because, as Irenaeus put it, "the glory of God is the living human," or "humanity alive."[21] It is critical to note that this knowledge—knowledge of God, and thus participation in the divine glory—is the ultimate missional goal in John's Gospel. When Jesus said that the disciples' love will cause others to know they are Jesus' disciples (13:35), he was speaking, not merely of a penultimate factual knowledge, for that knowledge points to the ultimate knowledge: knowing God intimately, covenantally. Similarly, in this chapter,

---

[*zēsometha*] before him [*enōpion autou*], and we shall have knowledge [*gnōsometha*]. We shall press on to know the Lord [*diōxomen tou gnōnai ton kyrion*]." It should be noted that in commenting on 17:3, Cyril's talk of participation in God and Christ, mentioned by Thompson, is fundamentally by means of the Eucharist, to which the Spirit "brings" us: "For this knowledge [of God] is life, laboring as it were in birth of the whole meaning of the mystery and granting to us participation in the mystery of the Eucharist, whereby we are joined to the living and life-giving Word." This knowledge is the opposite of "barren speculations" and is instead transformative, sufficient even to insure that the truth that "faith without works is death" is realized in actual living because this knowledge "dwells in our hearts, reshaping those who receive it into sonship with him [Christ] and molding them into incorruption and piety toward God through life, according to the Gospel" (*Commentary on the Gospel of John* 11.5, cited in Elowsky, *John 11–21*, 231).

19. Commenting on 17:3, Origen tries to make the distinction between being divine and sharing in God's divinity by distinguishing between God as *ho theos* and humans as *theos* (*Commentary on the Gospel of John* 2.17, cited in Elowsky, *John 11–21*, 232).

20. As we will see in the next chapter, this paradoxical truth will come to expression in part through Jesus' handing over of the Spirit from the cross.

21. "*Gloria enim Dei vivens homo, vita autem hominis visio Dei,*" the early Latin translation of the (unpreserved) Greek text in Irenaeus, *Against Heresies* 4.20.7. It is often interpreted as "the glory of God is man [or a person] fully alive," which for Irenaeus would mean alive to God, as the second half of the sentence indicates: "and the life of man [a person] is the vision of God." See Donovan, "Alive to the Glory of God."

the knowledge that God has sent Jesus and loved the world, a consequence of the disciples' unity (17:23), is not mere factual knowledge but a transformative knowledge that brings the recipients of it into relational, covenant, participatory knowing.

Jesus' own life-giving, knowledge-conveying mission—which was the dominant theme of chapters 1–12—is at its conclusion. But the mission of God will continue through his disciples. Accordingly, Jesus prays for them.

Jesus Prays for His Immediate Disciples and Their Mission (17:6-19)

This middle section of the prayer, the longest of the three, is actually a combination of declarations and petitions, the former giving rise to the latter. The topics in the passage move from revelation to response, and then from protection to consecration and mission—both that of Jesus and that of his disciples. The passage culminates in v. 18: "As you have sent me into the world, so I have sent them into the world." Jesus' intercessory prayer, especially its intense focus on protection, only makes sense in the context of his concern for the disciples' mission, for those who share in his mission will likely share in his persecution (v. 14), as we have seen in 15:18—16:4a. Hence the word "world" occurs thirteen (!) times in these fourteen verses, for the world is both the focus of God's mission and the source of opposition to it.[22]

Election and revelation (17:6–10)

The first cluster of declarations (17:6–8) is about God's election of the disciples, Jesus' revelation to them, and their response of faith. Jesus has completed his mission of revealing God ("your name," v. 6; i.e., the "I AM") to a group selected from "the world" and now distinct from it (cf. 15:19). Jesus speaks the scriptural language of election and its implicit corollary, holiness (separateness for God's purposes), not as a cause for pride but as a claim about identity that carries an inherent obligation to mission. (He will return to the topic of holiness later.) The disciples, it is implied, are ready to carry on the mission because of the divine call, their faithful response, and their consequent "unworldly" identity. In other words, this focus on the disciples

22. "World" appears in vv. 6, 9, 11 (2x), 13, 14 (3x), 15, 16 (2x), and 18 (2x). It occurs once in the previous section of the prayer (v. 5) and four times in the last section (vv. 21, 23, 24, 25). Of course, for John, there is an evil power behind the world's opposition to God's mission.

and their mission is about a certain kind of missional politics, or visible public witness—the church as an alter-culture representing the "unworldly" kingdom of Jesus (cf. 18:36, "My kingdom is not from this world").

The first actual mention of intercession in this section (17:9–10) therefore specifies the disciples, rather than "the world," as the concern of Jesus' prayer. Jesus does not thereby reject the world or forbid praying for it; rather, he is setting his disciples apart and praying for them to be in mission to the world from which they were drawn. The goal of that mission, implicitly, is the replication of the disciples' experience of being drawn from the world to Jesus: "the hope for the world is that it ceases to be the world by receiving the witness of Jesus' followers."[23] The disciples "belong" to both the Father and the Son, and in their mission they bring glory to the Son. The Son is glorified "in" or "among" them because they have become, and are becoming, his disciples and bearing fruit (15:8); "the disciples are so transformed by the formation he [Jesus] has given them that they will disclose *his* presence and identity when he is no longer physically in the world."[24] But the Son is about to leave, and so a major focus of this prayer is for protection of the disciples now that their protector, Jesus, is departing (17:11–16).

Protection and identity (17:11–16)

Jesus asks the Father to "protect [or "keep"; Gk. *tērēson*] them in your name that you have given me, so that they may be one, as (*kathōs*) we are one" (17:11; cf. 17:22). As v. 21, in the third section of the prayer, will make explicit, this unity is more than *imitation* of the Father-Son unity; it is *participation* in that divine unity. Even here, Jesus is asking that the disciples may continue faithfully to inhabit the space called "I AM," the divine name given also to Jesus,[25] the space where the life of Father and Son have the same name, the same character (17:12).[26] The disciples participate, and must continue to participate, in the unity of Father and Son—what Kent Brower calls participation "in the very mutuality of the Triune God"[27]—that enables unity in the community of the disciples. *Jesus' prayer implies that*

23. Lincoln, *John*, 436. See also the implicit call in 12:46, discussed in chapter 2, to move from the darkness, associated with "the world" in John, to the light (Jesus).

24. Byrne, *Life Abounding*, 284.

25. See the "absolute" I am (*egō eimi*) statements in 4:26; 6:20; 8:24, 28, 58; 13:19; 18:5, 6, 8.

26. We should recall that spatial language can be used to represent relationships.

27. Brower, *Holiness in the Gospels*, 74. Brower describes this life, using the term "theosis," as a life of dependence, joy, mission, peace, and protection (72–74).

unity requires prayer and divine assistance, and that disunity is something from which the disciples must be protected in order to be unworldly agents of God's worldly mission.[28] Because the Father and the Son are one, the Father's mission is the Son's mission, and vice versa. So too the disciples can share in that mission as they share in the unity of Father and Son. And they will also share in the world's rejection of the Father and the Son (17:14).

This petition for protection is not, however, a request for evacuation from the world, only protection from "the evil one" (17:15), who is the "ruler of this world" (12:31; 14:30; 16:11; cf. Matt 6:13) and, implicitly, the agent of ecclesial disunity.[29] There are plenty of other things from which the disciples need protection, according to the Gospel as a whole.[30] Most fundamentally, however, the issue here is not merely protection or even unity, but identity:

> I have given them your word, and the world has hated them because they do not belong to the world, just as I do not belong to the world *(ouk eisin ek tou kosmou kathōs egō ouk eimi ek tou kosmou).* (17:14)

> They [the disciples] do not belong to the world, just as I do not belong to the world *(ek tou kosmou ouk eisin kathōs egō ouk eimi ek tou kosmou).* (17:16).

Jesus will restate this twice-repeated claim about christological and ecclesial origin and identity, interpreting it in slightly different language, to Pilate:

> [36]My kingdom is not from this world *(ek tou kosmou toutou).* If my kingdom were from this world *(ek tou kosmou toutou),* my followers would be fighting to keep me from being handed over to the Jews. But as it is, my kingdom is not from here." [37]Pilate asked him, "So you are a king?" Jesus answered, "You say that I am a king. For this I was born, and for this I came into the world, to testify to the truth. Everyone who belongs to the truth *(ek tēs alētheias)* listens to my voice." (John 18:36–37)

The notion of identity in these texts is conveyed by the Greek preposition *ek,* meaning "from" or "out of" or "belonging to." We might synthesize these claims made by Jesus before his Father and Pilate by saying that the source

28. Similarly, Lincoln, *John,* 436. As Bultmann famously put it, the disciples are being charged, not to escape the world or to accommodate themselves to it, but to live in the world "in an unworldly manner" (*John,* 502; cf. 508).

29. I am rather certain Screwtape in C. S. Lewis' *Screwtape Letters* would concur.

30. Thompson (*John,* 353) remarks that "the disciples are in danger of falling away, of being scattered and devoured by wolves, of withering on the vine like the branches that failed to bear fruit—indeed, of perishing (see 3:16; 6:12, 27, 39; 10:10, 28; 11:50; 12:25; 17:12; 18:9)."

and shape of Jesus' kingship in the world—his identity and mission—is *outside* this world (i.e., it originates in his being with God, in the Father's bosom—1:1–18) but is precisely *for* this world.[31] So too the disciples who belong to Jesus' kingdom are determined by his identity and mission as an alter-culture for mission in the world. This will be a royal mission that does not operate according to the world's standards of kingdom-building, including especially the "normal" means of employing violence to protect or further the king and his kingdom (18:10–11, 36). (Of course, Peter does in fact use violence to attempt to stop Jesus' arrest and hence crucifixion, but Jesus repudiates the action [18:10–11].)[32]

Consecration and commission (17:17–19, focusing on v. 18)

It is precisely *as* this alter-culture, representing an alternative way of sovereignty or imperial rule, of "running the world," that the disciples reflect the unity of Father and Son, participate in the mission given by the Father to the Son, and potentially receive the hatred of the world for the Father and the Son as they, like Jesus, bear witness to the truth of this alternative kingdom. It is no accident, therefore, that in addition to the word "world," this middle and longest section of the prayer—as well as the third section (17:20–26), following on its theme—is heavily populated by the word "as" or, better, "just as"—Greek *kathōs*. Of particular importance is 17:18, the sending text, which is one of seven "just as" sentences in 17:11–23:

- so that they may be one, <u>as</u> (*kathōs*) we are one (17:11)

- the world has hated them because they do not belong to the world, <u>just as</u> (*kathōs*) I do not belong to the world (17:14)

- They do not belong to the world, <u>just as</u> (*kathōs*) I do not belong to the world. (17:16)

- <u>As</u> (*kathōs*) you have sent me into the world, so I have sent them into the world. (17:18)

- <u>As</u> (*kathōs*) you, Father, are in me and I am in you, may they also be in us, so that the world may believe that you have sent me. (17:21)

---

31. The Greek phrase *ek tou kosmou* can imply both origin/source and identity. The point is that something other than "the world" accounts for the source and shape of Jesus' identity and mission, and thus the same must be said of the disciples. According to Augustine, "he [Jesus] did not say: 'My kingdom is not *in* this world,' but 'is not *of* this world'" (*Homilies on the Gospel of John* 115.2). I owe this reference to Fritz Bauerschmidt.

32. On this incident, see the discussion in chapter 6.

- The glory that you have given me I have given them, so that they may be one, <u>as</u> (*kathōs*) we are one (17:22)

- I in them and you in me, that they may become completely one, so that the world may know that you have sent me and have loved them <u>even as</u> (*kathōs*) you have loved me. (17:23)

As we focus on 17:18 ("As you have sent me . . . so I have sent them"), therefore, we must see its *kathōs* phrase, or "just as" phrase, in connection with other, similar phrases. An important question about the actual content of 17:18 (and therefore also about 20:21) is this: does the initial word "As" (*kathōs*) suggest merely a bare fact—"I followed your precedent and sent them just like you sent me"—or does it imply something more robust, a like *manner*: "I sent them in the same manner and mode of activity that you, Father, sent me." That is, is the mimesis (imitation, similarity) simply of sentness or of actual substance—of shape? Is the verse speaking about natural sequence or profound similarity?

Everything we have already considered, especially the connection to Jesus' words before Pilate in chapter 18, as well as the other uses of *kathōs* in this chapter, suggests that this use of *kathōs* implies manner and substance. It should be translated "just as" (so NET). What Raymond Brown says about the parallel verse in 20:21 applies here, too: "The special Johannine contribution to the theology of this mission is that the Father's sending of the Son serves both as the *model* and the *ground* for the Son's sending of the disciples" (emphasis added).[33]

Withdrawal from the world, then, is not an option for Jesus' disciples, for it would not be "just as" Jesus; it would be the opposite of their master's life-narrative of being sent into the world (v. 18).[34] Retreat from the world would mean the cessation of mission, a failure to follow Jesus in bearing public testimony to the life-giving truth in word and deed, and it would contradict the very purpose of the disciples' election. That purpose is not simply to *be* God's elect, nor simply to *know* the truth, but to be sanctified and sent into the world just as the Father sanctified, or consecrated, Jesus and sent Jesus into the world:

> [17]Sanctify them in the truth; your word is truth. [18]As you have sent me into the world, so I have sent them into the world. [19]And

33. Brown, *John* 2:1036.

34. "If Jesus' own mission is the model for the disciples' mission, then that mission will lead them into deep engagement with, not withdrawal from, the world" (Thompson, *John*, 352). Disciples participate in the missional "trinitarian dynamism" (Rossé, *Spirituality of Communion*, 85).

for their sakes I sanctify myself, so that they also may be sanctified in truth. (John 17:17–19)

There is here, perhaps, an echo of the call of, and promise to, Abraham: "in
you all the families of the earth shall be blessed" (Gen 12:3). The self-conse-
cration or sanctification of Jesus is his commitment to the death he will soon
undergo, which will draw all people to himself (John 12:32), which will both
inspire and consecrate the disciples, and which will embody his way of "doing
kingdom." Johannine holiness is *other-worldly, this-worldly holiness* because
its *source* is not this world but its *focus* is precisely this world. Indeed, ironically, as we will see in the third section of the prayer, it is precisely the hostile
world, which forms the *context* for Jesus' prayer and for the disciples' holiness,
that is in fact the ultimate *goal* of both the prayer and the disciples' holiness:
"that the world may believe . . . that the world may know" (vv. 21, 23).

Here in vv. 17–19, once again in John, we have the chain of mission,
indeed a chain of sanctification and mission. This pattern of sanctification
and sending has already appeared in the words of Jesus, who described
himself as "the one whom the Father has sanctified and sent into the world"
(10:36).[35] Now it is the disciples' turn. In fact, as Richard Bauckham points
out, three key christological claims in John 10 reappear as the key components of Jesus' prayer for the disciples in chapter 17:

1. the oneness of Jesus and the Father in 10:30 yields the theme of unity
   in 17:11, 21–23;

2. Jesus as one consecrated/sanctified and sent by the Father in 10:36
   leads to the disciples' being consecrated/sanctified and sent in 17:17–
   19, 21, 23; and

3. the mutual indwelling of the Father and the Son in 10:38 becomes
   the mutual indwelling of the disciples with the Father and the Son in
   17:21, 23, 26.[36]

If we take the verb tenses in 17:18 as indicators of time, this sending
of the disciples has already happened, although it will not occur "formally,"

---

35. This statement occurs in the context of Jesus' presence in Jerusalem for the Feast
of Dedication, or Hanukkah, the celebration of the reconsecration of the temple, or perhaps the Feast of the Inauguration of the Altar (so Bauckham), following the desecra-
tion of the temple in 167 BC. Many scholars have seen in this text an allusion to Jesus as
the new temple of God, an important Johannine theme (see esp. Coloe, *God Dwells with
Us*). Bauckham, however, argues that Hanukkah celebrates the altar, not the temple,
and that Jesus is being depicted as the new altar, probably the altar of burnt offering,
anticipating his death. See Bauckham, "Holiness of Jesus and His Disciples," 98–108.

36. See the helpful table in Bauckham, "Holiness of Jesus and His Disciples," 109.

directly, until 20:22, when the Holy Spirit is given to make the mission possible.[37] Since the Gospel does not narrate a particular explicit point in time when an earlier commissioning occurred, we can assume that for Jesus in John, simply being with him as his disciple is inherently a sending out, as we suggested in considering 4:34–38. Discipleship is missional, as story after story in the first half of the Gospel makes clear. This inherently missional character of discipleship is, in fact, precisely the point of chapter 15, as we have also seen: election by, and abiding in, Jesus are for the purpose of bearing fruit. The important point is not the *timing* of the commissioning but its *content*.

The final request Jesus makes of his Father in 17:6–19 is for the consecration or sanctification of his disciples (v. 17). Immediately preceding the implicit commissioning of v. 18, this petition means that the community must maintain its distinction *from* the world even as it is engaged in mission *to* the world. The disciples constitute an alter-culture, just as Jesus was an alternative to other possible forms of being Israel's shepherd or king and to other forms of kingship more generally—Roman or otherwise. The disciples' sanctification, their holiness, is both missional and derivative, even participatory. Jesus asks that God "[s]anctify them in the truth," after which he adds, "your word (*logos*) is truth" (17:17; cf. 17:19). The christological echoes in these words are strong; it is Jesus who is God's word (*logos*; 1:1–18); it is Jesus who is the truth (14:6; cf. 1:17; 4:24; 8:32; cf. 18:37–38); it is Jesus whom the Father sanctified and sent into the world (10:36).[38] To be sanctified in the word of God and the truth is to participate in the missional holiness of Jesus the Word and the Truth, who is also God's Holy One (6:69). Jesus' holiness means his being set apart, "sanctified" by the Father who "sent [him] into the world" (10:36, echoed in 17:18–19). Jesus himself bore witness to the truth in the face of opposition until the end (8:45–46; 18:37), and he has already told the disciples that the soon-to-arrive Spirit of truth will testify on his behalf and guide them into all truth (15:26; 16:13) so that they too will bear witness (15:27)—implicitly, like Jesus.[39] Holiness is, in other words inherently derivative, participatory,

---

37. The text of 17:18 reads, *kathōs eme apesteilas eis ton kosmon, kagō apesteila autous eis ton kosmon*. Both verbs are in the aorist tense (*apesteilas, apesteila*), and the parallelism probably suggests that the second action, like the first, occurred in the past. It is possible, however, from the perspective of verbal aspect, that each action is being seen as a whole, irrespective of time, and may not imply past actions.

38. As noted in the discussion of chapter 10, the verb "to sanctify" occurs in John only in 10:36 and here, in 17:17 and 17:19 (twice).

39. So also Thompson (*John*, 355): "the mission of the disciples, like that of Jesus, springs from and expresses God's persistent will to bring life to the world, but their mission also anticipates an indifferent or hostile response. Nevertheless, they are sent

and missional—life-giving; it is Christoform and cruciform. Even at the point of death, Jesus consecrates himself to the Father for the sake of the disciples, so that they may share in his consecration, his sanctification, his witness to the truth (17:19).[40]

What is more, for the disciples to be sanctified in God's Holy One, Jesus (6:69), is also to be sanctified in God the Father, who is—as our passage alone tells us in John—the "Holy Father" (17:11), and in the Holy Spirit (1:33; 14:26; 20:22). As we will see in chapter 20, the direct commissioning of the disciples includes the giving of the Holy Spirit promised and described in chapters 14–16.[41] All of this means, then, that the alter-cultural, "political," and missional existence of the disciples is a participation in the holiness of the Father, the Son, and the Spirit—which is really one holy existence in three. "[T]he church's union with the triune God and with one another leans outward."[42]

Because of the immediate, imminent challenge of this missional life—death by crucifixion—Jesus rededicates himself to the Father's mission (17:19). The challenge of being sent by God may be immense, both to Jesus and to his disciples, but so also is the joy, for Jesus speaks the words of this prayer, which the disciples hear, in order to share his own joy with them (17:13; cf. 15:11; 16:24; see also 4:36). This joy is possible because of sharing in the divine life and thus also in the divine mission, of therefore having a holiness that is derivative and missional and full of life, even if its mission is inherently cruciform and dangerous because it derives from the crucifixion of Jesus.

---

and will be equipped by the Holy Spirit, the Spirit of truth, to persevere in their mission of speaking the truth in the world (16:8–13; 20:21–23)."

40. It seems to be unnecessary to choose between calling the language of this prayer either "consecration" or "sanctification," as some interpreters insist (e.g., Moloney, "To Make God Known," 301n.53), largely in reaction to the tradition of calling it Jesus' "high-priestly prayer." Jesus is indeed consecrating his disciples, setting them apart for their mission, but that consecrated mission requires their being made holy—their sanctification.

41. It is interesting, and perhaps highly significant, that John the Baptist describes Jesus as the one who baptizes with the Holy Spirit (1:33), which is an image of being *in* the Spirit, and then Jesus first promises that the Spirit will be in the disciples (14:17) before breathing the Spirit into them (20:22), which are clearly images of having the Spirit *within*. In other words, together these texts convey a joint image of mutual indwelling not unlike the idiom of John 15. Moreover, the images of water and the Spirit (3:1–7; 7:37–39; cf. 4:7–15, 23–24) and breath and the Spirit (3:8; 20:22) both suggest new life/new creation.

42. Flemming, *Why Mission*, 67.

Jesus Prays for His Future Disciples and
Their Mission (17:20–26)

The concluding section of the prayer in John 17 echoes much of the second section but brings a larger set of disciples into Jesus' petitions before the Father: those who (will) believe in response to the witness of the original disciples. It is interesting and significant that Jesus assumes the success of the original disciples' mission—specifically their *logos*, their "word."[43] This clearly means, at one level, the disciples' verbal testimony; their success in witness is parallel to that of Jesus: "And many more believed because of his [Jesus'] word" (4:41; cf. 4:50). To the degree that the disciples *abide in* and *keep* Jesus' word,[44] enabling them in turn to *spread* the word about Jesus, they share in his mission of extending life to others, because Jesus' words "are spirit and life" (6:63; cf. 5:24; 6:68; 8:51). At the same time, just as Jesus said, "The words that I say to you I do not speak on my own; but the Father who dwells in me does his works" (14:10; cf. 14:24; 17:14), so also the disciples' successful witness-bearing is participatory, a function of the indwelling Christ in the person of the speaking, witness-bearing Spirit (16:7–15). The disciples' word is really *Jesus'* word, which is really *the Father's* word, as we have repeatedly heard already in this prayer (17:6, 8, 14, 17), which is also really *the Spirit's* word. It is a divine word that is powerful and effective (see Isa 55:11).

At another level, the word "word" here, as in the earlier occurrences in this chapter, is closely connected to the reality that Jesus not only *speaks* the word of God but *is* the word of God, the Word made flesh. In a profound sense, when the disciples have successfully shared their word, which is the word of the Triune God, they have shared Jesus. What faithful disciples ultimately offer others is not their own utterances but the person of Jesus, who is ready to come and indwell those who receive and keep his word (John 14:23). And if the Word became flesh, this continuity between the word and work of Jesus and the words and work of the disciples suggests that the disciples' "word" (17:20) is something more than utterances, even powerful utterances: it is their entire missional, incarnational, "political" existence. The kind of word that faithfully testifies to the Word incarnate must in some sense participate in that Word's enfleshment in the world and

---

43. One could argue that John is composing this prayer of Jesus retrospectively, after the actual effectiveness of the original disciples' mission that produced, among other results, the "Johannine community." But this sort of interpretation runs counter to a fundamental Johannine theological perspective: certainty about the life-giving power of the divine word.

44. See 8:31, 51; 14:15; 15:7, 10; 17:6, 8.

to the alter-kingdom of Jesus. The life of holiness, unity, love, and joy for which Jesus prays in this chapter is an essential part of the disciples "word," for it is such a community of disciples, visible in and to the world, that Jesus is forming, indwelling, and empowering.

Unity, participation, and mission (17:20–23)

The focus in this section of the prayer is once again on unity, unity that is both *participatory* (in the divine unity) and *purposeful* (to bear witness to the world). Thus the inherently communal, participatory, and missional character of discipleship is reinforced once again in this section of the prayer.

The first sentences of this section of the prayer (17:20–23) are specifically a prayer for unity: "that they all may be one" (17:21), which includes both the original and subsequent disciples—an incipient theology of the communion of the saints. This human unity is a participation in the unity of Father and Son (a unity already affirmed in 10:30), and it is missional, as Jesus says twice (v. 21 and vv. 22–23):

Text	Unity as Participation in the Father and the Son	Unity as Missional
17:21	²¹that they may all be one. As (*kathōs*) you, Father, are in me and I am in you, may they also be in us,	so that (*hina*) the world may believe that you have sent me.
17:22–23	²²The glory that you have given me I have given them, so that they may be one, as (*kathōs*) we are one, ²³I in them and you in me, that (*hina*) they may become completely one,	so that (*hina*) the world may know that you have sent me and have loved them even as (*kathōs*) you have loved me.

Once again we have participatory mission, or missional theosis. Yet two interpretive errors need to be avoided in considering this passage.

First, the threefold use of "as," or "just as" (*kathōs*), in these verses might suggest that there is simply a lot of parallel activity and imitation going on: "this should be like that," so to speak. But, similarly to what we saw in 17:18, this sort of interpretation would be a misreading of the thrust of the passage. The greater context once again helps in addressing this question. Given the explicit divine motivation of love in sending the Son (especially 3:16), the implicit and explicit missional love of Jesus (e.g., laying down his life: 10:11–18;

13:1), the strong motif of mimetic, participatory love (ch. 13 plus 15:12–17), and the call to abide in Jesus' love (15:9–10), it seems highly likely that there is more than a bare fact of sequence stated here. This text is therefore better understood as referring to the disciples' *participation* in a divine relationship, an "extension of the fellowship between Father and Son."[45] This is particularly clear in 17:21, where Jesus does not pray for the disciples merely to be in *him*—which would in fact set up a parallel that could be depicted analogically as "Son : Father :: disciples : Son"—but he prays that they would be in "*us.*" That is, Jesus wants his disciples to join an existing relationship, not to start a new, parallel one. This is reaffirmed, in slightly different language, almost the language of "nesting," in 17:23: the Father is in the Son, who is to be in the disciples, thereby making the Father-who-indwells-the-Son to indwell the disciples, too—inseparably from the Son. The language could hardly be more intimate or participatory.

Second, one might be tempted to understand the phrase "and [you, Father] have loved them [i.e., the disciples rather than the world] even as you have loved me" in v. 23b as creating a mood of self-satisfaction and exclusion vis-à-vis the world, rather than mission. But this interpretation is ruled out both by the second half of v. 21—"so that the world may believe" and by the Gospel's larger context, in which the words "world" and "believe" indicate the scope of the *missio Dei* and the hoped-for response of faith. Nowhere is this clearer than in 3:16. "Because God's love is universal it is inescapably missiological";[46] accordingly, to participate in that divine love means to participate in the divine mission. The unity of the disciples has one primary purpose: so that they may bear effective witness to God's life-giving love for the world.

Jesus has already said much the same thing in chapter 13: "By this everyone will know that you are my disciples, if you have love for one another" (13:35). In a sense, the disciples are a "community whose love is a magnetic force to a watching world."[47] In other words, the love and unity within the community of the disciples is not an end in itself but bears witness to God's love and God's desire to draw, or "sweep" (so Moloney), the world into that divine community of love.[48] This means, then, that the "magnetic" force" is

---

45. Schnelle, *Theology of the New Testament*, 665.

46. Culpepper, "Creation Ethics," 87.

47. Köstenberger, *Theology*, 541.

48. So also Köstenberger: "Love, service, and unity were not to be ends in themselves" but "to enable mission" ("Sensitivity to Outsiders," 182); similarly, Lincoln, "Johannine Vision," 116. Nissen (*New Testament and Mission*, 83), commenting on both John 15 and John 17, also stresses the missional character of love in the community of disciples, but he sees the mission only as "centripetal"—"mission by attraction," failing

not only an attracting, gathering force, but also a *moving* force, as we saw in considering the (mobile) vine image in chapter 15. The community "is meant to be an embodied witness to the truth about Jesus," the truth that God loves the world, and it is to be such on the assumption that conversion is possible, that "the world is not seen as in such a permanently hostile state that mission would be futile."[49] But the witness, both by attraction and (especially) by dissemination, may be difficult and costly, as Jesus has earlier warned (esp. 15:18—16:4), and as his own fate will demonstrate.

Costly love, participatory mission, and glory (17:24–26)

The costly character of the disciples' mission is obviously going to be the case if, as we have already seen, Jesus' glorification is in fact his loving, self-giving crucifixion—and vice versa. One way of describing theosis is as participation in the glory of God—God's transcendent splendor. In this section of the prayer, Jesus indicates that the disciples' participation in the unity of Father and Son is due to Jesus' having shared the divine glory given to him (17:22)—which he actually has had "before the foundation of the world" (17:24; cf. 17:5)—with his disciples. Since the Father's sharing of glory with the Son was a manifestation of the Father's love for the Son (17:24), two things are implied. First, the nature of divine love and the nature of divine glory cohere; to experience one is to experience the other. Second, divine glory manifests itself in love, even in costly love. The Father's sending of the Son and the Son's willingness to die constitute a salvific drama of sharing divine glory and love within the Godhead and with the world. As Andy Johnson remarks:

> In John's gospel . . . divine glory has a cruciform shape that explicates divine holiness in terms of the depths of divine love. It may surprise us to find out that the disciples themselves— in all their humanity—are granted a share in this very divine glory (17:22). Participating in this glory means that their corporate life together as well as their individual lives must take

---

to see the explicit and implicit "centrifugal" dimensions of mission in John.

49. Lincoln, *John*, 439. Cf. Rossé (*Spirituality of Communion*, 87), who notes that the missional message is not only words: "[John] sees believers as themselves in a state of mission by reason of their being one." Brower (*Holiness in the Gospels*, 79–80) adds, from a broader theological perspective but in keeping with the Johannine point of view, that a self-centered love "would not replicate the love in the Holy Trinity," for though the Trinity "is complete in itself, God has from eternity freely chosen to love outside the Trinity" with a love that "has always been outward looking, never self-absorbed." For this God is "a triune, social being of relationality, a perpetual movement of love."

a similar cruciform shape that will explicate divine holiness in term[s] of the depths of the divine love that they themselves have experienced. This divine love is to be mirrored in relationships in human communities (13:34–35; 15:12–17) and replicated in missional patterns of redemptive activity for the world God loves.[50]

The missional God sent the Son out of love, the Son's mission was motivated and shaped by love, and the disciples are sent to continue that mission in the same spirit of love. Jesus' request in 17:26 confirms this conclusion: "I made your name known to them, and I will make it known, so that the love with which you have loved me may be in them, and I in them." This echo of 15:9–10 about abiding in Jesus and his love reinforces the claim of chapter 15 that mission—there described as bearing fruit—requires both *abiding in* Jesus and *loving like* Jesus. The two are, in fact, inseparable, as chapter 15 implies and 17:26 states explicitly. Moreover, the end of chapter 17 makes it quite clear that the only way that the world, which currently does not know God, will come to know God is through the disciples' practicing unity and love by means of their mutual indwelling with the Father and the Son. *Mission, in other words, requires a communal spirituality of unity and love that comes only by the reciprocal residence of the community and God, a profound participation in the life of Father, Son, and Spirit. It requires, in other words, a trinitarian ecclesial politics.*[51]

Thus, we have here an implicit extramural, or centrifugal, love command. To receive the love of God by participating in the divine life is itself a witness to the reality of that love (17:23). To bear public witness to that love is de facto to pass it on, for if the world is going to "know"—i.e., come to intimate, personal knowledge of—the love of God that sent the Son and that animates the disciples (17:23), this intimate, divine, covenant love can only be known experientially and hence in the company of those who are already indwelt by that love (17:26). Accordingly, the disciples are to engage the world in love, indeed in the kind of self-giving love that was expressed in God's gift of the Son and that led Jesus first to wash his disciples' feet and then to die on the cross. Chapter 17, in other words, should alleviate any remaining doubts we may have about the missional thrust of chapters 13 and 15, while chapters 13 and 15 should alleviate any doubts we might have about the loving character of the missional task.

---

50. Johnson, *Holiness and the Missio Dei*, 88.

51. Although the Spirit is not specifically mentioned in chapter 17, we know from chapters 14 and 20 that the "coming" or presence of the Father and Son into the disciples is by means of the Spirit.

Verses 24–26 focus not only on the disciples' present mission but also on their future reality, "their eschatological communal destiny."[52] Jesus desires that his disciples be present with him and share in the divine glory (*doxa*) that the Father shared with him before creation (17:24; cf. 17:5).

Udo Schnelle helpfully defines *doxa* in John as "both the divine mode of being in Jesus Christ and his appearance in this world in a way that can be experienced by human beings."[53] He finds four forms of Christ's glory: preexistence glory, incarnational glory, glory manifested in signs, and postexistence [post-resurrection/exaltation] glory, to which we should add the glory of the cross.[54] However, it is questionable whether these are really four (or five) *different* forms of glory, as if the divine glory and thus the divine nature were changeable. If the cross is the hermeneutical key to the semantic content of glory,[55] then all of the "forms" of glory in John must be related to the cross. In other words, the incarnation, signs, and death of the Son reveal the singular, eternal glory of God that can be described as self-giving, life-giving love. God, in short, is cruciform. Of course, Jesus' self-giving death is also the loving act of a "truly human life."[56] Accordingly (if paradoxically), true humanity, true discipleship, is participation in this cruciform divine life and love.

The petition in 17:24–26, then, expresses what will later be called the final state and ultimate goal of theosis: sharing fully in the glory of God. It is the natural continuation of present participation in the love and unity of Father and Son described in 17:21–23, for Jesus—remarkably—has said that this unity is the result of his having already shared the divine glory with his disciples (17:22). Just as the Father's love led to sharing his glory with the Son, so also that love now leads the Son to share the divine glory with the disciples. The disciples' "glorification," then, is both present and future; it is known as the experience of God's unifying, self-giving (cruciform) love in the present, which Jesus has already described in vv. 21–23 (focusing on unity) and which he will reiterate in v. 26 (focusing on love): "I made your name known to them, and I will make it known, so that the love with which you have loved me may be in them, and I in them." Yet its full realization is future, a future of the fullness of God's life, of God's self-giving love.

---

52. Lincoln, *John*, 439.

53. Schnelle, *Theology of the New Testament*, 675.

54. Schnelle, *Theology of the New Testament*, 675. Schnelle curiously omits the glory of the cross here, though it is noted on 699–700.

55. See Koester, *The Word of Life*, 120–23.

56. Schnelle, *Theology of the New Testament*, 697.

It is within this context that Jesus applies the chapter's opening definition of eternal life (17:3) to the disciples: the knowledge of God comes through his Sent One, Jesus. To know God, to have eternal life, is to be part of a community of disciples who have a relationship of mutual abiding in the divine words, love, and glory found in Jesus. It is a present glory that leads eventually to a far greater glory. But this is not a self-centered glory, a selfish love. It is a glory and love that goes to the cross, literally for Jesus and at least metaphorically for his disciples (though perhaps literally, too; cf. 16:2; 21:19). It is a missional love, and if the presence of divine glory means the presence of this kind of love, then participation in God—theosis—is both cruciform and missional. This must be the case, furthermore, if the cross is the moment of Jesus' glorification (12:23–34; 13:31–32; cf. 3:13–15; 8:28). As Craig Koester puts it, "If glory defines what the crucifixion is, the crucifixion defines what glory is. The crucifixion manifests the scope of divine power by disclosing the depth of divine love."[57] The glory of God is known in this life by participating in the missional love of God that reaches into the world. The purpose of the disciples' unity is nothing other than the display of God's love for the world, demonstrated most dramatically on the cross, and the drawing of the world into that life-giving love by coming to know the Son and sharing in his cruciform love for others.

To conclude: *Jesus' prayer in John 17 presents us with a corporate spirituality for faithful witness.* More specifically, as the imminent death of Jesus is associated with the glorification of both the Father and the Son, and also of the disciples, the logical conclusion is that it is the disciples' sharing in the cross—that is, in the love that is embodied on the cross—that constitutes their sharing in both the holiness and the glory that belong to God. It is this participation in that specific sort of divine holiness and glory that permits the disciples to be agents of the divine mission. As with Paul, then, *Johannine missional theosis is, in its present manifestation, cruciform.*[58] Mission, therefore, is derivative, communal, participatory, and cruciform. "The Holy Father consecrates Jesus the Holy One, who consecrates himself [to death] so that the disciples may also be consecrated, participating in the holiness of Jesus and the Father through the Holy Spirit."[59]

This communal cruciformity defines theosis for John, just as it did for Paul, because to speak of God's holiness is to speak of God's own cruciform, communal identity. Accordingly, the disciples will be a sort of alter-culture in the world, though not an isolated sect. For as Richard Bauckham has said

---

57. Koester, *The Word of Life*, 122.

58. See especially Gorman, *Inhabiting the Cruciform God.*

59. Bauckham, "The Holiness of Jesus and His Disciples," 112.

about the disciples in John, "God makes them holy, dedicated to him, not in order to remove them from the world, but in order to send them into the world to make God known. . . . [T]hey are consecrated in order to continue Jesus' own mission in the world."[60]

John depicts Jesus' prayer of consecration and commissioning as a "one-off" event just prior to his passion. Yet there is every reason to think that John believes the resurrected Jesus continues to sustain his disciples, as chapters 20–21 will attest. As Raymond Brown puts it, the disciples' mission "is to continue the Son's mission; and this requires that the Son must be present to them during this mission, just as the Father had to be present to the Son during His mission."[61] Moreover, if in fact in this chapter Jesus is presented, at least to some degree, retrospectively, through the lens of his death and resurrection, then the prayer of the pre-passion Jesus is also the prayer of the post-passion Jesus. This suggests that John wants us to know that Jesus *continues to pray* for the unity, holiness, and protection of the church in its loving, life-giving mission to the world.

Summary of John 17

According to John 17, the deepest desire of Jesus is to create a community of disciples who participate in and manifest the unity of God, who continue the mission of God, and who will one day know the full glory of God. More specifically, we can say:

1. The unity of disciples is both a parallel to and a participation in the divine unity of Father and Son.

2. Mutual indwelling, unity, and mission are inextricably interrelated; there cannot be one without the other. The relationship of the disciples to the Father and Son, this "sharing in the life of the triune God . . . spawns the mission."[62] The disciples' love for one another "is shaped by and participates in the relationship of love between Jesus and the Father."[63]

3. Unity is the prerequisite for mission and mission the natural fruit of unity.

---

60. Bauckham, "The Holiness of Jesus and His Disciples," 113.

61. Brown, *John* 2:1036.

62. Flemming, *Recovering*, 122.

63. Lincoln, *John*, 388.

4. The disciples' similarity to Jesus consists of "other-worldly" belonging-ness and holiness combined with "this-worldly" sentness and mission, meaning—above all—love.

5. The missional shape of this participatory communal holiness, unity, and love is cruciform.

6. The purpose, or perhaps even the content, of sanctification/holiness is covenantal loyalty to and intimacy with God in community, loving unity with one another in God, and joyful participation in the *missio Dei*.[64]

All of this has contemporary ecumenical and missiological implications. To update the language of John 17: *there is no ecumenism without mission, no mission without ecumenism, no mission without community; and there is none of this without a corporate spirituality of participatory cruciformity.*[65]

Conclusion to the Mission Discourse

In John 15, with its image of a mobile vine in which disciples abide, we have what is perhaps the most potent symbiosis of spirituality and mission in the New Testament, the quintessence of a participatory missiology. Chapter 15 is rooted in chapters 13–14. It is further developed in chapter 16 (with its elaboration of the witness-bearing role of the *alter Christus* [14:16], i.e., the Paraclete [15:26; 16:13]) through the end of chapter 17, Jesus' prayer of consecration and commissioning for himself and the disciples. The shape of the missional life is given by the icon of foot washing; it is self-giving, life-giving love. We have characterized this participatory missional spirituality, or missional theosis, as "abide and go."

The varied uses of the common verb "to do" (*poiein*) link much of the Mission Discourse together to give voice to this missional theosis:

- Jesus answered, "You do not know now what <u>I am doing</u>, but later you will understand." (13:7)

- After he had washed their feet, had put on his robe, and had returned to the table, he said to them, "Do you know what <u>I have done to you</u>? (13:12)

- For I have set you an example, that <u>you also should do as I have done to you</u>. (13:15)

---

64. Similarly, Brower, *Holiness in the Gospels*, 81.
65. So also for Paul.

- If you know these things, you are blessed <u>if you do them</u>. (13:17)

- Do you not believe that I am in the Father and the Father is in me? The words that I say to you I do not speak on my own; but <u>the Father who dwells in me does his works</u>. (14:10)

- Very truly [Amen, amen], I tell you, the one who believes in me <u>will also do the works that I do</u> and, in fact, <u>will do greater works than these</u>, because I am going to the Father. (14:12)

- <u>I will do</u> whatever you ask in my name, so that the Father may be glorified in the Son. (14:13)

- If in my name you ask me for anything, <u>I will do it</u>. (14:14)

- Jesus answered him, "Those who love me will keep my word, and my Father will love them, and <u>we will</u> come to them and <u>make</u> ["<u>do</u>"; *poiēsometha*] our home with them. (14:23)

- But <u>I do</u> as the Father has commanded me, so that the world may know that I love the Father. Rise, let us be on our way. (14:31)

- I am the vine, you are the branches. Those who abide in me and I in them bear much fruit, because <u>apart from me you can do nothing</u>. (15:5)

- You are my friends <u>if you do</u> what I command you. (15:14)

- I do not call you servants any longer, because the servant does not know <u>what the master is doing</u>; but I have called you friends, because I have made known to you everything that I have heard from my Father. (15:15)

- I glorified you on earth by <u>finishing the work that you gave me to do</u>. (17:4)

How do we synthesize these texts? It is certainly not a matter of a Johannine "works righteousness" in which salvation (or theosis) is earned by doing. Rather, this is about missional participation. To be sent as Jesus was sent is to be in a relationship of mutual indwelling with the Sender such that the works one does are the works of the indwelling one. For Jesus, there was an ontological unity with the Father that, in a sense, guaranteed his doing the Father's works. It was impossible for him not to do the works of God. His works were God's works (*erga*), his mission God's mission (*ergon*). Nonetheless, being fully human, Jesus needed to *willingly* do his Father's will. Like Jesus, disciples are in a relationship of mutual indwelling. Jesus has finished his work, as he will say again from the cross, and yet he continues his work in and through his disciples.

But even more than Jesus, since they are not God by nature, the disciples need to depend on Jesus (and thus also on the Father and the Spirit) by constantly abiding and praying. As they do, they will share so deeply in Jesus' passion for bringing life to the world that they will become Jesus' friends (15:14–15). At the same time, they will always remain his disciples. In fact, as suggested in the previous chapter, disciples will become disciples as they participate in this divine missional life of bearing fruit: "My Father is glorified by this, that you bear much fruit and *become* my disciples" (15:8; emphasis added). And all of this is dependent on the presence and power of the resurrected Christ present by the Paraclete. For that reason, we turn now to John 20–21.

5

As the Father Has Sent Me (II)

Missional Theosis in John 20–21

In the previous chapters, we have seen the missional characteristics of the Gospel of John as a whole, looked at aspects of mission in the first half of the Gospel, and considered in depth the profound missional spirituality and theology contained in the Mission Discourse that is John 13–17. We turn now to the last two chapters of the Gospel to see what missional theosis looks like in light of the resurrection and the gift of the Spirit.

As noted in the discussion of the missional structure of the Gospel in chapter 2, a consideration of John as a whole literary and theological piece ought to keep chapters 20 and 21 together, and not separate out chapter 21 as an appendix or epilogue. We referred to the contents of these last two chapters as "The Resurrection of the Son and the Mission of the Spirit-Empowered Disciples." As in John 17, here mission implies a commissioning. Two of the three Synoptic Gospels conclude with commissioning scenes: Matt 28:16–20 and Luke 24:44–49.[1] Similarly, in several episodes and in several ways, in John 20–21 the risen Jesus commissions the disciples, both individually and corporately, to continue his mission.

Of course, on the cross Jesus knew his mission was completed, saying, "It is finished" (19:30; cf. 19:28). But his unique and effective work of giving

---

1. It appears that later scribes felt that Mark, too, needed a commissioning scene to be a complete gospel (the longer and shorter additional endings). Perhaps the original text of Mark had such a scene, if Mark 16:8 is not the end (so Lunn, *The Original Ending*). If that verse actually is the end, then the commissioning of Mark's audience is probably implicit in the silence of the women.

life to the world by dying for the world had to be embodied and proclaimed by witnesses. Jesus' life-giving mission, in its fullest sense of abundant life, was going to continue through his disciples, as he said it would (14:12; 17:18, anticipating 20:21).

John 20

John 20 begins with Mary Magdalene's discovery of the moved stone at Jesus' tomb, prompting her to find Peter and "the other disciple" and announce the bad news of his body's (supposedly) having been taken (20:1-2). Already Mary Magdalene is functioning as a sort of "apostle to the apostles" (see below). After the somewhat humorous (and puzzling) account of the two disciples running, entering Jesus' tomb, and then going home (20:3-10), the rest of chapter 20 consists of a triad of appearance narratives, each concluding with an explicit or implicit commission. The risen Lord (vv. 13, 18, 20, 25, 28) appears to Mary Magdalene (20:11-18), to the gathered disciples minus Thomas (20:19-23), and to Thomas himself (20:24-29, followed by a missional coda in 20:30-31). Each individual or group bears witness to the encounter and to Jesus' identity (vv. 18, 25, 28): he is Lord, indeed Lord and God, as the Gospel has been telling us in various ways since the very beginning.

The triad of appearance narratives is full of echoes of chapters 14–17 of the Mission Discourse:[2]

Mission Discourse (chs. 14–17)	Post-Resurrection Appearances/ Commissionings (ch. 20)
I am coming to you. (14:18)	[S]he turned around and saw Jesus standing there. (20:14)
[A]gain a little while, and you will see me. (16:16)	Jesus came and stood among them. (20:19)
I will see you again . . . (16:22)	
Peace I leave with you; my peace I give to you. (14:27)	Peace be with you. (20:19, 21, 26)
I have said this to you, so that in me you may have peace. (16:33)	

---

2. Adapted and expanded from Talbert, *Reading John*, 263, who relies on the work of A. M. Hunter.

Mission Discourse (chs. 14–17)	Post-Resurrection Appearances/ Commissionings (ch. 20)
As you have sent me . . . so I have sent them (17:18)	As the Father has sent me, so I send you. (20:21)
I appointed you to go and bear fruit, fruit that will last . . . (15:16)	Go to my brothers and say to them . . . (20:17)
[Y]our pain will turn into joy. (16:20) I will see you again, and your hearts will rejoice. (16:22)	Then the disciples rejoiced when they saw the Lord. (20:20)
[16]And I will ask the Father, and he will give you another Advocate, to be with you forever. [17]This is the Spirit of truth . . . and he will be in you. . . . [26]But the Advocate, the Holy Spirit, whom the Father will send in my name, will teach you everything, and remind you of all that I have said to you. (14:16–17, 26) [26]When the Advocate comes, whom I will send to you from the Father, the Spirit of truth who comes from the Father, he will testify on my behalf. [27]You also are to testify because you have been with me from the beginning. (15:26–27) [I]f I go, I will send him [the Spirit] to you. (16:7b)	Receive the Holy Spirit. (20:22)
[8]And when he comes, he [the Advocate] will prove the world wrong about sin and righteousness and judgment: [9]about sin, because they do not believe in me . . . (16:8–9)	If you forgive the sins of any, they are forgiven them; if you retain the sins of any, they are retained. (20:23)
And this is eternal life, that they may know you, the only true God, and Jesus Christ whom you have sent. (17:3)	But these are written so that you may come to believe that Jesus is the Messiah, the Son of God, and that through believing you may have life in his name. (20:31)

This table clearly indicates that the missional emphasis and some of the particular missional themes continue in the three appearance narratives, which we will now examine, with special emphasis on the appearance to the disciples as a group.

Mary Magdalene: apostle to the apostles (20:11–18)

The appearance to Mary (20:11–18) is noteworthy, of course, because the first such resurrection appearance/commissioning in the Gospel involves a woman. It is "possibly the most poignant and heartwarming [scene] in the entire gospel."[3] When the personal, covenantal bond between Jesus and Mary is affirmed as he speaks her name (20:16; cf. 10:3–4), she is ready, perhaps like another Mary in another Gospel (cf. Luke 1:26–55), to be charged with a mission. She will do so not as one who clings to the physical body of her Lord, but as a member of the family of God (20:17), as a child of God (cf. 1:12).[4] To become children of God, then, is to participate in the divine family business, so to speak; it is inherently missional. Jesus commissions Mary as the first witness to him as risen Lord, and she fulfills the commission (20:17–18). The first "missionary"—the "apostle to the apostles"[5]—bears witness to Jesus the risen Lord and thus also to the church's first missional task. The episode also bears emphatic witness to the critical role of women in that task.

The disciples as joyful agents of shalom (20:19–23)

The appearance to, and commissioning of, the disciples as a group (20:19–23) is significant in several ways, not least because the scene takes up multiple missional themes—some implicit, others explicit—from the Gospel narrative, suggesting that the entire narrative has had the disciples' mission in view. First, Jesus twice speaks peace (20:19, 21). The most immediate reason for Jesus' word of peace is obviously to allay the disciples' fright, to reassure them that he is not one of the feared authorities from whom they are hiding. The "proof" that he is the crucified Lord, now risen, is the evidence of his hands and side (20:20); the risen one remains the crucified one.[6] Fear of status-quo religious authorities is a common reason for not speaking openly about Jesus in this Gospel (see 7:13; 9:22; 12:42; 19:38), so the implication is also that henceforth the disciples should not be afraid to bear public witness to Jesus. Indeed, the pre-crucified Jesus had also offered

---

3. Byrne, *Abounding Life*, 331.

4. Brown (*John* 2:1016) suggests that the "my/your Father/God" language in 20:17 is more about inclusion in the family (like Ruth 1:16) than about differentiation.

5. Dorothy Lee (*Flesh and Glory*, 226) traces this phrase back to Hippolytus (d. 235).

6. Bosch (*Transforming Mission*, 525–26) stresses the missional significance of this reality.

peace to his disciples as they were preparing for the mission of continuing his work in his absence (14:27; 16:33).

The words of peace, the affirmative version of the common biblical prohibition "Fear not," also connote a theophany.[7] This crucified but risen Jesus is also "Lord and God," as Thomas will eventually confess. The missional responsibility of the disciples is heightened by these final scenes of identifying precisely who Jesus is, the identity of the one whose mission they continue and to whom that mission will bear witness.

But there is more. As Dean Flemming writes, "This peace—God's wide-ranging *shalom*—signifies more than simply a conventional greeting or a calm state of mind. In the context, it speaks forgiveness of their failures, a restored relationship, and freedom from fear of the hostility of others."[8] Ultimately, the word of peace signals the wholeness and the harmony associated with God's coming kingdom, which begins with forgiveness of the people's sins. The disciples are going to be commissioned with a ministry of the forgiveness of sins (20:23). But first they must themselves be recipients of forgiveness. "Rather than coming with condemnation on his lips for the disciples' abandoning him in his arrest and death," remarks Andy Johnson, "Jesus comes with open arms that embody human and divine reconciliation, speaking words of peace that imply that the disciples are forgiven even before they ask to be."[9] Their reaction is one of joy (20:20b), as they know they have seen—and heard—the risen crucified Lord.

Implicitly, this word of peace in 20:19 is also, then, a word of mission. This connection becomes clearer in the second peace-pronouncement (20:21a), which immediately precedes the explicit commission (20:21b). To quote Dean Flemming again:

> Jesus' followers not only *experience* God's *shalom*; they also give it away. Jesus' second bestowal of peace introduces his commission to participate in his own sending mission (Jn 20:21). What's more, Jesus promises that, by the Spirit, they will extend the *shalom* of forgiveness to others (Jn 20:23). In other words, Jesus calls them to live as both a reconciled and a reconciling community, to share the peace and restoration they have received.[10]

In concert with Flemming's last observation, Ross Hastings perceptively outlines John 20:19–23 as follows:

7. See, e.g., Gen 26:24; Judg 6:23; Matt 14:27; Mark 6:50; Luke 1:30; 2:10; Rev 1:17.

8. Flemming, *Why Mission?* 63.

9. Johnson, *Holiness and the* Missio Dei, 98.

10. Flemming, *Why Mission?* 63.

Vv. 19–20: The church *discovering* [or, better, *receiving*] shalom through

1. the presence and influence of the risen Jesus (v. 19)

2. the redemptive nature of the once-crucified One (v. 20)

Vv. 21–23: The church *disseminating* shalom through

3. the trinitarian and participatory nature of the commission (v. 21)

4. the impartation of the Spirit (v. 22)

5. the privileged task of pronouncing forgiveness (v. 23)[11]

We will further consider this passage about receiving and disseminating shalom in terms of three missional dimensions: the mode, the means, and the content of mission. But the main point is simple: "Mission as participation in the life of God is the key tenet of this whole passage."[12]

The mode of mission: Christlikeness

The first explicitly missional dimension of this story is the general commission, the (Johannine) Great Commission:[13] "As the Father has sent me, so I send you" (20:21), echoing 17:18.[14] This is the *mode* of mission: Christlikeness. The adverb *kathōs* ("as," "just as"), as in 17:18, should be interpreted to mean "in the same manner that" the Father sent the Son. This means that the Father's love that motivated and shaped the sending of the Son is being passed along as the Son's love, which is now to motivate and shape the disciples' mission. "For John, the church's 'sent-ness' is a continuation of Jesus' sent-ness."[15] Moreover, just as the Sent One (the Son) reveals the Sending One (the Father), "the disciples must now show forth the presence of Jesus so that whoever sees the disciples is seeing Jesus."[16]

The best language to describe this Christlikeness must bring together the strong sense of similarity to Jesus (imitation, or mimesis) and the

11. Hastings, *Missional God*, 26 (emphasis added). "Receiving" is my adjustment.

12. Hastings, *Missional God*, 269. See also Koshy, *Identity*.

13. So also Nissen, *New Testament and Mission*, 79–80. Hastings calls it the "Greatest Commission" because it "connects the mission of the church deep into the eternal purpose of the Godhead" (*Missional God*, 27).

14. "The mission of Jesus, to carry out the Father's work, is the mimetic basis for the disciples' mission to continue the divine work (17:18; 20:21)" (Bennema, *Mimesis*, 80).

15. Flemming, *Why Mission?* 62.

16. Brown, *John* 2:1036. The plural "disciples," indicating the community, is significant.

equally strong sense of the need for enabling (dependence, empowerment). This makes the word "participation" especially appropriate, and connects the mode of mission to its means.

The means of mission: the Spirit

Jesus' earlier offering of peace in John was specifically associated with the Spirit.[17] The second missional dimension of this passage, then, is the missional theme of the Spirit who empowers and emboldens the disciples' witness. This is the *means* of mission: the presence and power of the Paraclete, the *"alter Christus"* (see 14:16) who makes Christ present and therefore makes Christosis, or missional theosis, possible. Immediately after the words of commission, Jesus performs the physical act of directed breathing, accompanied by additional words that interpret the act and give substance to the words of commission. After the words explain the means, or the "how," of the mission—by the power of the Spirit—they will then explain the "what."[18]

Jesus' gesture of breathing is a kind of "acted parable" and "prophetic action,"[19] something not unlike his washing of the disciples' feet. It recalls the creation story, suggesting new creation. Indeed, in 20:22 John picks up on the exact word "breathed" from Genesis 2:7 LXX:

> *ho theos . . . enephysēsen eis to prosōpon autou pnoēn zōēs kai egeneto ho anthrōpos eis psychēn zōsan.*

> God . . . breathed into his face [nostrils] the breath of life and the man became a living soul/being. (my translation)

> *kai touto eipōn enephysēsen kai legei autois, labete pneuma hagion*

> and having said that, he breathed into [them] and said, "Receive the Holy Spirit." (my translation)[20]

17. See especially 14:26–27; see also 16:33 in the context of 16:7, 13.

18. The following paragraphs draw on my article "The Spirit, the Prophets, and the End of the 'Johannine Jesus.'"

19. Harris, *Mission in the Gospels*, 176 ("acted parable"); Manning, *Echoes of a Prophet*, 167 ("prophetic action").

20. It is unfortunate that all translations I have consulted, and most commentators, understand the breathing here to be "on" rather than "into" the disciples. Although "breathe on" is the common definition (so BDAG [Danker, *Lexicon*]), the parallels between this text, on the one hand, and the Ezekiel and Genesis texts, on the other (where

The new-creation allusion is also parallel to new birth from the Spirit (1:12; 3:1–8; cf. Ezekiel 37), rooted in the promise of the life-giving Spirit in Ezekiel:

> [9]And he said to me, "Prophesy, human one, prophesy to the breath/spirit (*pneuma*) and say to the breath/spirit (*pneumati*): Thus says the Lord: From the four winds (*pneumatōn*) come and breathe into (*emphysēson eis*) these dead ones, and they will live." [10]And I prophesied just as he commanded me, and the breath/spirit/Spirit (*to pneuma*) entered into them, and they lived, and they stood on their feet, a very large assembly. (Ezek 37:9–10 LXX [my translation]; cf. Ezek 11:19; 18:31; 36:26; 37:14; 39:29)

In fact, in the entire Bible, the verb *emphysaō* ("breathe") is used with *pneuma* ("breath," "wind," "s/Spirit") only three times: Wis 15:11 (a brief reference to human ignorance of the Creator) plus Ezek 37:9 and John 20:22, suggesting that Ezekiel may be the primary intertext in play here.[21] The image is of new creation in the sense of new life, of revivification, for the Spirit gives life (John 6:63).

The new-creation/revivification allusion also indicates the deep, participatory relationship the disciples now have with the Spirit. The Spirit is no longer merely *with* them but is *in* them, as happened in the original creation, as prophesied by Ezekiel, and as Jesus had promised (14:17). The parallels between the two main intertexts (Gen 2:7; Ezek 37:9–10) and John 20 suggest that the gift of the Holy Spirit is the gift of life in a new way, as Jesus had also promised (7:37–39). Furthermore, this gift of the Spirit is the gift of the life-giving presence of God and Jesus, which now inhabits the disciples so that they can be conduits of this divine life to others. Indeed, all the promises in the Mission Discourse about the Spirit's activity in and through the disciples will now, we may assume, come to fruition. Moreover, we now implicitly learn what the promised baptism by Jesus in the Holy Spirit (1:33) is intended to lead to: not merely receiving new birth (John 3) and the gift of life (as important as they are), but also continuing the life-giving mission of Jesus. This ongoing mission can only be accomplished by those who are immersed in the life-giving Spirit—that is, baptized with or in the Spirit—and whom the life-giving Spirit fills, just as it remained with Jesus (1:32–33).

"into" [*eis*] is specified), suggest that "breathe into" is implied in John. In any case, the Spirit ends up "in" the disciples, as the Genesis and Ezekiel texts both make clear.

21. Peterson, *John's Use of Ezekiel*, 173. Peterson (167–82, with a list on 167–68) argues convincingly for narrative parallels between Ezekiel 37 and John 20, culminating in John with the divine breath being given, as in Ezek 37:9–10. See also Manning, *Echoes of a Prophet*, 165–71. (Neither Peterson nor Manning mentions Wis 15:11.) The somewhat similar Gen 2:7 LXX uses *pnoēn*, not *pneuma*.

That is, the disciples' relationship to the Spirit is like their relationship to Jesus: mutual indwelling for empowerment in mission.[22] And through such disciples the Spirit will flow (7:37–39), originating in Jesus and furthering the presence of the divine life in the world.

It would be easy to under-estimate the significance of this moment here in chapter 20. We are accustomed to seeing the death-resurrection-ascension sequence of the Jesus story as the goal of the Johannine narrative because it is the time of the exaltation of Jesus, the return of the Son to the Father. But the Johannine narrative is not merely focused on the Father and the Son. In fact, the gift of the Spirit is central to Jesus' mission and thus to the narrative. But this narrative significance of the Spirit is often missed, ironically, because there has been so much focus on the distinctive Johannine nomenclature for the Spirit as Paraclete (*paraklētos*; 14:16, 26; 15:26; 16:7) and, implicitly, as *alter Christus* ("another" *paraklētos*; 14:16).

We of course should not minimize this special language for and role of the Spirit in John, but we must also focus on the Spirit as a character in the narrative. Indeed, the goal of the Johannine story is not merely the departure of Jesus but *the departure of Jesus so that the Spirit may come*. Jesus himself says as much in the Mission Discourse: "Nevertheless I tell you the truth: it is to your advantage that I go away, for if I do not go away, the Advocate will not come to you; but if I go, I will send him to you" (16:7), a point that the narrator had already made in 7:39—"as yet there was no Spirit, because Jesus was not yet glorified." In other words, the glorification of Jesus is the *penultimate*, not the *ultimate*, goal of the story. This is because the entire ministry of the Spirit-endowed Jesus may be summarized as endowing others with the same Spirit,[23] as we see in the words of the Baptist early in the Gospel:

> [32]And John testified, "I saw the Spirit descending from heaven like a dove, and it remained on him. [33]I myself did not know him, but the one who sent me to baptize with water said to me, 'He on whom you see the Spirit descend and remain is the one who baptizes with the Holy Spirit.' [34]And I myself have seen and have testified that this is the Son of God." (John 1:32–34)

22. The disciples are in the Spirit by baptism, and Spirit is in the disciples by in-breathing. In both cases, Jesus is the actor, the disciples the recipient of his action.

23. Of course Christians have debated over the centuries about whether the Spirit proceeds from the Father and the Son, or only from the Father. In my view, John is clear that both the Father and the Son send the Spirit, though the Father is the ultimate source (14:26; 15:26). Theologically, then, we might "compromise" and say that the Spirit proceeds *from* the Father *through* the Son, as a number of theologians have suggested.

The connection between the death/glorification of Jesus and the giving of/baptizing in the Spirit is likely made by John himself in 19:30, 34,[24] which read as follows in the NRSV:

> When Jesus had received the wine, he said, "It is finished." Then he bowed his head and gave up his spirit (*paredōken to pneuma*). . . . [O]ne of the soldiers pierced his side with a spear, and at once blood and water came out.

With some other interpreters, I take the last phrase of 19:30 to be not, or not merely, a euphemism for dying,[25] nor a return of the Spirit to the Father,[26] but a reference to the giving of the Spirit to the disciples.[27] Thus, it should be translated "He handed over the Spirit." In a sense, this event is a proleptic, or perhaps even symbolic, giving that will be reenacted in the presence of the remaining, fearful disciples in the appearance/commissioning story itself in chapter 20.[28] But at Jesus' actual death we have a powerful iconic moment confirming what the foot-washing scene, another powerful iconic moment, also revealed: that Spirit-empowered discipleship and mission are cruciform. In other words, we have here an icon of what Myk Habets, echoing Jürgen Moltmann, has called a *pneumatologica crucis*—a pneumatology

---

24. The following paragraphs draw from my essay "The Spirit, the Prophets, and the End of the 'Johannine Jesus.'"

25. So Smit, "The Gift of the Spirit in John 19:30?" For Smit, the spirit is both human and divine—and Jesus is therefore fully dead. He does allow, however, for intertextual links to the promised and actual gift of the Spirit to the disciples, though this event (death) is not the time of the gift.

26. So, e.g., Crump, "Who Gets What?"

27. E.g., Brown, *John* 2:1082; Moloney, *John*, 504–5, 508–9. Lincoln (*John*, 47), is at first more cautious but finds 7:38–39 as likely support for a reference to the Spirit. (I am less convinced that Matt 27:50 and Luke 23:46 have the same force or double entendre, though perhaps they do.) See also Dunn, "'The Lord the Giver of Life,'" 14–15; 15n.27. Dunn (15) says that both 19:30 and 20:22 show that "the giving of the life-creating Spirit was the immediate and direct consequence of Jesus' passion."

28. For a rich, succinct reading of this text, see Sánchez, *Receiver, Bearer, and Giver*, 68–69 (cf. also 191). He also adds (107), "In John's Gospel, the cross anticipates Jesus' breathing of the Spirit on the disciples as the risen Lord." See also Bennema, "The Giving of the Spirit" (esp. 200–201), who describes 19:30 as "a proleptic symbolic reference" to the gift of the Spirit. More recently, Bennema speaks of 19:30 as a reference to "the start of the process of the giving of the Spirit," with 20:22 referring to the actual giving ("One or Two Pentecosts?" 100): "The condition of 7:39, then, is fulfilled in 19:30 (symbolically) and 20:22 (in reality)." Moloney (personal correspondence, December 30, 2017) suggests that the key to understanding these two texts is "the unity of 'the hour,'" within which "there is a foundational gift of the Spirit (19:30), and a missionary gift of the Spirit (20:22–23)" that "belong together as 'one' in the 'oneness' of the hour."

of the cross.[29] The flow of blood and water from Jesus' spear-pierced side (19:34)—water being a "pneumatic image" throughout John[30]—symbolizes that in his death comes life, as we have heard throughout the Gospel.[31]

Even if this reading of 19:30 were found to be incorrect, the important point is still this: the Spirit is not a Johannine *footnote* to the body of the Gospel; rather, the gift of the Spirit for the ongoing mission of God through the disciples is the *climax* of the Gospel's narrative.

The content of mission: forgiveness and life

The third missional theme in this text is the "what" of the mission, its content: the forgiveness of sins. "If you forgive the sins of any, they are forgiven them; if you retain the sins of any, they are retained" (20:23).[32] These words of Jesus have provoked not a few controversies about their significance for Christian faith and especially ministry.[33] But a few things are quite clear.

For one thing, in John's Gospel, Jesus himself is "the Lamb of God who takes away the sin of the world" (1:29, 36; cf. 19:14, 31–37). Accordingly, the fundamental mission of the disciples is to proclaim and mediate the efficacious saving death of Jesus as the means of forgiveness, rather than to be the actual source of forgiveness themselves. The Fourth Gospel clearly attests to the significance of the forgiveness of sins to Jesus' ministry; it is critical to his mission of giving life, for those who are not in proper relationship with the source of life will "die in their sins" (8:21, 24). The implicit corollary of this reality is that the forgiveness of sins is the gateway to life, the abundant life (10:10) Jesus came to bring.

Moreover, the work of the Spirit includes convicting the world about sin (16:8–9). Thus, the ministry of forgiving sins is *derivative*, grounded in the ministry and death of Jesus and in the work of the Spirit, and it does

---

29. See Habets, *The Anointed Son*, 162, 165–68, 173, 243, 253–56, 264, 270.

30. Sánchez, *Receiver, Bearer, and Giver*, 68.

31. E.g., chapter 1 about taking away sins and baptizing with the Spirit; chapter 3 about baptism in water and the Spirit and receiving healing and eternal life by looking on the exalted, serpent-like one. In John, says Sánchez (*Receiver, Bearer, and Giver*, 69), Jesus is the Lamb of God who bears [the Spirit] and baptizes with the Spirit to take away the sin of the world."

32. For an extended, insightful discussion, see Brown, *John* 2:1041–45.

33. Significantly, Raymond Brown concludes (*John* 2:1044) that this ministry of forgiveness is not here confined to a particular rite, such as baptism or penance, but that such rites "are but partial manifestations of a much larger power, namely, the power to isolate, repel, and negate evil and sin, a power given to Jesus in his mission by the Father and given in turn by Jesus through the Spirit to those whom he commissions."

not exist in a vacuum.[34] As Andy Johnson puts it, "Almost assuredly, the language in the second part of each of these clauses in the passive voice (they are forgiven/released/they are retained) is an example of the divine passive. In other words, the implied actor in the second part of each clause is God while the community . . . is the actor in the first part of each clause."[35] Forgiveness is ultimately *God's* work, not that of the disciples, who are certainly agents but *only* agents. "If you forgive the sins of any" in 20:23 should therefore not be interpreted as dispensing to the disciples either ultimate control over, or a carte blanche for, the forgiveness of sins. Forgiveness, according to this Gospel, is dependent on acknowledging sin and confessing Jesus—each in response to the Spirit's ministry through the disciples—but God, not the community of disciples, is the one who has been offended and from whom forgiveness is needed. This response, of course, cannot be coerced, and rejection of Jesus is always a possibility. Forgiveness is the *gateway* to life, which is the ultimate goal (20:30–31).

Furthermore, this larger context for the disciples' ministry of forgiveness suggests that their ministry is not *limited* to the granting (or withholding) of forgiveness. Just as Jesus the Lamb of God was sent to do more than die for the world's sins, so also the disciples, sent "just as" (*kathōs*) Jesus was sent, will do more than extend forgiveness. If forgiveness for sins and liberation from them (8:34) constitute the *sine qua non* of escaping divine condemnation and receiving Jesus' gift of abundant life, these critical elements do not constitute the *entirety* of that life. The story of the healing of the man born blind in chapter 9 illustrates, for John, the close relationship among forgiveness, healing, restoration, and discipleship. Salvation, or life, is multi-dimensional.

Finally, and very importantly, the ministry of forgiving sins and all of its associated practices is not limited in scope: it is a ministry for all: "if you forgive/retain the sins of *any*" (20:23; emphasis added). This is not merely "congregational care"; it is external mission, too.

Summary of 20:19–23

In this part of chapter 20, then, we have a major statement about mission. In the words of Lucien Legrand: "Spirit, sending, peace and forgiveness of sins, judgment and binding of sins—here we have a synthesis of missionary

---

34. Okure's general point (*Johannine Approach*, 193) is specifically true here: Jesus' mission is "ultimately . . . the one and only mission in the Gospel; all the other missions are in function of it." We might also say, "are means of participation in it."

35. Johnson, *Holiness and the* Missio Dei, 100.

theology woven about the gift of the Spirit. From the outstretched hands and open heart of Jesus exalted, the Spirit spills out on the world, to be received in peace or rejected in judgment. Here, in its entirety, is the profound reality of mission."[36]

The witness to and of Thomas, and beyond (20:24–31)

Finally, the appearance to Thomas comes following the witness of the disciples (20:25) that echoes the words of Mary (20:18). The same Jesus appears: speaking peace; presenting evidence that he, the risen one, remains the crucified one; inviting Thomas to replace faithlessness with faith (20:26–27). Thomas' famous answer is the "right" answer, the answer that the entire Gospel narrative wishes to engender, not only from Thomas but from all who receive the witness about Jesus, especially without seeing him (20:29). The confession of Thomas that Jesus is "God" forms an inclusio with the Gospel's Opening (1:1–18), in which the Word was said to be God, the unique God. Perhaps more importantly, Thomas' confession that Jesus is "*my* Lord and *my* God" (emphasis added) indicates that he embodies the missional goal of the Gospel: the personal embrace of Jesus as God-in-the-flesh and therefore the source of all love, light, and life. This, too, is an echo of the Mary Magdalene narrative, in which Mary speaks of "my Lord" (20:13). Thomas, then, is offered as a sort of ideal seeker-turned-disciple, who had questioned Jesus and been told about Jesus' divine identity (14:5–7), doubted (20:24–25), and finally come to faith (20:27–28). But he is paradigmatic partly in an ironic sense, for he is meant to inspire those who will not and cannot physically see Jesus as he did (20:29).

Thus, the benediction Jesus pronounces on all who do believe without seeing is an implicit call to mission, which is then made more explicit in the missional coda of 20:30–31. The purpose of the Gospel, like the purpose of the disciples, is to bear witness to the life-giving Son of God Jesus, so that more may come to Thomas-like faith and thus to life. The connection of believing and life makes it clear that belief, even right belief and confession, is not merely an *assent* but an *embrace*, and specifically an embrace of the covenant life, the intimate family life of mutual indwelling that Jesus has described as the life of his disciples in relation to him, and thereby to the Father and to the Spirit.[37]

---

36. Legrand, *Unity and Plurality*, 140.

37. Cornelis Bennema calls "family" the "primary Johannine theological category"; the divine family invites humans into its relational intimacy (*Encountering Jesus*, 33); "people continue in the divine family through appropriate [Spirit-enabled] family

Conclusion to John 20

Chapter 20 has given the disciples the commission, the missional mode (Christlikeness), the means to carrying out the commission (the Spirit), and the content of the mission (forgiveness of sins and new life in relationship with Jesus as Lord and God). Theologically speaking, this is once again missional theosis. The giving of the Spirit to the disciples in John 20 is a scene, says Paul Fiddes, "characterized by movement, as the narrative is told of a Father sending a Son who breathes out a Spirit, the source of whose activity (forgiveness) lies in the Father. In the language of later Trinitarian reflection, the Spirit issues from the Father through the Son."[38] Fiddes continues, very much in sync with the argument we have been making, in words that merit quoting at length:

> It is into these interweaving currents of mission that the disciples are drawn. The signs of the ministry of Jesus, represented by the written signs of the Gospel text, are to be reproduced in their own lives in a multiplicity of new ways so that others will believe without seeing the historical Jesus (20:29–31). What is being portrayed here is not mere imitation of the ministry of Christ, not simply a modelling of human community on the relations in God. Participating in the movement of sending, disciples *represent* the actions of Jesus in their acts. There is an identification not of substance but of act and event; i.e., humans don't become God. It is surely in the light of this open-ended continuation of the reconciling and redemptive activity of Jesus that we should read what commentators have dismissed as over-exaggerated hyperbole at the conclusion of the Gospel, the claim that the world is not large enough to contain the books that could be written about the "many other things which Jesus did" (21:25).[39]

In other words, it is the disciples' missional spirituality, their participation in the Spirit, by which they will do greater works than Jesus (14:12), deeds that continued in the evangelist's day and that continue in our day.

This mention of the last verse of the Gospel, 21:25, by Fiddes brings us of course to chapter 21 itself.

---

behavior in terms of ongoing loyalty expressed in or as discipleship" (35). See also his *Mimesis*, 155–65. For him, as for van der Watt (e.g., *Family of the King*), family is the context of Johannine ethics and mimesis is "family behavior." Cf. Koshy, *Identity*.

38. Fiddes, *Participating in God*, 51.

39. Fiddes, *Participating in God*, 51–52.

John 21

John 21 has proven a challenge to interpreters. A number have referred to it as an ecclesiastically oriented ending to the Gospel, even if some of its themes are hinted at earlier,[40] and some would contrast this focus with the "strongly 'christological' focus" of the rest of the Gospel, including chapter 20.[41] Some have naturally, but too narrowly, interpreted the chapter as focused on Peter and the beloved disciple simply as individuals, whether historical or literary.

As the proposed outline of this Gospel suggests, however, the first two of these interpretive suggestions draws too thick of a line between the first twenty chapters and chapter 21, while the second probably draws too rigid a distinction between the disciples as a whole and one or two individuals. Indeed, if we see the Gospel as fundamentally a document meant to reflect and encourage the disciples' mission of continuing the mission of Jesus, then chapter 21 becomes not an anomaly but the zenith of the Gospel—that to which it has been pointing all along. Accordingly, chapter 21 is best seen, not as an epilogue, but as a summary of the Gospel's missional spirituality and a peroratio to remain faithful to the mission of Jesus in dependence on him. Teresa Okure rightly calls this chapter the demonstration of the Johannine understanding of mission, parallel to the mini mission discourse in chapter 4 and fleshing out the themes of John 13–17. "John 21 summarily dramatizes the central points made in the discourses" about the disciples' relationship with Jesus "for personal life and missionary fruitfulness."[42]

The risen Jesus and the disciples' mission (21:1–14)

According to Alan Culpepper, John 21:1–14 "draws upon multiple genres and therefore serves multiple functions."[43] Culpepper convincingly shows that here we have a miracle story, an appearance story, a meal story, a recognition story, and a beloved-disciple-and-Peter story.[44] To this list we must add one other genre: the passage is another of Jesus' acted or living parables (like the foot washing in chapter 13 and the Spirit-breathing in chapter 20) that we find in the Gospel.[45] The subject now is the disciples' mission as

---

40. E.g., Brown, *John* 2:1082.

41. E.g., Byrne, *Life Abounding*, 343.

42. Okure, *Johannine Approach*, 219–26 (quotations from 219).

43. Culpepper, "Designs for the Church," 373.

44. Culpepper, "Designs for the Church," 373–79.

45. As with the foot washing and several other events, Craig Koester (*Symbolism*,

fishers of people, a theme also present in the Synoptic Gospels.[46] (Earlier, as also in the Synoptics, the disciples' mission, like that of Jesus, was described in terms of harvesting.)[47] The story is full of allusions to earlier parts of the Gospel as well as "ecclesial imagery."[48]

Abiding and abounding

The disciples number seven, certainly symbolic of wholeness. Five of them are named (Simon Peter, Thomas, Nathanael, the sons of Zebedee [not so named previously in John]), while the beloved disciple is later mentioned (21:7). These seven represent not only Jesus' first disciples, but all disciples of all times and places—hence perhaps the one unspecified disciple. Their failure to catch any fish (21:3) until they follow Jesus' directive (21:6) symbolizes the need to depend on Jesus for their mission. The episode is, in other words, a dramatic (and effective) parabolic commentary on Jesus' strong words regarding mission in chapter 15:

> [4]Abide in me as I abide in you. Just as the branch cannot bear fruit by itself unless it abides in the vine, neither can you unless you abide in me. [5]I am the vine, you are the branches. Those who abide in me and I in them bear much fruit, because apart from me you can do nothing (*chōris emou ou dynasthe poiein ouden*). (15:4–5).

Apart from Jesus, the disciples "caught nothing (*ouden*)" (21:3), as Jesus had forewarned in chapter 15. The theme of "doing nothing" is an important missional motif in John, indicating, by negation, the dependence of the sent

---

134–38) calls the catch of fish a "symbolic action"—Jesus' last. Each symbolic action, Koester says (134), focuses first on Christology and then on discipleship.

46. Matt 4:18–22; Mark 1:16–20; Luke 5:1–11. All of the Synoptic stories are about the initial call of the disciples to share in Jesus' kingdom activity during his earthly ministry. It seems likely that John knew a version, or versions, of the Synoptic accounts, above all Luke's, which is most like John's. The location of the account at the *end* of John's Gospel implies the continuity of the disciples' mission with that of Jesus after his physical departure and his "replacement" by the Spirit. It also implies that the work of ministry will in fact resemble that of Jesus—"just as"—to use Johannine language. Lincoln (*John*, 511) points out that fishing and catching people with nets was occasionally an image of eschatological divine judgment in the OT and at Qumran; Jesus has transformed the image into one of salvation.

47. John 4:35–38; cf., e.g., Matt 9:35–38; 13:1–9, 18–33.

48. Culpepper ("Designs for the Church," 379–402) discusses fishing, "drawing" and the untorn net, night, the boat, the number 7, the charcoal fire and other details, the 153 fish, the meal of bread and fish, and fish in general as ecclesial images.

one on the sender as the source and paradigm of the sent one's mission. The theme begins christologically (occurrences of "nothing" are underlined):

- "the Son can do <u>nothing</u> on his own (*ou dynatai . . . poiein aph' heautou ouden*), but only what he sees the Father doing; for whatever the Father does, the Son does likewise (*homoiōs poiei*)" (5:19)

- "I can do <u>nothing</u> on my own (*ou dynamai egō poiein ap' emautou ouden*)" (5:30)

- "When you have lifted up the Son of Man, then you will realize that I am he, and that I do <u>nothing</u> on my own (*ap' emautou poiō ouden*), but I speak these things as the Father instructed me" (8:28)

- "If this man were not from God, he could do <u>nothing</u> (*ouk ēdynato poiein ouden*)" (9:33)

In chapter 15, the christological truth of the sent one's dependence on the sender is applied by Jesus to the disciples' abiding in him as the key to their missional existence; that truth is played out here in chapter 21. Peter, the leader, and others had effectively ceased abiding in Jesus, symbolized by their going fishing (21:3). Jesus, however, though unrecognized by the disciples (21:4), acted to restore the covenantal relationship and to recall the disciples to their mission—and its power-source.

The "flip side" of the results of failing to abide in Jesus is the success promised to those who do abide:

> ⁷If you abide in me, and my words abide in you, ask for whatever you wish, and it will be done for you. ⁸My Father is glorified by this, that you bear much fruit and become my disciples. (15:7–8)

By heeding Jesus' directive to cast the net in a certain place, the disciples demonstrate their obedience to his words, similar to Jesus' own obedience to the Father's instructions; in having success, they relearn their dependence on him, as he depended on the Father; and in experiencing fishing as a parable of their own discipleship, they are recognizing that their ministry is actually Jesus' ministry, even as Jesus' ministry was his Father's. In effect, then, Jesus is here portrayed as the "great fisherman."

With obedience to and dependence on Jesus, the disciples catch many fish: 153 (21:11). Whatever the 153 fish symbolize precisely,[49] they are cer-

---

49. For various interpretations of this interesting number, which is both triangular and the sum of all the numbers from 1 to 17, see, inter alia, Lincoln, *John*, 513, and especially Culpepper, "Designs for the Church." After surveying all the various kinds of interpretations over the centuries, Culpepper concludes that its symbolism is clearly "related to the church, even if we cannot decipher it with confidence" (402). For a

tainly a sign of the missional abundance (more than the disciples could ever ask or imagine) that will transpire when the disciples abide in Jesus, of the universality of the "catch," and perhaps also of the unity-in-diversity of that catch, symbolized by the untorn net (21:11). Moreover, the fish likely represent the fulfillment of Ezekiel's prophecy that life-giving waters will flow from the eschatological temple; the result will be "a place for the spreading of nets; its fish will be of a great many kinds, like the fish of the Great Sea" (Ezek 47:10):[50]

> its fish [will be] . . . very, very great in number (LXX *hoi ichthyes autēs . . . plēthos poly sphodra*) (Ezek 47:10 LXX; my translation)
>
> they were not able to haul it in because of the great number of fish (*apo tou plēthous tōn ichthyōn*) (John 21:6; my translation)

The explicit associations among water, life, and the Spirit in John (3:3–8; 7:37–39; cf. 19:28–30), together with the implicit associations among these motifs in Ezekiel,[51] suggest furthermore the connection between plenteous fishing-catches and the work of the Spirit. The image of plenteous fish in Ezekiel is part of a larger image of abundant life, including much fruit (Ezek 47:1–12):

> On the banks, on both sides of the river, there will grow all kinds of trees for food. Their leaves will not wither nor their fruit fail, but they will bear fresh fruit every month, because the water for them flows from the sanctuary. Their fruit will be for food, and their leaves for healing. (Ezek 47:12, echoed in Rev 22:2)

Could there be allusions to the promises of such abundant life and much fruit in John 10 and John 15? Whether or not the answer to that question is "yes," the image here in John 21 is almost certainly one of Spirit-empowered fishing. If we were tempted to think that the Spirit had "disappeared" after chapter 20, then, such is not the case. To rely on Jesus is to rely on the Spirit. If it is true that the Spirit is the promised *alter Christus* (14:16), then it is also

---

survey that offers a political interpretation, see Oakman, "Political Meaning."

50. See *Lincoln, John*, 511–12.

51. In Ezekiel, the Spirit takes the prophet to the temple (ch. 8, where the prophet sees abominable worship practices; ch. 11, when God's glory therefore leaves the temple; and ch. 43, when God's glory returns to the temple). It is at the temple where God promises to give the people a new heart and a new spirit (11:19; cf. 36:26–27; 39:29), and the Spirit will give the people new life (ch. 37); it is from the (eschatological) temple that the life-giving waters flow, implying the gift of the Spirit promised earlier in the book.

true that Jesus is the *alter Spiritus*. Or, more precisely, the work of Jesus in and through the disciples is the work of the Spirit, and vice versa.

Hauling and eating

The disciples' catch of fish was such that "they were not able to haul (*helky-sai*) it in" (21:6). This is the same verb (used also in 21:11, discussed below) that John has used to speak of the Father drawing people and the Son drawing people from the cross:

> No one can come to me unless the Father who sent me draws (*helkysē*) them . . . (6:44 NIV)

> And I, when I am lifted up from the earth, will draw (*helkysō*) all people to myself. (12:32 NRSV)

That is to say, the disciples are now continuing the mission of Jesus, which is the mission of the Father (articulated this way in the Bread of Life discourse), to draw people—"haul fish"—into the divine life that is made possible by Jesus' death on the cross. That is participatory mission, or missional theosis.

The same verb, *helkō*, found in 21:6 is also used in 18:10 of Peter's drawing the sword to cut off the ear of the high priest's slave (*heilkysen*). This instance might suggest that the use of the verb in chapter 21 has nothing but a mundane sense. But two aspects of chapter 21 as a whole make it likely that the occurrences of *helkō* in this chapter do indeed echo 6:44 and 12:32 and have the missional sense just proposed: (1) the overall missional thrust of the chapter and (2) the presence of other echoes in the chapter from earlier parts of the Gospel.

Moreover, it is not coincidental that it is *Peter* who hauled out a sword (18:10) and *Peter* who hauled the net of fish ashore (21:11). This double reference to Peter as a "hauler" also suggests mission and hints at the restoration of Peter that is coming in the narrative. Peter, who has denied Jesus with his words and also with his deed of drawing a sword (18:10), is being portrayed as one whose mission is to draw people to Jesus, as a participant in Jesus' peace (20:19, 21, 26), not one whose mission is to draw the sword in violent acts of protecting or promoting Jesus. Furthermore, to the degree that Peter is a representative figure, his hauling "can be seen as the disciples' involvement in the mission of God and Jesus in drawing people to Jesus."[52] ("Drawing" them to Jesus sounds better than "hauling" them to Jesus!) For

---

52. Lincoln, *John*, 513.

the Gospel's audience, Peter's two episodes of hauling represent two different ways of understanding participation in Jesus' mission. One is the way of violence, of defending and promoting Jesus' kingdom with the sword. The other is the way of peace, the way of the Spirit: abiding in Jesus and drawing in fish at his command just as (*kathōs*) Jesus himself did.

After the fishing episode, Jesus' actions at breakfast (21:9–13) recall the Bread of Life discourse and the distribution of the loaves and fish (6:11) which that discourse interprets:

Chapter 6	Chapter 21
There is a boy here who has five barley loaves (*artous*) and two fish (*opsaria*). (6:9)	When they had gone ashore, they saw a charcoal fire there, with fish (*opsarion*) on it, and bread (*arton*). (21:9)
Then Jesus took (*elaben*) the loaves (*artous*), and when he had given thanks, he distributed (*diedōken*) them to those who were seated; so also (*homoiōs*) the fish (*opsariōn*), as much as they wanted. (6:11)	Jesus said to them, "Come and have breakfast." . . . Jesus came and took (*lambanei*) the bread (*arton*) and gave (*didōsin*) it to them, and did the same (*homoiōs*) with the fish (*opsarion*). (21:12a, 13)

Interestingly, although forms of the Greek words for bread ("loaves/loaf"), "fish," "take," and "distribute/give" from John 6 reappear in chapter 21, there is no reference to thanksgiving (*eucharistēsas* in 6:11), the most obvious word for the Christian sacrament that is often thought to be the referent (whether primary or secondary) of the event narrated in chapter 6 and, possibly, also chapter 21. But the absence of a reference to thanksgiving, and thus Eucharist, suggests that the primary emphasis here is not on the meal as symbolic of the *Eucharist* but on the meal as symbolic of the disciples' *missional mandate*, including their dependence on Jesus as they go about offering him, the Bread of Life, to the world. This symbolic meal further suggests that the disciples are not merely eating fish and ordinary bread, but consuming the bread of life, the "food" needed for abiding (6:56) and hence missional success. Such consumption symbolizes taking Jesus in, or one half of the relationship of mutual indwelling.

The charcoal fire (21:9; *anthrakian*) is a clear echo of the scene of Peter's denial around the same kind of fire (18:18; *anthrakian*). (The word *anthrakia* is used nowhere else in the New Testament.) With this detail, the narrative is further transitioning to a moment of restoration for Peter, the denier and quitter who "unfriended" Jesus, and hence a time of renewal both for him and for all the disciples whom he represents.

The risen Jesus and the disciples' mission, continued (21:15–23)

The scene of Peter's restoration and the prediction of his future (21:15–23) highlight both the nature and the cost of ministry in Jesus' name. The brief conversation between Jesus and Peter (21:15–19), rich in vocabulary and literary artistry, is a Johannine rhetorical gem—and another commissioning scene.[53] Peter's earlier threefold denial (predicted in 13:38, narrated in 18:15–27) is matched by his triple affirmation of love in response to Jesus' threefold inquiry about his love, or covenant faithfulness, and the corollary threefold charge from Jesus to feed his sheep/lambs (21:15–17).[54] The mission of catching fish is presumed successful; the fish have become sheep, and so they must be nurtured. Evangelization must become pastoral ministry. But shepherding by nature is not merely centripetal missional activity; searching for stray sheep and gathering the flock together implies a centrifugal missional dimension to shepherding.[55]

Peter and other disciples will now participate in the "shepherding" ministry of Jesus the Good Shepherd (ch. 10), an image also drawn from Ezekiel, as we saw in chapter 2, and which also makes Jesus the shepherd of Israel in the tradition of Moses, David, and indeed Yhwh.[56] Just as Moses

---

53. Most scholars agree that the various words for love, lambs/sheep, and tending/feeding do not have great exegetical significance in terms of indicating important nuances (e.g., Brown, *John* 2.1102–6), but this conclusion should not detract from our appreciation of the profound theology and impressive aesthetics of the passage.

54. The parallel between the predicted and the enacted triple denial, on the one hand, and the triple interrogation-response, on the other, is literarily and theologically satisfying in many ways. Although the parallel could have been created, not by the author of chapters 1–20 but by a later author (i.e., the author of chapter 21), it is more likely that the parallel is intended and constructed by one author. Years ago Paul Minear argued that "it is highly probably that the same author intended from the outset to balance the triple denial . . . with the triple pledge of love" ("The Original Functions of John 21," 92). The text in which the denial is predicted (13:30–38) also has significant parallels to 21:15–23. Jan van der Watt ("Ethics Alive," 442) points to the similar settings (a meal); the focus on love, loyalty, and knowledge; the mention of Peter's death; and the presence of the title "Lord" for Jesus.

55. In the postmodern context, and perhaps at other (all?) times, there is not always a clear division between fish and sheep, those being "caught" and those being nurtured. Stanley Skreslet (*Picturing Christian Witness*, 155–90) argues that the shepherding ministry presented here is "missionary shepherding" because, based on and John 10 and its Old Testament precedents, it includes a "gathering" function (e.g., John 10:16) and thus overlaps to a degree with fishing.

56. For the connections between Jesus as shepherd and both Moses and David, see Aus, *Simon Peter's Denial and Jesus' Commissioning Him*, 192–98.

selected Joshua as his replacement (Num 27:12–23), Jesus selects Peter to be his "shepherd successor."[57]

The sheep, however, are not Peter's, or any of the disciples'; the sheep belong to Jesus ("my" sheep/lambs), the Good Shepherd. Peter exercises his ministry as Jesus' agent. As (sub-)shepherd, that is, Peter—and all those Peter represents—participates in the shepherding ministry of Jesus, which is in fact the shepherding activity of God. "As the Father has sent me to be the shepherd," Jesus might have said in John, "so also I send you to be shepherds in my name." Moreover, just as Jesus the Good Shepherd laid down his life for the sheep (ch. 10), so also will Peter lose his life (21:18–19) as a faithful disciple ("Follow me" in 21:19, 22) and sub-shepherd. He will be the focused fulfillment of Jesus' predictions about the disciples' being hated and even killed (15:18—16:4a). Peter's concern about the beloved disciple (21:20–21) is narrated with another flashback, this time to the farewell supper, an additional appropriate reminder that sharing in Jesus' ministry means sharing in his fate, even if it brings glory to God (21:19), as did Jesus' death. That is, the ministry of shepherding in Jesus' name is cruciform.

It is the witness of the beloved disciple that brings the long narrative we call the Gospel of John to a close (21:24). Yet even the beloved disciple's truthful testimony, somehow preserved in this Gospel, does not and cannot tell the whole story of what Jesus did (*epoiēsen*; 21:25). The world itself could not hold the required tomes if all that Jesus did were recorded. This claim is more than a hyperbolic conclusion to the Gospel narrative. It is an implicit reminder that Jesus promised his disciples would accomplish still "greater works" (14:12). Of course, they will not supplant Jesus and his works, but they will continue his mission, using his *modus operandi*, and doing so by means of prayer in his name as they abide in him (15:7, 16). Indeed, this will actually be *Jesus* continuing to do the sorts of things narrated in the Gospel: "I will do (*poiēsō*) whatever you ask in my name" (14:13); "If in my name you ask me for anything, I will do (*poiēsō*) it" (14:14); "If you abide in me, and my words abide in you, ask for whatever you wish, and it will be done for you" (15:7). The last text includes a sort of divine, and even christological and pneumatological, passive: "it will be done—by my Father and me through the Spirit—for you." The reality of "you [disciples]

---

57. Aus, *Simon Peter's Denial and Jesus' Commissioning Him*, 196–98. Aus finds supplemental intertexts in Song of Solomon 1:7–8 and Hos 11:1 (197, 200–207), and he finds the three texts connected in rabbinic sources. I would stress, however, (1) that unlike Moses, Jesus selects his successor after his death (and resurrection), not before; (2) that Jesus has already commissioned the entire group of disciples in chapters 17 and 20; and therefore (3) that Peter is a representative figure, not merely an individual, in this commissioning scene.

can do nothing" has become the new reality of "I [Jesus] can do everything." The "things Jesus did (*epoiēsen*)" (21:25) are amazing, but they are not over; they have only just begun. The disciples continue the witness of the beloved disciple, not merely by sharing his witness, but by their own participation in the same Father-conceived, Jesus-shaped, Spirit-empowered mission.

Synthesis of John 20–21

We have found in John 20–21 narratives about the resurrection of the Son and the mission of the Spirit-empowered disciples, as our outline of the Gospel indicates. As Jesus appears to and addresses Mary, the disciples as a group (twice), Thomas, and Peter, he explicitly or implicitly commissions them, sending them just as the Father had sent him.

This is not to say that the earthly mission of Jesus and the mission of the disciples is identical, but there is continuity between them as the Spirit works a Jesus-like mission in and through the disciples. Jesus is the Lamb of God who takes away the sins of the world (1:29) and dies to give people life, so the disciples are missionally charged with the forgiving of sins (20:21–23) that will lead to life; Jesus is the savior of the world (4:42), so his disciples are missionally charged to fish for all sorts of fish until their nets are full (21:1–11); Jesus is the Good Shepherd who gives his life as bread for the world (10:10–18; 6:51–55), so the disciples are missionally charged with the feeding of Jesus' lambs (21:15–19); Jesus washes feet as an icon of his death and the love that motivates him (ch. 13), so the disciples face the possibility of death themselves (21:18–19).

We come, then, to the end of John's Gospel, and of our treatment of some of its major sections sequentially, focusing on the expressions of missional theosis in those various parts of the Gospel. It is time to step back and have a look at the Gospel as a whole, and in so doing to focus on the theme of love that has emerged at so many points in our treatment of the Gospel to this point.

6

Extreme Missional Theosis

John's Implicit Ethic of Enemy-Love

In the previous chapters we have looked in detail at discrete parts of the second half of John after considering the Gospel as a whole and portions of the first half of the book. In this next-to-last chapter we once again look at John as a whole, taking up the topic of love and, particularly, an issue that has surfaced now and again: What are the implications of missional theosis not only for loving outsiders, or "the world," but specifically for loving the world *as John portrays it*: in opposition to God, Jesus, and the disciples? In other words, what are the implications of John's Gospel for the love of enemies? It is hard to imagine a more difficult or more relevant question in the early part of the twenty-first century. It has to do with Jesus' "extreme" form of love—love "*eis telos*" (John 13:1), meaning both "to the end" and "*in extremis*," and with his disciples' participation in that extreme love.

Introduction

It is commonly stated that the Fourth Gospel has little in the way of explicit ethics. Some interpreters find this lacuna rather troubling,[1] while others remind us that commandments and other forms of explicit ethical teaching are not the only way to convey moral concerns.[2] The "ethos" of a biblical

1. E.g., Meeks, "The Ethics of the Fourth Evangelist."
2. E.g., for the New Testament generally, van der Watt, *Identity, Ethics, and Ethos*; Zimmermann, "The 'Implicit Ethics' of New Testament Writings."

writing (i.e., the attitudes and corollary practices it reflects), its narrative world, its portrayal of characters, its central metaphors and images, its allusions to Scripture and to oral tradition, and its theology—claims about God and all things in relation to God—are all possible vehicles of ethical teaching. Such vehicles advocate moral values and practices in more *implicit* than *explicit* ways.[3]

Furthermore, as we noted in earlier chapters, what the Gospel of John actually says *explicitly* on the subject of human love seems, to many interpreters, restricted to love within the community of disciples: "love one another" (13:34–35; 15:12, 17; cf. 13:14). There appears to be no explicit commandment to love outsiders, much less enemies. This apparent omission has given rise to some stark claims about John by scholars both "conservative" and "liberal." Recalling what we saw in chapters 2 and 3, we need to note what the evangelical Robert Gundry wrote:

> Just as Jesus the Word spoke God's word to the world . . . so Jesus' disciples are to do. But they are not to love the unbelieving world any more than Jesus did. . . . It is enough to love one another and dangerous to love worldlings.[4]

Even more scathing are the oft-cited words of the critical scholar Jack Sanders that we quoted in chapter 2. He complains about the alleged "weakness and moral bankruptcy" of Johannine ethics. Unlike the Good Samaritan in Luke 10, contends Sanders, the Johannine Christian asks the man left half-dead,

> "Do you believe that Jesus is the one who came down from God?" The Johannine Christian then tells him, "If you believe, you will have eternal life" . . . while the dying man's blood stains the ground.[5]

The claim of this chapter is that, in spite of these apparent gaps and these sorts of criticism, the Gospel of John possesses an implicit love ethic, not merely of love toward outsiders generally, but of *enemy*-love.[6] This

---

3. See, e.g., van der Watt and Zimmerman, *Rethinking the Ethics of John*; Brown and Skinner, *Johannine Ethics*; van der Watt, "Radical Social Redefinition and Radical Love." For the same point much earlier, see Hays, *Moral Vision*, 4.

4. Gundry, *Jesus the Word*, 61.

5. Sanders, *Ethics in the New Testament*, 99–100.

6. I assume a common definition of "enemy": someone who opposes, strongly dislikes, or hates someone or something and may seek to harm that person or thing. I also acknowledge that someone who is not generally perceived as an enemy, and does not perceive the other as an enemy, may become an enemy of sorts by engaging in an act of betrayal or other form of harm. (I am grateful to Michelle Rader for conversation

ethic is grounded in the divine act of sending the Son into a hostile world to save it, drawing people into the sphere of the love that exists between the Father and the Son. It is further grounded in the acts of Jesus narrated in the Gospel that embody such love of enemy.[7] Moreover, this ethic of enemy-love is implied in the Son's similar sending of the disciples into the same hostile world with him as their example of love, and with the gift of God's shalom and God's Spirit to empower them. The result is an ethic and spirituality of extreme missional theosis: participation in the extreme love of God.

Reading a Gospel, Reading John

We have, of course, been reading the Gospel of John throughout this entire book. However, this chapter's overall claim is dependent in part on a particular understanding of what we are reading when we read a New Testament gospel, and especially the Fourth Gospel.

Although a gospel is certainly *more* than an ancient biography, it is not *less* than one. The main purpose of an ancient biography was to remember a person by telling the story of the person from the perspective of the biographer. The individual's ethical concerns were conveyed not only by reporting words, but also by narrating deeds, in part so that those deeds might be imitated (or, if bad, avoided).[8] Thus a "major purpose" of ancient biography was imitation, or *mimēsis*. A common ancient cultural belief was that good teachers and deities should be imitated; Jews connected these two, believing that imitating holy teachers was imitating the holy God.[9]

Richard Burridge insightfully describes John as "a biography about the love of God breaking into our world in the person of Jesus the Jew."[10] John's apparent lack of ethical material, therefore, need not dismay us, for Jesus' activity expresses the divine love and life that he offers. Thus, we need to link the activity of Jesus, as God the Father's Son and designated agent, with claims the Gospel makes about God—especially God's love—and with the overall implicit, and sometimes explicit, exhortation for the disciples to imitate Jesus' practices of divine love as they participate in it.[11]

---

about this subject.)

7. For a similar approach to love in John, though without specifically speaking of enemy-love, see Moloney, *Love in the Gospel of John*.

8. See especially Burridge, *Imitating Jesus*, 19–32.

9. See Burridge, *Imitating Jesus*, 77–78.

10. Burridge, *Imitating Jesus*, 322.

11. On imitation (and participation) in John, see especially Bennema, *Mimesis*.

The Gospel of John, then, is not just a story of a good, heroic figure, not even of the perfect exemplary human figure; it is a narrative about God: the Word that became human (1:14) *was* God (1:1) and *explained* God (1:18). Jesus is not merely *a* revelation of God but *the* divine self-revelation; he "fully interprets God" and "unveils God's character absolutely."[12] This incarnate Word, "the self-exegesis of God,"[13] is "one" with his Father (10:30; 17:11, 22; cf. 5:17–27, 30). Recognizing John as a narrative about God, while thinking about ancient ethics as imitation of the divine, correlates well with a common early Christian conviction that we have returned to again and again in this book: that God (or Christ) became what we are so that we might become what God (or Christ) is. Affirming this "marvelous exchange" led certain church fathers, and others since their era, to speak of the purpose of the incarnation as deification, or theosis—becoming like God by participating in the life of God. As interpreters from Irenaeus to Martin Luther to Marianne Meye Thompson have said, this purpose is expressed in the Opening of the Gospel in the language about the Son of God becoming flesh (1:14, 18) so that we might become children of God (1:12).[14] Similarly, Jesus the light of the world (8:12; 9:5; 12:46) has as his mission that people might believe in the light and become children of [the] light (12:36).[15] Theosis is also Christosis.[16] As we have repeatedly stressed, this is more than imitation; it is participation.

Although theosis means more than becoming like God ethically, for it includes, by divine grace, sharing in God's immortality and eternal glory, it most definitely encompasses a robust moral dimension. Accordingly, reading John in light of the Opening (1:1–18)—the Gospel's own "reading guide"[17]—means taking the transformation of humans into God-like, Christlike persons as one of the Gospel's chief purposes—and the mission of its divine protagonists.[18] We might say this goal is for people to share in the divine "DNA."

---

12. Keener, *John*, 1:424.

13. Schnelle, *Theology of the New Testament*, 674.

14. See Thompson, *John*, 32.

15. For Jesus and/as light, see also 1:4–9; 3:19–21; 11:9–10; 12:35.

16. The term "Christosis" has recently been used especially by Ben Blackwell. See, e.g., his *Christosis*.

17. Calling 1:1–18 the Gospel's "reading guide" does not contradict the claim of chapter 2 that these verses constitute more than a prologue; the unit introduces the narrative from within that narrative.

18. For a similar overall approach to John as a text about theosis, see Byers, *Ecclesiology and Theosis*, though Byers does not focus on the missional dimension of theosis.

The approach taken to John in this chapter is once again to look at the final form of the text as a literary whole, from the Opening to chapter 21. We will not consider the (largely older) approach to John that looks at its alleged compositional, or redactional, history. Nor will we consider the purported phases of the Johannine community that various stages of composition might have reflected. It is tempting to many, however, to pursue such approaches, as they *might* explain the centrality of "love one another" and the alleged absence of "love your enemies" in John (specifically in the Mission Discourse, chapters 13–17) as the product of a beleaguered community in need of internal harmony and mutual care. But such an approach is ultimately unsatisfying historically, literarily, and theologically. Accordingly, our goal will be to continue focusing "not on the community that *produced* John's Gospel, but on the sort of community John's Gospel *seeks to produce.*"[19]

With these principles of reading John as a whole in hand, we will look at what John *states* about God's enemy-love, *narrates* about Jesus' enemy-love, and *infers* about the disciples' enemy-love. Only a very few interpreters have suggested that the Gospel implicitly enjoins love of enemies.[20] The goal of this chapter is to strengthen their case, and perhaps to increase their number.

"For God so loved the world": God and the Hostile *Kosmos*

"For God so loved the world that he gave his only Son, so that everyone who believes in him may not perish but may have eternal life" (John 3:16). If, as 1 John says (cf. 4:8–10, 16), God *is* love, then this well-known Gospel text claims that God *does* love, *practices* love; divine being and action are inseparable.

For John, the demonstration of divine love is obviously the gift of the Son, sent by the Father to bring the divine love, light, and life to humanity. This divine mission is displayed in various "signs" and culminates in the Son's healing, saving death, as the immediate context of 3:16 makes clear: "And just as Moses lifted up the serpent in the wilderness, so must the Son of Man be lifted up, that whoever believes in him may have eternal life" (3:14–15). Jesus reaffirms this mission of giving life through death in several

---

19. Byers, *Ecclesiology and Theosis*, 3 (emphasis added).

20. A brief but significant example is Smith, "Ethics and the Interpretation of the Fourth Gospel": the command to love one another is "capacious, capable of infinite expansion" (111; cf. 116).

places, but perhaps no more dramatically than he does in 12:32—"And I, when I am lifted up from the earth, will draw all people to myself." That is, as we saw in chapter 2, his mission is that people may be "swept" into the eternal relationship of love shared by the Father and the Son.[21]

"The world" (*kosmos*) in 3:16 refers to humanity: humanity as a whole, and each individual: the "whoever" of 3:15, the "all people" of 12:32. This world of human beings was, John 1 implies in its echo of Genesis 1, created by God (through the agency of the Son; 1:3) as good—indeed, "very good" (Gen 1:31). But the very good, created world is hostile toward both God the Father and his primary agent, or emissary, the Son, as well as toward his secondary agents, namely Jesus' disciples, who are sent out by the Son as the Father had sent him (17:18; 20:21).[22]

The word "world" (*kosmos*) appears seventy-eight times in John. Sometimes "the world" means "the created order" (1:10; 12:25; 16:21, 28; 17:24); occasionally it refers especially to Jesus' own people (e.g., 7:4; 18:20) who, by and large in John, reject Jesus. But on the whole, even in the latter sorts of instances, the world for John is humanity, and the treatment of Jesus by his own people, especially their leaders, is representative of the world's treatment of God—its hatred (e.g., 15:18–25).[23] As a character in the drama of John, "the world" is the antagonist, the God-hater.[24]

Several texts illustrate this situation of divine loving activity in the face of human ignorance, hostility, and hatred toward the Father and the Son. John 1:10 says, "He [the Logos/Word] was in the world, and the world came into being through him; yet the world did not know him," while in 12:47 Jesus declares, "I do not judge anyone who hears my words and does not keep them, for I came not to judge the world, but to save the world"—an echo of 3:16–19. In John, the world is ruled by an anti-God figure (Satan) and is itself in a profound state of anti-Godness.[25] Yet God the Father and the Son still love the world (humanity), for Jesus was both sent by the Father (3:16) and willingly came (12:47) to save the very world that hates them. *This is nothing other than divine love for enemies.* As Craig Koester puts it:

21. See Moloney, *Love in the Gospel of John*, 61–64 et passim.

22. See Marrow, "Κόσμος in John." The *kosmos*, argues Marrow, "comes to embody . . . the rejection of the revelation, the opposition to the Revealer [Jesus], and the resolute hatred" of all who do receive the Revealer (98). On the sending motif, see chapter 4 above.

23. See Marrow, "Κόσμος in John," 100–101.

24. See Skinner, "The World: Promise and Unfulfilled Hope," 64–65.

25. Satan is three times called "the ruler of this world" (12:31; 14:30; 16:11).

> John's ominous portrayal of "the world" gives depth to his understanding of the love of God and the work of Jesus. . . . [I]n John's Gospel God loves the world that hates him; he gives his Son for the world that rejects him. He offers his love to a world estranged from him in order to overcome its hostility and bring the world back into relationship with its creator (3:16).[26]

In Pauline language, we could say that "in Christ God was reconciling the world to himself" (2 Cor 5:19); that "God proves [manifests] his love for us in that while we still were sinners Christ died for us," for "while we were enemies, we were reconciled to God through the death of his Son" (Rom 5:8, 10). For John, as for Paul, the gift of the Son is a gift *for enemies.*

If the "mission" of the Fourth Gospel, and of the God to whom it bears witness, is to engender children of God who resemble their Father (John 1:12), sharing the divine DNA, then it would seem inevitable that such children will share the fundamental divine character trait of love for the world, which means also love for enemies.

We turn next to the Son, and particularly to the narrative theme of his love for enemies—God's enemy-love in the flesh.

"The Logos Takes the Side of His Adversaries"

This brief quotation about the Logos from the great theologian Karl Barth[27] sums up one key claim of the Gospel's Prologue noted above:

> [10]He was in the world, and the world came into being through him; yet the world did not know him. [11]He came to what was his own, and his own people did not accept him. [12]But to all who received him, who believed in his name, he gave power to become children of God. (1:10–12)

Although the word "love" does not appear in this passage, it is clearly about Christ's love for the world. This is a text about grace—a word that will occur four times just after these lines (1:14–17). And this grace is the grace of enemy-love.

How does this love play itself out in the Gospel narrative itself?

---

26. Koester, *The Word of Life*, 81.

27. Karl Barth, *Erklärung des Johannes-Evangeliums (Kapitel 1–8)*, edited by Walter Fürst, Gesamtausgabe II (Zurich: TVZ, 1976), 110, quoted in Hengel, "The Prologue of the Gospel of John," 284.

Jesus brings life to enemies

John 3:1—4:54 portrays three individuals who encounter Jesus, illustrating the Son's offer of life to all and various responses to him. The three include a Jew, the Pharisee Nicodemus (3:1–21); an unnamed Samaritan woman (4:1–42); and an unnamed "royal official" (*basilikos*—4:46, 49). The overall flow of the narrative in this section of the gospel—from Jew to "half-Jew" (Samaritan) to royal official—strongly suggests that this royal official should be understood as a non-Jew: a gentile, or at least a gentile sympathizer and hence functionally a gentile (4:46–54). These three figures—a Jew, a half-Jew, and a non-Jew (gentile/gentile sympathizer)—together symbolize and emphasize the universality of Jesus' mission mentioned in 1:10–12 and the universal scope of God's love noted in 3:16.[28] Together they illustrate that Jesus is "the Savior of the world" (4:42). Moreover, the two unnamed figures also represent Israel's enemies: the Samaritans and the Romans.

John 4:1–42 narrates Jesus encountering the Samaritan woman at the well and offering her "living water" (4:10), even though "Jews do not share things in common with Samaritans" (4:9b). The no-contact policy existed because the two groups were religious enemies; Craig Keener observes that "[t]he opposition between the two peoples was proverbial."[29] Indeed, the book of Sirach claims that the Samaritans were even *God's* enemies:

> Two nations my soul detests, and the third is not even a people:
> Those who live in Seir, and the Philistines, and the foolish people
> that live in Shechem [in Samaria]. (Sir 50:25–26)[30]

Moreover, in John 8:48 Jesus is accused of being a Samaritan and being demon-possessed—evidence of the strongly negative view of Samaritans assumed by the Gospel to be "normal." Thus, the typical interpretations of Jesus interacting with the Samaritan woman as boundary breaking—ethnic, cultural, religious, gender, and perhaps even ethical (given the woman's "history")—is not wrong, but it is inadequate.[31] Jesus is transgressing the boundary between friend and enemy in a profound act of loving the

---

28. Köstenberger (*Theology*, 546) finds a parallel between these three figures and the Jerusalem/Judea—Samaria—ends of the earth pattern of Acts 1:8.

29. Keener, *John* 1:599.

30. For more on Jewish-Samaritan relations, see Keener, *John* 1:599–601; Knoppers, *Jews and Samaritans*. Relations ebbed and flowed with various degrees of animosity, and the "no-contact" policy was not always strictly observed. Nonetheless, characterizing Samaritans as the Jews' "enemies" is on the whole accurate for the first century and, for John (as for Luke), theologically significant.

31. On breaking boundaries, see, e.g., Keener, *John* 1:591–98.

despised. This Savior of the world, representing the God of Israel, does not hate the enemy but loves the enemy.

The claim that Jesus "had to go through Samaria" (4:4) on his way back to Galilee from Judea is incorrect with respect to itinerary, for there were other possible routes.[32] The claim is a theological one; the necessity is related to God's plan and Jesus' mission.[33] Jesus has to travel into Samaria, not merely because his mission is to the world, but also because God loves the world that opposes God, and this divine enemy-love is incarnate in Jesus. Furthermore, implicitly, God in Jesus is also reconciling human enemies to one another, represented by Jews and Samaritans and by their coming together to worship the one Father in (the) Spirit and the Truth, Jesus (4:23; cf. 14:6).[34]

The subsequent short episode (4:46–54) involves someone, notes Keener, "who to some [in the first century] will appear as suspicious as the Samaritan woman."[35] A "royal official" is clearly a member of the powerful elite. In light of the apparent narrative progression of characters Jesus engages in John 3–4, noted above, he is likely a gentile. But whether a gentile Roman official, a member of the Herodian family, or a Jew in the service of Herod Antipas (tetrarch of Galilee and Perea), this man would have been viewed by the people of Jesus' (and John's) day as a member of, or collaborator with, the Roman oppressors—the enemies.

From the "human" side of John's narrative, in view of the various persons who encounter Jesus in John, the point of this story is that even unexpected characters (as with the Samaritan woman) can have faith in Jesus and receive the life he came to bring: the man's son, the man himself, and his "whole household" (4:53). This sign of life has occurred at Cana (4:46), the site of the wedding episode (2:1–11), symbolizing the eschatological gift of abundant life.

From the "divine" side of John's narrative, with a focus on Jesus as God's agent and God's self-revelation, the point of this story (once again in parallel with the story of the Samaritan woman) is God's love for enemies. The Roman official could not be more a part of "the world"—the world in opposition to God, the world of oppressors and even killers. After all,

32. See, e.g., Brown, *John* 1:169.

33. Brown, *John* 1:169; see also, e.g., Keener (*John*, 1:590), who notes other references to divine "necessity."

34. See also Swartley, *Covenant of Peace*, 277, 304–23. Some scholars believe John 4 represents a "Samaritan mission" phase in the Johannine community's history. The chapter is at least an impetus for both cross-cultural mission and reconciliation with enemies.

35. Keener, *John*, 1:630.

it will be Roman soldiers, under the direction of a Roman official of the highest order—Pontius Pilate, procurator (governor) of Judea—who will execute Jesus as an act of fidelity to royalty itself: the emperor (19:12–16). For Jesus, according to the Jewish authorities, had made himself royalty—Greek *basilea*—in direct competition with the emperor (19:12, 15), who was the true *basilea* of the empire, and the one whom the *basilikos* (royal official) ultimately served.[36]

Jesus washes the feet of enemies

As we saw in chapter 3, the story of Jesus washing his disciples' feet in John 13 symbolizes both the unique salvific (cleansing, forgiving) effect of his upcoming death and its paradigmatic character as an act of self-giving love. Jan van der Watt claims that the foot washing is an act of "socially deviant behavior" (not normally performed by hosts, or masters) that "defines the focal point" of John 13.[37] Some would contend, however, that even if there is a narrative of love for others and perhaps even enemies early in John, when we arrive at the narrative of Jesus' death (his consummate act of love), beginning with the foot-washing scene, Jesus restricts his love to his disciples and teaches his disciples to act similarly—to love *one another*. Period.

More specifically, the phrase "Having loved his own who were in the world, he loved them to the end [and/or 'to the uttermost'[38]]" in 13:1 has sometimes been interpreted in an exclusive way as a reference to Jesus' disciples who are "in the world" (17:11). After all, Jesus washes the feet of his gathered disciples, whom he will soon call his "friends" (15:13–15); he does not go out into the streets and invite others in to have their feet washed as a symbol of his undying (and dying) love for them. This Jesus would be the founder of an isolationist, "sectarian" group.

Yet—apart from the utter incomprehensibility in John's Gospel of the Son not loving and dying for the whole world, as the agent of the Father's universal love—the verbal echo of 1:10–11 ("the world [3x] . . . his own . . . his own people") in 13:1 ("his own who were in the world") raises questions about a narrow interpretation.[39] The similarity of language in these two places could well imply that Jesus' love of "his own" in 13:1 is not re-

---

36. On this and similar themes in John, see Carter, *John and Empire*.

37. Van der Watt, "Ethos and Ethics," 169.

38. The Greek construction (*eis telos*) can mean either, or perhaps—for John the expert in double entendre—both. Anticipating Jesus' words from the cross, *Tetelestai* (19:30), the phrase *eis telos* in 13:1 could almost be translated "to the finish line."

39. See discussion in chapter 3.

stricted to the circle of disciples but is inclusive of all his own people and, by extension, the rest of the world.[40]

The indiscriminate love implied in 13:1 receives confirmation by the mention of Judas in the very next verse, 13:2. Why is Judas mentioned here? And why does Jesus not speak to his traitor or reveal his identity until *after* the foot washing (13:21–30)? Since the narrator tells us both in 6:70–71 and here in 13:2 (cf. 13:27) that Judas will be inhabited by Satan—"the ruler of this world" (12:31; 14:30; 16:11)—and is going to betray Jesus, his presence during the meal has powerful symbolic value. Judas represents the hostile world that is ruled by Satan and does not accept Jesus. In fact, this Judas-world persecutes Jesus, handing him over to death.

The verb *paradidōmi*, which means "hand over" or "betray," occurs three times in chapter 13—in vv. 2, 11, and 21. John will use the same verb in the passion narrative (chapters 18–19) to tell us not only that Judas hands Jesus over to death (18:2, 5; 19:11), but also that the Jewish leaders (18:30, 35–36) and the Roman Pilate (19:16)—representing the Jewish and gentile halves of the world—do the same. Jesus washes the feet even of his betrayer, not in ignorance or accidentally, but *with full knowledge of his betrayer's identity* (13:11, 18–19, 26–27). Accordingly, Jesus' death is meant to benefit the entire world (12:32), the world that participates in Judas' handing over of Jesus.[41]

Also present at the meal, of course, is Peter, who wholeheartedly embraces Jesus' mission (6:68) and wants to share fully in it, even if he does not really understand it or its possible implications for him (13:6–10, 36–38). But Peter the Jesus-enthusiast will soon become Peter the Jesus-denier (13:38; 18:15–18, 25–27).

Here, then, once again, is enemy-love.[42] Jesus washes the feet of his betrayer, the "archetype of the evil disciple."[43] He washes the feet of his enthusiastic friend turned friend-renouncing enemy, representative of all of

---

40. "In context 'his own' (*tous idious*) refers to Jesus' disciples but does not deny that the people of Israel are 'his own'" (Thompson, *John*, 284, referring to her comments on 1:11). It is also possible that "his own" and "his own people" in 1:11 refer to all of humanity ("the world," as in 1:10), which would make the phrase in 13:1 even more certainly inclusive. See Skinner, "The World," 63–64. As we saw in chapter 3, this kind of interpretation dates at least to the fifth century in the commentary of Cyril of Alexandria on John, cited in Elowsky, *John 11–21*, 84.

41. Cyril of Alexandria wrote that although Jesus "knew that Judas was full of devilishly bitter poison . . . Jesus honored him as much as the rest of the disciples . . . continually exhibiting his own unique love," which sort of love is "distinctive of the divine nature" (*Commentary on the Gospel of John*, 9, cited in Elowsky, *John 11–21*, 94).

42. So also Köstenberger, "Sensitivity to Outsiders," 180.

43. Moloney, *Love in the Gospel of John*, 112.

Jesus' faithless friends, both then and subsequently. The foot washing is a counter-cultural and counter-intuitive act of grace, of enemy-love. And, as we saw in chapter 3, because Jesus is the "unique self-exegesis" of God,[44] then *Jesus'* love in motion, as he stoops to wash feet, is *God's* love in motion. The foot washing tells us something profound, not only about the self-emptying, self-giving enemy-love of *Jesus*, but also about the gracious, self-giving enemy-love of *God*. In John 13, we find "the extraordinary revelation of God—'God at our feet.'"[45] This is the God of whom Jesus' disciples are to become children, sharing in such divine DNA.

In John, then, Jesus is not only a "friend of sinners";[46] he is a "lover of enemies." He willingly gives life *to* the world (6:33), and he does so by giving his flesh *for* the world (6:51, 57) despite its hostility toward him, his Father, and his disciples. As Jan van der Watt rightly contends, "Sharing meals has definite ethical implications."[47] Accordingly, Jesus' decision to share this last meal with sinners and enemies like Judas and Peter, and to wash their feet, is an implicit example and exhortation for Jesus' followers to act missionally, in analogous ways, toward their own enemies.

Jesus rejects violence toward enemies as he prepares to die for them

Judas and Peter reappear in the dramatic scene of Jesus' arrest, in which Peter commits an act of violence just after Jesus twice identifies himself as the divine "I AM":[48]

> [10]Then Simon Peter, who had a sword, drew it, struck the high priest's slave, and cut off his right ear. The slave's name was Malchus. [11]Jesus said to Peter, "Put your sword back into its sheath. Am I not to drink the cup that the Father has given me?" (John 18:10–11)

This incident is also narrated in the other Gospels (Matt 26:51–54; Mark 14:47; Luke 22:49–51). In Matthew (26:52) and Luke (22:51), as in

---

44. Udo Schnelle's term in light of 1:18 (*Theology of the New Testament*, 674).

45. Byrne, *Life Abounding*, 228. Similarly, Moloney, *Love in the Gospel of John*, 108.

46. Burridge, *Imitating Jesus*, 334–44.

47. See Van der Watt, "Radical Social Redefinition and Radical Love," 121 and "Ethics and Ethos," 166, though he does not make the connection to enemy-love.

48. See 18:5, 8 (cf. 18:6), and Exod 3:11–15; Isa 43:10–13. The "I AM" (which is helpfully typeset this way, not simply as "I am," in the NAB) is often mistranslated as "I am he."

John, Jesus rejects violence on his behalf against his enemies. In all three Synoptic Gospels, the incident itself and/or its immediate aftermath is interpreted either as the fulfillment of Scripture (Matthew, Mark) or as the dramatic climax of the power of Satan (Luke); that is, the event itself is bigger than the actions of the human characters. So too in John. Immediately before Peter's attack on the slave, Jesus' request to let his disciples go is interpreted as the fulfillment of Scripture (18:9). Moreover, in his response to Peter, Jesus reaffirms his need to "drink the cup that the Father has given me" (18:11)—that is, to fulfill his Father's will by going to the cross.

The irony in the Johannine narrative is palpable. Only in John is Peter—as well as the slave, Malchus—named. The man who would "lay down my life for you" (13:37) may now be dangerously close to taking someone else's life for Jesus' sake. Peter thinks he is *defending* Jesus, but his violent deed is an act of *denying* Jesus, a preamble to his flat-out denial to come. His violence is a repudiation of Jesus' example of loving enemies (chapter 13), of his gift of peace in the midst of hostility from the world (14:27; 16:33), and his guarantee that what he is doing and how he is doing it is a victory over the hostile world (16:33)—though not by means of worldly ways (cf. 18:36, discussed below). Furthermore, this victorious Jesus is not merely able to call for his Father's angels; he is the very presence of God, as his double "I AM" statement implies just before the sword incident (18:5, 8). The Son who is one with the Father, the agent of creation, hardly needs a disciple, a sword, or even a multitude of the heavenly host for protection or battle. Yet the powerful Word, who can knock soldiers to their knees with a word, "does not destroy his captors; instead, he gives himself to them."[49]

Jesus' penetrating rhetorical question to Peter, "Am I not to drink the cup that the Father has given me?" (18:11b), is much more than acceptance of his fate. Jesus is stating that he is going to fulfill his saving mission that gives ultimate expression to God's love for the world and draws people to himself—even people like the high priest and his slave. (Malchus' name is known because he likely became a follower of Jesus.) The image of "drinking the cup" is found only here in John, but it appears also in the Synoptic tradition as a reference to Jesus' suffering and death and to the meal that both precedes and commemorates that death.[50] In Mark and Matthew, the cup imagery is first used as a word-picture, not only for Jesus' death, but also for his disciples' "drinking the same cup," that is, sharing in Jesus' mission and fate (Matt 20:22–23; Mark 10:38–39[51])—which is clearly

---

49. Thompson, *John*, 364.

50. Matt 20:22–23; 26:27–29, 39; Mark 10:38–39; 14:23–25, 36; Luke 22:17–20, 42.

51. Luke lacks the explicit text ("i.e., "You will drink my cup"), but implies the idea

participatory, and which, in concrete terms, means taking up their own cross, even to the point of suffering and death.[52] Even if John does not know one or more of the actual Synoptic Gospels, John 18:11 is a clear echo of the Synoptic Jesus tradition, oral or otherwise. Thus, Peter is implicitly being invited not only to accept Jesus' death, and Jesus' non-violent response to his persecutors, but also to accept his own participation in that dying and nonviolence—that is, receiving rather than inflicting violence. In 21:18–19, this implicit invitation will become an explicit call to discipleship for Peter, and a prophecy concerning him.

The Christology of this narrative in its context is critically important. Eleven times in chapters 18 and 19 Jesus is referred to as a "king."[53] The question at the heart of the passion narrative in John is "What *kind* of king is Jesus?" The answer? He is an otherworldly king, meaning not that his reign is invisible and spiritual, but that it is defined by its source: heaven, the abode of God the Father, who *is* love and *does* love—even toward enemies. "My kingdom is not from [or "of"] this world," says Jesus. "If my kingdom were from this world, my followers would be fighting to keep me from being handed over to the Jews. But as it is, my kingdom is not from here" (18:36). His is a kingdom that is not shaped, propagated, or defended by the violence of human kingdoms.[54]

The incident in the garden, then, is at once revelatory of God (it is a theophany of sorts, as all fall down); of Jesus the godly king, the nature of his mission, and his commitment to that mission; and of the *inappropriate* way to participate in that mission (with violence), which also means, implicitly, the *appropriate* way: by forsaking violence and taking up the cross that draws all kinds of people, even enemies, to the Crucified One. This scene therefore implicitly reflects the theme of, and constitutes an invitation to, missional theosis.

Jesus offers his disciples shalom and the Spirit, and rehabilitates the violent Peter

As we saw in the previous chapter, John 20 and 21 narrate the resurrection appearances of Jesus and the implicit and explicit episodes of commissioning

---

in several ways, not least in the narrative of the Last Supper.

52. Matt 10:37–38; Mark 8:34—9:1 par.; 9:33–37 par.; 10:35–45 par.

53. See Swartley, *Covenant of Peace*, 284. The references are 18:33, 37 (2x), 39; 19:3, 12, 14, 15, 19, 21 (2x).

54. See also Swartley, *Covenant of Peace*, 299–300. On the whole passage and its implications, see Scheffler, "Jesus' Non-violence at His Arrest."

the disciples. Each chapter contains numerous connections to earlier parts of the Gospel, too.

The disciples as a group are literarily central to chapter 20, which begins and ends with a focus on individuals (Mary Magdalene and Thomas). At the supper, Jesus had promised the Spirit, or Paraclete/Advocate (14:15–17, 25–27; 15:26–27; 16:7–15), to his disciples, together with his gift of peace, or shalom (14:27; 16:33), as the disciples were about to be sent into a hostile world to bear witness and fruit. When Jesus appears to his disciples after the resurrection, he reaffirms the gift of peace (20:19, 21, 26) and breathes the Spirit into them so they can continue the "chain" of mission: Father → Son → disciples:

> [21]Jesus said to them again, "Peace be with you. As the Father has sent me, so I send you." [22]When he had said this, he breathed on them and said to them, "Receive the Holy Spirit. [23]If you forgive the sins of any, they are forgiven them; if you retain the sins of any, they are retained." (20:21–23)

As in the Mission Discourse, the gifts of the Spirit and shalom are for the work of mission, specifically mission that is continuous in character with the mission of Jesus, which can only mean embodying the love of God for the hostile world. In that mission, the disciples are to practice peace by offering not condemnation, but forgiveness—just like their heavenly Father—though there is no guarantee that their mission as Spirit-empowered agents of the Father and the Son will always be accepted and forgiveness thereby granted (cf. 3:18). The gift of shalom should therefore not be construed narrowly as "inner tranquility." It is a *missional* peace, a gift that implicitly continues the message to Peter in the garden: the kingdom of Jesus does not come through or give rise to violence.[55]

Peter is explicitly the main subject of chapter 21 (though he has a representative role), and many interpreters have noted the connections between it and earlier chapters. Two details in the episodes involving Peter are echoes of earlier episodes and are of particular interest to us once again in this chapter.

First, there is the Greek verb *helkō*, "draw, haul," which occurs five times in John: to signify the activity of the Father and the Son in drawing people to themselves (6:44; 12:32), the hauling in of fishing nets (21:6, 11—the latter referring specifically to Peter), and Peter's drawing his sword to cut off the ear of Malchus (18:10). Apart from this last occurrence, the verb is employed in John to express mission, whether the outreach of the Father

---

55. See also Swartley, *Covenant of Peace*, 288.

and the Son or, symbolically, the disciples' mission of fishing for people. In chapter 21, Peter is being portrayed as one whose task is to draw people to Jesus, as a participant in Jesus' shalom-filled mission, rather than one whose mission is to draw the sword in violent acts against enemies to protect or promote Jesus. The contrast between Peter's two types of hauling/drawing invites auditors and readers of the Gospel to consider the two missional options and to choose the appropriate one.

Second, the charcoal fire (21:9—*anthrakian*) that is associated with the presence of the risen Jesus in chapter 21 recalls the scene of Peter's threefold denial around another charcoal fire (18:18—*anthrakian*). The charcoal fire anticipates the imminent restoration of Peter, through an appropriate three-fold question-and-affirmation session with Jesus (21:15–17). The renewal of Peter implicitly includes his leaving behind "worldly" ways of establishing the kingdom of the Father and the Son, particularly by means of violence, and embracing the worldwide mission of "fishing" for people (21:1–14), feeding the resulting "sheep" (21:15–17), and—like the Good Shepherd himself (10:11–18)—being willing to sacrifice one's own life in the service of that divine, life-giving mission (21:18–19).[56]

Summary: John's narratives of enemy-love

Our examination of aspects of the Johannine narrative has strongly suggested that Jesus both practiced enemy-love and implicitly taught it to his disciples. The question before us now is how this *implicit* ethic relates to the *explicit* ethic simply to "love one another."

"I Have Set You an Example"

A basic text from the Dead Sea Scrolls, Rule of the Community (1QS), begins with a requirement to love God wholeheartedly by *loving* whatever God has chosen and *hating* whatever God has rejected (I,1–4). Specifically, this means to "love all the sons of light" and "hate all the sons of darkness" (I,9–10). Moreover, at some future date, according to the War Scroll (1QM, 4QM), the sons of light will destroy the chief sons of darkness, the gentile rulers (*Kittim*).[57] Is this possibly what "love one another" implies in John— love the children of light, but hate the children of darkness ("the world")?

---

56. Similarly, Byers (*Ecclesiology and Theosis*, 222–23) finds in Peter an example of a "divinized," or Christlike, character who, as an "under-shepherd," shares in the suffering of Jesus the Good Shepherd.

57. See the helpful summary in Meier, *Law and Love*, 537–39.

One often hears that, unlike the Synoptics, John contains neither the general exhortation to love one's neighbor nor the particular command to love one's enemies (as Jesus requires in Matt 5:44; Luke 6:27, 35). It is also normally said, however, that at least John, unlike the Dead Sea Scrolls, neither describes nor prescribes reciprocal hatred of enemies.[58] While true, the latter observation does not really get to the heart of the matter, or of the fundamental difference between John and such texts from the Scrolls. For in each case, the root question is this: what does it mean to be children of the light, children of *God*, and thus to *become like God*? As John Meier explains, the rationale for the Scrolls' promoting hatred of the children of darkness is that "only in that way can one align oneself with God, who likewise hates them and dooms them to eternal destruction."[59]

Since the purpose of a Gospel as an ancient biography is, in part, to narrate its audience into the story and way of life of its protagonist, and since for John Jesus in motion is in fact God in motion, then the ethics implied by Jesus' activity—including his enemy-love—is, in part, what it means implicitly in John to become like God (theosis). But does the *explicit* ethic of "love one another" in chapters 13 and 15 contradict this compelling, but only *implicit*, ethic of imitating God?

No greater love

In John 15:13, Jesus famously declares, "No one has greater love than this, to lay down one's life for one's friends," describing his friends as those who obey him (15:14). Does this automatically limit Jesus' love and its corollary ethic to one's friends? Two points need to be made.

First, the maxim in v. 13 is one of *definition* rather than *exclusion*. Jesus is not *limiting* his own love or that of his disciples to friends. Rather, he says that *self-giving* love, even to the point of giving up one's life, as he himself is about to do, is the essence of friendship.

Second, ever since the patristic period, some commentators have interpreted this text in connection with Jesus' example of enemy-love and his injunction to his disciples to love their enemies. For example, Augustine calls to mind Paul's words about God's enemy-love in Romans 5, noted earlier in this chapter:

---

58. E.g., Burridge, *Imitating Jesus*, 334; Swartley, *Covenant of Peace*, 277, adapting an earlier work.

59. Meier, *Law and Love*, 539.

So there you are. In Christ we do find greater love, seeing that he gave up his life not for his friends but for his enemies. How great must be God's love for humanity and what extraordinary affection, so to love even sinners that he would die for love of them![60]

Does Augustine mute the distinctive voice of John? The narrative of John's Gospel suggests not. As we have seen, Peter will soon disobey and thereby "unfriend" Jesus, yet there is every evidence that Jesus dies for, forgives, and rehabilitates Peter. That is, Jesus loved and died for Peter in spite of Peter's betrayal; he loved and died for the friend-turned-enemy so that the enemy could once again become a friend. Peter, in this narrative capacity, is both an individual and a representative of all disciples, past and present.

Gregory the Great reads 15:13 similarly, connecting it to Luke 23:34 ("Father, forgive them; for they do not know what they are doing") and focusing on its ethical implications:

The Lord had come to die even for his enemies, and yet he said he would lay down his life for his friends to show us that when we are able to win over our enemies by loving them, even our persecutors are our friends.[61]

Emissaries of enemy-love

There will be no ears lopped off of slaves—or anyone else—by the new Peter, the disciple re-friended by Jesus, and all he represents. Instead, they will be emissaries of enemy-love. The context of the love command supports this claim.

Earlier we argued that if the activity of Jesus is also the activity of God, then when Jesus tells the disciples that he has given them an "example" (13:15), he is telling them not only that such foot washing imitates him, but also that it imitates the Father. Moreover, if God has washed not only the feet of friends but also the feet of enemies, then the action to which the foot washing points is not merely servant-love for *friends* (so 15:13–15), but also servant-love for *enemies*. The context, therefore, of "love one another" when Jesus first pronounces the words (13:14, implicitly; 13:34–35) is itself the example of enemy-love.

The context of "love one another" in both John 13 and John 15 is also mission, as we saw in chapter 3. The exhortation to "love one another," and

60. Augustine, *Sermon* 215.5, quoted in Elowsky, *John 11–21*, 174.

61. Gregory the Great, *Forty Gospel Homilies* 27, quoted in Elowsky, *John 11–21*, 173–74.

to the unity such love produces, is never far from words about the disciples' being sent and bearing witness. An important table from chapter 3 bears reconfiguring and expanding here:

"One another"	Missional context
So if I, the Lord and Teacher, have washed your feet, you also ought to wash one another's feet. (13:14; my translation)	[A] slave is not greater than his or her master, nor is a sent one (*apostolos*) greater than the one who sent that person (13:16; my translation)
	[W]hoever receives one whom I send receives me; and whoever receives me receives the One who sent me (13:20; my translation)
[L]ove one another. Just as I have loved you, you also should love one another. (13:34)	
	By this everyone will know that you are my disciples . . . (13:35a)
. . . if you have love for one another. (13:35b)	
[L]ove one another as I have loved you . . . love one another (15:12b, 17b)	I chose you. And I appointed you to go and bear fruit, fruit that will last (15:16)
As you, Father, are in me and I am in you, may they also be in us . . . (17:21a)	. . . so that the world may believe that you have sent me. (17:21b)
. . . that they may be one, as we are one, I in them and you in me, that they may become completely one . . . (17:22b–23a)	. . . so that the world may know that you have sent me and have loved them even as you have loved me. (17:23b)

Loving one another does not require disciples to go anywhere, but loving a hostile world certainly does (15:16; "go"). Thus, Jesus' love command and example do not end with love among the disciples, nor do they have internal unity as their ultimate goal. Such love and unity are meant to bring others—*including specifically others who are hostile toward God and God's agents in the world*—into the divine love and life.[62] "As you have sent me into the world, so I have sent them [his disciples] into the world," prays Jesus (17:18). That is, the disciples are sent out of divine love, shared among themselves, to bring others, even haters and persecutors, into the love of the Father, Son, and community. A Brian Wren hymn summarizes the Johannine

---

62. See also Moloney, *Love in the Gospel of John*, 129–32.

sentiment: "[W]e'll go with joy, to give the world, the love that makes us one."[63] And that world, in John's Gospel, is a *hostile* world.

These two essential contexts of the love command—enemy-love and mission—come together in the warnings Jesus issues about hostility. The disciples' witness will also have negative consequences (15:18–25; cf. 13:16) simply because Jesus' own love for the world—for enemies—had such results. Parallel to the chain of mission, there is a chain of hatred and hostility similarly focused on Jesus as the center link, flanked by the sending Father and the sent disciples (15:18, 20–21, 23–24; cf. 16:33; 17:14–16; cf. 1 John 3:13).[64] This chain can be depicted, as with other chains, like this: (hatred/rejection of) Father → Son → disciples. Perhaps the actual "flow" of hatred, however, is best represented as follows: Father ← Son → disciples. That is, the hostility is focused on Jesus and spreads from him to the Sender and the sent ones.

In context, then, "love one another" includes love for the world and for enemies. Ultimately this is because "God so loved the world," and because Jesus, as Richard Burridge remarks, "shows us what the divine love is like, so that we can imitate him and so participate in the divine life."[65] This is clearly a spirituality of participation, even of theosis, that is inherently missional in character. To participate in the life of God, according to John, is to love others, including enemies.

John's *explicit* ethic, then, does not contradict its *implicit* ethic. But does Jesus' own behavior contradict it?

"You Are from Your Father the Devil" (John 8:44)— Counterfactual Evidence?

If the Fourth Gospel implicitly advocates enemy-love, is not the hate speech we find in it, even on the lips of Jesus (especially in John 8), a telling counterfactual proof of just the opposite? If an ancient biography was supposed to encourage imitation of the subject, then what do we do with John when the behavior of the divine subject(s)—the Son and the Father—looks unworthy of imitation?

One answer would be to take such behaviors as negative examples, which would be appropriate for a standard ancient biography, but hardly so—at least for most Christians in either the first or the twenty-first century—for a biography of Jesus the Son of God. Another answer, commonly

---

63. The last lines of "I Come with Joy" (1971).

64. See also Thompson, *John*, 355.

65. Burridge, *Imitating Jesus*, 345.

offered by commentators on John, is to interpret the strong critique of "the Jews" in light of the proposed historical situation of a community under fire from the synagogue, together with the purported normalcy of invective speech in ancient rhetoric. In that social and rhetorical context, it has been argued, such strong language placed on the lips of Jesus is at least somewhat understandable, even if it is ultimately deemed inappropriate or worse. In this scenario, the "historical" Jesus is exonerated and the community or social world blamed.

But this explanation does not satisfy, either historically or theologically. Historically, there is significant doubt about what we can know about the Johannine community and its situation.[66] And theologically, we are still left wondering, "How can Jesus, remembered by the Johannine Christians as representing the God who loves the world, even the hostile world, spew such venom?" Furthermore, we must wonder, "How can Jesus' disciples then or now be expected to imitate Jesus if the Jesus they imitate does such things?"

The answer to how we can explain Jesus' strong language literarily and theologically lies in at least two dimensions of the phenomenon of "enemies" in Johannine perspective.

First of all, in the poetic and prophetic traditions of Israel, enemies are regularly identified by name and/or activity.[67] Enemies must first be *identified* before there can be an appropriate response to them. Throughout the Fourth Gospel, Jesus identifies those who reject him and thereby reject God—what the Scriptures of Israel refer to as the enemies of God. And yet, even as those enemies are *identified* by Jesus in John, they are not ultimately *rejected*. Despite all the rejection of Jesus (and thus of God the Father) by "the world," and most especially by his own people, Jesus dies for all. In addition to the manifestation of this universal love in the foot washing as an icon of the cross, this universal love for the hostile world is displayed—literally—on the cross itself. The inscription on the cross, "in Hebrew, in Latin, and in Greek" (19:20), not only announces Jesus as king, but also indicates the *kind* of king he is—the king of suffering love, in radical contrast to the king of oppressive power (the emperor and his representative, Pilate) and in radical continuity with the God revealed in the foot washing. "In this is love, not that we loved God but that he loved us and sent his Son to be the atoning sacrifice for our sins" (1 John 4:10). In other words, the naming of Jesus' enemies does not negate the fact that he loves

---

66. See especially Lamb, *Text, Context and the Johannine Community.*

67. E.g., Pss 9–10, 14, 35–36, 74, 83; Isa 13–24; Amos 1–2. See Motyer, *Your Father the Devil?* 134–40.

them on behalf of the Father; the inscription on the cross is in "Hebrew" (possibly Aramaic) because "the Jews"—whatever the precise referent (the Jewish people, the Judeans, Jewish leaders, Jewish opponents of Jesus, synagogue members)—are still the object of God's love, of Jesus' love. Perhaps the Pharisee Nicodemus, the seeker turned defender turned friend (3:1–10; 7:50–52; 19:38–40), is a narrative sign of that reality.[68]

Second, the Gospel of John depicts an apocalyptic conflict between two fathers and their children: God, the Son of God, and the children of God, on the one hand, versus Satan and his children, on the other. As in the Synoptics and Paul, and as already noted, the ultimate enemy of God and Jesus (and therefore of humanity) is Satan, the ruler of this world, "the evil one" (17:15).[69] For John, calling those who oppose the Father and the Son children of "your father the devil" (8:44) is not hate speech. It is, within the Johannine perspective, naming the enemies—a statement of fact. Tom Thatcher calls it "an essentially neutral" observation "about the natural course of affairs, not . . . hateful or unloving accusations."[70] For "the Johannine premise" is that "actions reveal ancestry."[71] Indeed, what is remarkable, in contrast to the Dead Sea Scrolls that also depict a conflict between the children of God/light and the children of darkness, is that neither Jesus himself nor the narrator calls on the children of light to hate—much less exterminate—the children of darkness. The implicit theology in the Scrolls, as we saw earlier, is essentially one of deification—sharing in the divine character: if you hate your enemies, you will be like God! The implicit theology and ethic of John is also one of theosis, but a theosis that is antithetical to that of the Scrolls: although you have enemies, do not hate them but love them, because you are disciples of God's Son and children of God the Father.[72] If you love your enemies, you will be like God! This participatory love, this sharing in the divine DNA, is at the heart of John's apocalyptic spirituality and ethic of theosis.[73]

68. See also Culpepper, "Nicodemus."

69. Jesus of course defeats Satan in the cross and resurrection, an act of "cosmic exorcism" (Swartley, *Covenant of Peace*, 280).

70. Thatcher, "Cain the Jew the AntiChrist," 372.

71. Thatcher, "Cain the Jew the AntiChrist," 354.

72. Thatcher, "Cain the Jew the AntiChrist," 356.

73. For a compelling argument that the Gospel of John is neither anti-Semitic nor supportive of violence, see Anderson, "Anti-Semitism and Religious Violence."

Conclusion

Not all that is important in a text is explicit. As Jan van der Watt points out, in John believers are never called to love God, yet everything about the Gospel indicates the presumption that believers will live in loving obedience to their Father.[74] Similarly, although the Fourth Gospel never declares "Love your enemies," it implies precisely that in its presentation of God, the activity of Jesus, the love command, and the Spirit-empowered mission of the disciples.

In the Dead Sea Scrolls, we find an explicit exhortation to hate enemies. Its theological grammar is "Hate your enemies, and you will be like God." The well-known theological grammar of Matthew and Luke is "If you love your enemies, you will become like your (perfect/merciful) heavenly Father" (see Matt 5:43–48/Luke 6:27–36). We have discovered that the theological grammar of John is "If you are children of God, enlivened with his Spirit, you will love as your heavenly Father does and as Jesus the Son did, which means loving enemies." The fundamental issue in all of these cases is becoming like God, or deification (theosis). For Matthew and Luke, on the one hand, and John, on the other, the theological grammar is slightly different, but the net result is the same: Godlike love of enemies. And throughout John, Jesus is the one who incarnates, models, and enjoins this sort of divine love for his disciples then and now. Missional theosis, in other words, includes within it love for enemies, a love that may sweep them, by grace, into the breadth and depth of God's love in Christ.

The entire Gospel of John has been about extreme divine love. And the corollary of that extreme divine love is extreme participation in that love. Such is the challenge, as well as the promise, of missional theosis.

---

74. Van der Watt, "Ethics and Ethos," 160.

7

Conclusions and Hermeneutical Reflections on Contemporary Missional Theosis

This final chapter will first summarize the preceding chapters and place them in dialogue with certain other interpreters. It will then offer some hermeneutical reflections about missional theosis, based in part from this study and in part from my having observed missional theosis in practice.

Summarizing the Present Book

The central thesis of this book has been the following:

> Johannine spirituality fundamentally consists in the *mutual indwelling* of the Triune God (Father, Son, and Spirit) and Jesus' disciples such that disciples *participate* in the divine love and life, and therefore in the life-giving mission of God, thereby both *demonstrating their likeness to God as God's children* and *becoming more and more like God as they become like his Son by the work of the Spirit*. This spirituality can be summarized in the phrase "abide and go," based on John 15.

This thesis has been developed in six chapters.

Chapter 1, "Reading John Missionally and Theotically," considered this book as a work of missional hermeneutics and a reading of John in terms of theosis. The first part of the chapter defined missional hermeneutics as reading Scripture to discern and participate in what God is doing in Christ by the Spirit in general as well as in the readers' particular time and place (the *missio Dei*). Of the various approaches to, or streams of, missional hermeneutics, this book's approach is primarily text-centered. The chapter then stated the book's thesis and discussed the meaning of both theosis and missional theosis; it also briefly responded to objections to theosis. The final part of the chapter developed the notion of missional theosis in more detail, interacting with some recent work on theosis in John. One way to summarize missional theosis is to say that participation in the divine mission effects transformation into the likeness of God, who is by nature love and thus missional.

Chapter 2, "Missional Theosis in John: Structure, Theme, and Chapters 1–12," provided the book's basic perspective on the Gospel of John. The first part of the chapter considered and began to answer certain objections to the claim that John is in fact a spiritual and missional/ethical gospel. The next section argued for the centrality of mission to the Gospel's structure, challenging the traditional Prologue, Book of Signs, Book of Glory, Epilogue approach. Especially important were the following: renaming the Prologue as the Opening; designating chapters 13 to 17 the Mission Discourse rather than the Farewell Discourse, and uniting chapters 20 and 21 into a coherent unit about the resurrection and mission. The third part of the chapter considered the Gospel's theme of "life," tracing its significance in the Gospel and in its canonical context, with special reference to Ezekiel 34. The next part of the chapter explored the meaning of becoming children of God, gifted with the Spirit to become like God, in the first half of the Gospel, focusing on its implicit expectation that disciples participate in the divine mission. The final sections of the chapter focused on the life-giving intent of Jesus' signs, relating them as well to his discourse and to his life-giving death.

Chapter 3, "Abide and Go: Missional Theosis in John 13–16," focused especially on John 13 (the foot washing) and John 15 (abiding in the vine, bearing fruit) in terms of missional theosis. The chapter argued that intra-community or centripetal love in these chapters is ultimately centrifugal—outward-oriented. Spirituality, love, and mission are all united. The chapter began, however, with a look at the theological starting points of participation, namely the participation within the Godhead (perichoresis) and the participation of God with humanity (the incarnation). John portrays a missional, mutually indwelling God who has participated in human life and is forming a missional people who will be in a mutually indwelling relationship with that incarnate God. Next, the chapter considered the nature of John 13 to 17 as the Mission Discourse, including its relationship to the first half of the Gospel and to the "hour," the imminent death and exaltation of

Jesus. It stressed the claim that when the disciples participate missionally in Jesus' loving death, they are, paradoxically, participating in God's life. The discussion of John 13 emphasized the participatory and missional character of the iconic foot washing episode, concluding that theosis for John is both missional and cruciform. The section on John 15 highlighted the centrality of the verb "abide" but also the presence of the verbs "bear fruit" and "go/depart," meaning that the vine (the community of disciples in Christ) is a missional community, a "mobile vine," characterized by the paradoxical imperative "abide and go."

Chapter 4, "As the Father Has Sent Me (I): Missional Theosis in John 17," argued that John 17 is Jesus' commissioning prayer that concludes the Mission Discourse. The prayer focuses on the mission of Jesus himself, his immediate disciples, and his future disciples. Its main theme is participation in the divine unity and holiness such that the disciples can bear appropriate witness to the loving mission of the Father through the Son. That is, the disciples' unity will be both *participatory* (in the divine unity) and *purposeful* (to bear witness to the world). Jesus' prayer in John 17 presents us with a corporate spirituality for faithful witness. The chapter ends with a look at the word "do" as a unifying feature of the Mission Discourse; the disciples, by "doing," continue the "doing," the work, of the Father in the Son.

Chapter 5, "As the Father Has Sent Me (II): Missional Theosis in John 20–21," considered what missional theosis looks like in light of the resurrection and the gift of the Spirit. Following the structure of the Gospel proposed in chapter 2, this chapter kept John 20 and 21 together, seeing within them narratives of appearance and commissioning. The discussion of John 20 examined the narratives of Mary Magdalene as apostle to the apostles, the disciples as Spirit-infused agents of shalom, and Thomas as ideal believer and witness. Within the narrative of the disciples receiving the Spirit, the chapter explored the mode (Christlikeness), means (the Spirit), and content (shalom, forgiveness, life) of the disciples' mission. The analysis of chapter 21 noted the themes of the Gospel that are resolved or otherwise reprised as Jesus encounters and commissions the disciples. As fishers and as shepherds, the disciples are called to participate in a Father-conceived, Jesus-shaped, Spirit-empowered mission that will have a cruciform shape.

In chapter 6, "Extreme Missional Theosis: John's Implicit Ethic of Enemy-Love," we took a look back at the entire Gospel to see the prominence of the implicit but clear theme of enemy-love in John as missional theosis. The chapter examined what John states about God's enemy-love, narrates about Jesus' enemy-love, and infers about the disciples' enemy-love. After reviewing the concerns of some scholars that John lacks an ethic of outsider- or enemy-love, the chapter reviewed the nature of a gospel as ancient biography that presents a character to be imitated. The next part of the chapter traced the themes of God's love for a hostile humanity. The following section considered the enemy-loving actions of Jesus, particularly in washing the feet of Judas and Peter; in rejecting violence; and in offering forgiveness and the Spirit to the disciples, including Peter. This was then connected to the claim of Jesus that he is an example for his disciples, who are to be emissaries of enemy love. After examining some possible objections to the chapter's thesis, the chapter concluded with a comparison of theosis in the Dead Sea Scrolls and in John. To be like God is to love enemies, not hate or kill them. In this chapter, and throughout much of the book, we concluded that missional theosis is a costly participationist spirituality; it is, in other words, cruciform.

Having summarized the preceding chapters one by one, we can synthesize the book's conclusions from another angle: by returning to the three general questions we identified with missional hermeneutics in chapter: What does the Gospel of John say about the *missio Dei?* What does it say about the condition of humanity and the world, about the need for God's saving mission? and What does John say about the nature and mission of God's people as participants in the *missio Dei?*

What does the Gospel of John say about the missio Dei?

The God of the Gospel of John is the God of love, light, and life. As a divine community, indeed a divine family, of mutually indwelling communion, the Father, Son, and Spirit desire to include "the world"—humanity—within that divine family of love, light, and life. This gracious desire, or purpose, was begun in the creation of the world through Jesus the Word; expressed in the covenantal relationship with Israel; maintained in spite of human hostility; promised through the prophets to be renewed, deepened, and expanded in the eschatological age; and fulfilled in the incarnation, ministry, and death/resurrection (exaltation) of the Son. In his incarnation, the Son, sent by the Father, became like us so that we could become like him. The heart of the love shared within the divine family is manifested in Jesus' self-giving, life-giving death.

This divine mission of salvation is most commonly referred to in John as "life," or "eternal life," meaning both the divine life and the prophetically promised life of the age to come, which can be (partially but really) experienced in the present. This life is holistic and abundant, both "spiritual" and material—an embodied wholeness. It is entered into by encountering Jesus and acknowledging him and his death as the means of attaining life. This encounter is described as a new birth from above, a complete immersion in the life of God by means of baptism by the Spirit. Those who believe and are baptized in the Spirit enter the divine family and begin the process of becoming like the Son, which means also becoming like the Father who sent him, by the enabling work of the Spirit. This life is experienced not merely individualistically but communally, as branches in the vine. God's mission is to engender a family of children who share in the divine "DNA" (identity and behavior) and thereby participate in the "family business" as a unified, holy community sharing in the unity, holiness, and mission of the divine family.

What does the Gospel of John say about the condition of humanity and the world, about the need for God's saving mission?

The Gospel of John portrays humanity as in desperate need of the life offered by God. People are characterized as lacking faith, living in darkness, and existing in a state characterized by both sin and death. They are in a condition of hostility toward God and God's agents, especially the Son. They are thereby in a state of self-inflicted condemnation. In spite of all of this, however, they are loved by God the Father and Jesus the Son.

What does the Gospel of John say about the nature and mission of God's people as participants in the missio Dei?

As God's children and participants in the divine family, Jesus' disciples constitute the branches of a "mobile vine" that are expected to abide in Jesus even as they depart and bear fruit. Their commission is to "abide and go," becoming more like the Son as they participate in his ongoing ministry enabled by the *alter Christus*, the indwelling Spirit/Paraclete. They have been infused with this Spirit to bear faithful witness to Jesus, extending his shalom, forgiveness, and life to the world, to all. Because the life Jesus offers through them is the holistic life of the age to come, their ministry, or mission, will also be comprehensive and holistic, both "spiritual" and material. The nature of this mission is portrayed as participating in the "fishing" and "shepherding" mission of Jesus, in dependence on him.

The disciples' faithful participation in this divine mission depends on their corporate participation in the unity and holiness of the divine family. Foot washing is the symbol of their life together and in the world. That is, the shape of their mission will be like that of the Son in his self-giving, life-giving, friend-and-enemy-loving death. Together the disciples of all times and places constitute the sent one—the *apostolos*—of the Sent One. Their mission is not their own, but rather that of the Father, Son, and Spirit, in which they participate. And as they participate in this self-giving, life-giving mission, they become more and more like the God in whose life and mission they participate: disciples becoming disciples.

The spirituality we find in John's Gospel *is in no sense whatsoever "sectarian," fostering a community turned in on itself*. Rather, we find a missional spirituality that can be summarized as missional theosis: transformative, communal participation in the life and mission of the Father, Son, and Spirit. It is a mission that is *comprehensive* in its life-giving quality, *Christlike*—indeed cruciform—in its shape, and *charismatic* (or pneumatic) in its actual operation. "Jack Sanders' (in)famous caricature of Johannine ethics could not be further from the truth."[1]

Dialoguing with Other Interpreters

As we conclude our study, it might be valuable to set it in the context of the wider study of John with respect to its main topics: mission and theosis, and especially their connection to each other. How does the approach taken here compare to the work of other scholars? As noted early on, this book is, in a sense, part of the "movement" toward taking Johannine ethics (which can include mission and participation) more seriously. Interpreters with this sort of interest include Jan van der Watt, Ruben Zimmerman, Kobus Kok, Christopher Skinner, Sherri Brown, and a growing number of others. With respect to mission specifically, many others, including scholars of previous generations, have of course thought about mission in John. Language about theosis in John, though more ancient, is—ironically—much newer in contemporary biblical studies. We cannot possibly review all the interpreters mentioned in the previous six chapters, but we may briefly consider a few scholars we have encountered along the way as examples of important similarities and differences.

Some examples of a missional focus

Raymond Brown contends, in commenting on John 20:21–22, that "the special Johannine contribution" to the church's missional theology is its having

---

1. Moloney, "God, Eschatology, and 'This World,'" 215. For the Sanders quote, see chapters 2 and 6.

the Father's sending of the Son as both "the model and the ground" for the Son's sending of the disciples.[2] We would be in error to quarrel with the significance of the sending motif in the Fourth Gospel, but although many interpreters of John would concur with Brown's assessment, the question pursued in this book concerns how this missional motif relates to the Gospel's profound spirituality of indwelling and participation.

In his *New Testament and Mission*, Johannes Nissen offers five hermeneutical perspectives on the character of mission in John: it is trinitarian, incarnational, pneumatological, and contextually sensitive by being dialogical with various religious traditions, while also ultimately discontinuous with them ("I am the way . . .").[3] While I do not concur with every detail of his interpretation of these five points, they are a helpful summary of certain aspects of John's missional theology, moving out beyond the obvious central motif of sending identified by Brown. With respect to the trinitarian character of mission in John, Nissen rightly speaks of both divine perichoresis and a divine missional ontology, since God is love. He stresses the incarnation as the full and unique revelation of God, and he focuses on the free but Christocentric work of the Spirit. And on the subject of other religious traditions—a topic we have not explored in this book—he rightly maintains an attitude of respect and dialogue while holding fast to his trinitarian and christological convictions.

What was missing from Brown's brief claim is also absent from Nissen's summary: mission as participation. Brown does say that the disciples "continue the Son's mission" and that this "requires that the Son must be present to them during this mission"—which is approximating participation, but it is not quite there.[4] And, to be sure, Nissen says that the church's mission is "Spirit-empowered,"[5] and that the same Spirit brings about transformation through rebirth.[6] But he is wary of terms like "divinization" because of the ancient (and perhaps also modern) misunderstandings of such terms.[7] Andrew Lincoln, on the other hand, though not using theosis language, identifies the disciples as, at its core, "a community that participates in the divine

---

2. Brown, *John* 2:1036.

3. Nissen, *New Testament and Mission*, 92–96. I have re-ordered his list and used some of my own language to summarize his points. He is particularly attentive to the potential John has for understanding mission in a religiously pluralistic world.

4. Brown, *John*, 2:1036.

5. Nissen, *New Testament and Mission*, 96.

6. Nissen, *New Testament and Mission*, 88–89.

7. Nissen does, however, describe the results of new birth as "new life of divine quality" (*New Testament and Mission*, 79).

mission to the world."[8] This community's "present experience of eternal life constitutes an embodied witness of love, service, and unity."[9]

In his voluminous work on the Fourth Gospel, Francis Moloney sees the purpose of Jesus, and of the Gospel, as enabling human beings to be "swept" into the divine love and life.[10] This is the language of participation, both spiritually and missionally, and much closer to the argument of this book than is the language of Brown and even Nissen. Disciples, according to Moloney, are called to share the divine love and life—manifested most fully on the cross—with others. This is a cruciform understanding of Christian life, love, and mission. It requires deeds as well as words.

In her older but oft-quoted book *The Johannine Approach to Mission*, Teresa Okure makes the point that, according to John, the true missionary is Jesus, and the disciples are his instruments for effecting that mission.[11] What are the implications of this (correct) claim that Okure hints at but does not fully develop?

Mission, participation, and mimesis

If Jesus is the true missionary in John, then the disciples of Jesus participate in his mission, which is of course the Father's mission. And since Jesus' mission is his life, and since that life reveals and thereby participates in the life of his Father, when the disciples participate in Jesus' missional life they are participating in the missional life of God the Father. That is, in part, what it means to be children of God. The sending Father shares both his DNA and the family business (so to speak) with the children, who have the privilege of manifesting that divine DNA by participating in that divine business.

What I have proposed, following this line of thinking, is that participation in the missional life of the Father, the Son, and the Spirit is at the heart of John's missional theology and spirituality. I have contended that the best (though not the only) language for this missional spirituality of participation in the missional life of God is missional theosis. Ross Hastings, working from John 20 for a more pastoral audience, has likewise used the language of theosis in interpreting mission in the Fourth Gospel. He speaks specifically of it in terms of *discovering* and then *disseminating* God's shalom. The main elements of his understanding of theosis are (1) speaking what the sending Father says; (2) doing what the sending Father does; (3) judgment;

8. Lincoln, "Johannine Vision," 100.

9. Lincoln, "Johannine Vision," 116.

10. See especially his *Love in the Gospel of John*.

11. Okure, *Johannine Mission*, 219–26.

(4) servanthood and sacrifice; (5) intimate communion with the Father; (6) reflecting the likeness of the Sender through communion as contemplation and imitation; (7) being sanctified; and (8) being one with the Father and with one another.[12] Many of these themes from Hastings have actually emerged in our own study as well.

In a more academic treatise, Andy Byers has recently produced the first full-length study of theosis in John: *Ecclesiology and Theosis in the Gospel of John*. Byers takes a narrative approach to the Gospel, finding within it a "narrative ecclesiology of participation and deification" that is not only taught (e.g., in John 17) but also exemplified (e.g., in the man born blind of John 9). Like Jan van der Watt and Cornelis Bennema (the latter discussed below), Byers finds family language to be critical to understanding identity and behavior. Unlike Bennema, however, he finds the lines between divinity and humanity in antiquity a bit porous, allowing for participation and thus deification. Although Byers does not omit mission from his analysis of theosis, he insists that theosis in John is more than mission.[13] It is a communal life of participation in the one God of Israel revealed as Father, Son, and Spirit.

The present book has much in common with the work of Byers. But perhaps the scholarly work that is, in certain ways, closest to my own is that of Cornelis Bennema, especially in his book *Mimesis in the Johannine Literature: A Study in Johannine Ethics*.[14] Bennema's interest is ethics and moral transformation (including mission), and his fundamental claim is that the heart of Johannine ethics is mimesis (imitation) made possible by belonging as a child of God to the divine family of Father, Son, and Spirit. Mimesis is "the primary ethical instrument for directing appropriate character and conduct in the divine family."[15] Writing about divine, or Father-Son, mimesis in John, Bennema says, "the divine life that the Father and Son share is extended to believers who are subsequently drawn into this life-giving

---

12. Hastings, *Missional God*, 276–84.

13. See, e.g., his comments on John 17 (*Ecclesiology and Theosis*, 152): "Jesus does not just pray that the disciples will share in his mission; beyond a task-oriented or functional unity, Jesus prays that this new social entity *will actually share in his preexistent divine glory.*"

14. Bennema's book was published after I had completed most of the work on this volume. Fortunately, I was able to return to the manuscript and interact with it.

15. Bennema, *Mimesis*, 194–95. Cf. 162: "The Johannine concept of mimesis is primarily a form of family behaviour where God sets the example for Jesus, and Jesus largely sets the example of appropriate family behaviour for believers to imitate."

relationship with the Father and Son"; as a result, "Jesus' salvific mission" is "continued through the disciples' salvific mission."[16]

Although Bennema discusses indwelling and uses the language of participation,[17] these concepts are less central to his project than imitation: "*mimesis is instrumental for the God-human relationship.*"[18] Moreover, he is hesitant about the words theosis and deification.[19] For these reasons, Bennema's exploration of John at times feels a bit at odds with the argument of this book. Despite these differences from the present study, however, both Bennema's overall thesis and his proposal for how to understand the term theosis rightly are quite in sync with this book: "If one wants to use the term 'theosis' for the believer's transformation, it should perhaps be understood in terms of participation in God's life and character in order to become like God (*homoiousios*) rather than participation in God's essence in order to become God (*homoousios*)."[20] The following passage from Bennema's discussion of John 17 is particularly noteworthy:

> This relationship of life, light, love, truth and honour between the Father and Son is not exclusive; believers are drawn into this divine relationship through a birth "from above" and participate in the divine identity as "children of God" and Jesus' "siblings." ... Believers do not so much possess this divine identity as they participate or share in it by virtue of their union with God. As believers share in the divine identity of a perpetual communion of life, light, love, truth and honour, it is only natural that this communion will affect the believers and transform them in their thinking and behaviour. Thus, the believers' identity is shaped along the lines of the divine identity because sharing in the divine identity has a transformative effect.[21]

What Bennema is discussing here is what I refer to as transformative participation in the life of God, or theosis—indeed missional theosis.

16. Bennema, *Mimesis*, 74.

17. For "indwelling," see Bennema, *Mimesis*, esp. 126–27, 155–59. "It would be safe to conclude that communion (fellowship, oneness, unity, indwelling) is the most significant identity marker of the divine family" (156), meaning both within the Godhead and among the persons of the Godhead and the human family members. For participation, see 66, 97, 115, 130, 132n.64, 135, 146, 152, 154, 155–61, 164, 168, 173–74.

18. Bennema, *Mimesis*, 80.

19. Bennema, *Mimesis*, 127, 130, 132, 156.

20. Bennema, *Mimesis*, 132n.164. This comment is in connection with 1 John 3–4, but Bennema clearly implies its relevance to the entire Johannine corpus and even beyond.

21. Bennema, *Mimesis*, 130.

Whereas Bennema prefers the language of mimesis (imitation), communion, and relationality, and I the language of participation and theosis, the substance of our interpretations of John 17 and of John more generally is quite complementary.

At the end of his book, Bennema suggests the need for further research on the relationship between mimesis and theosis.[22] Whether or not Bennema's hope is even partly fulfilled by the present book, I would suggest that further research on the relationship between mimesis and mission is also needed. Bennema's own emphasis on *moral* transformation could itself be more consistently and explicitly *missional*.

By way of conclusion to this discussion of situating this book within the scholarly conversation, I am tempted to say that the present work is something of a marriage between the approaches and findings of Byers and Bennema (with support from the more pastoral work of Hastings). I actually read the studies by Byers and Bennema after completing most of the writing of this book. Perhaps this is a moment of convergence: several books trying, within a larger development toward ethics, mission, and participation in Johannine studies, to say things that can be brought together constructively as the scholarly conversation continues.

Some Initial Hermeneutical Reflections for the Life of the Church

The conversations in which I participate are not merely academic in the traditional sense of that term, but also deliberately theological and, indeed, practical. The contents of this book are intended for the church as well as the academy. As a proponent of missional hermeneutics, I take the discoveries I have found in the Gospel of John as part of the process of participating in, discerning, and further participating in the *missio Dei*. In other words, this study is not an analysis to be held at a distance; it invites embrace and self-involvement, both individually and communally. As Andrew Byers asks, what sort of community of disciples does this Gospel seek to produce?[23]

Rather than repeating the various summaries offered above, I simply wish now to highlight several key components of John's missional theosis, or missional spirituality, for the contemporary Christian church.[24]

---

22. Bennema, *Mimesis*, 204.

23. Byers, *Ecclesiology and Theosis*, 3.

24. For recent perspectives on missional spirituality more generally, see, e.g., Finn and Whitfield, *Spirituality for the Sent*. For John in particular, see Hastings, *Missional God*.

1. Christian *discipleship* is inherently *missional*; it involves being sent.

2. Christian mission is *derivative*, an extension of the Son's work on behalf of the Father in the power of the Spirit, and *participatory*, a sharing in the communion and missional life of the Triune God.

3. Christian mission is *holistic*: life-giving in the fullest sense of the word, addressing spiritual, emotional, physical, economic, and other human needs.

4. Intensive, intentional, alter-cultural Christian community is not at odds with intensive, intentional mission. In fact, these two elements of the church's life, the centripetal and the centrifugal, reinforce each other. Communal holiness and mission are inseparable.

5. Similarly, Christian unity and mission are inseparable. There is no true ecumenism without mission, no complete mission without ecumenism.

6. The church's mission—the integrity of its witness to the world and its ability to be a conduit of God's love, light, and life—depends on its holiness and unity, which makes both Christian integrity and Christian unity at every level and in every place matters of the utmost importance.

7. Finally, this study of John coheres with and confirms the thesis I have argued with respect to Paul in my book *Becoming the Gospel*: "Theosis—Spirit-enabled transformative participation in the life and character of God revealed in the crucified and resurrected Messiah Jesus—is the *starting point* of mission and is, in fact, its *proper theological framework*."[25] This framework of theosis may also be further described as communal, cruciform, life-giving, missional theosis.

It is imperative that work on the Gospel of John continue in ways that stress its implicit ethics and its missional dimension such that charges of its "sectarianism" can be laid to rest once and for all, and its rich treasure of spirituality and mission can be recognized and embodied. A spirituality of missional theosis, or "abide and go," will seem to many like another name for contemplation and action. Of many sources for this sort of spirituality, we may call on Mother Teresa, who speaks with a Johannine voice:

> We are called to love the world. And God loved the world so much that He gave Jesus. Today He loves the world so much that He gives you and me to be His love, His compassion, and

25. Gorman, *Becoming the Gospel*, 4 (emphasis added).

His presence. . . . The response that God asks of you is to be a contemplative. . . .

Our lives must be connected with the living Christ in us. If we do not live in the presence of God we cannot go on.

What is contemplation? To live the life of Jesus . . . , [t]o love Jesus, to live His life in us, to live our life in His life.[26]

All of this leads us to the question of the embodiment, or actualization, of Johannine missional theosis. For that subject, we turn briefly to some contemporary examples.

Some Examples of Contemporary Missional Theosis

As I was researching this book, I had the opportunity to visit several kinds of Christian communities in various parts of the United States and abroad.[27] To discuss all of them, or any of them in depth, would require another book. This brief section of the chapter briefly describes some living examples of Johannine missional spirituality: intense, intentional communities that are not merely focused on themselves. These include a traditional church with varied ministries, communities with a liturgical dimension that are not traditional churches, and a ministry born out of a church. Of course, many more examples could be brought forward. These are included merely as examples of communities that have self-consciously reflected on the relationship between their internal life and their external mission, and on the relationship of both to the Gospel of John. I report briefly here on conversations with some of their leaders and members, focusing on three geographical locations: Chicago, Illinois; Durham, North Carolina; and Taizé, France. Afterward, I will conclude this chapter with some additional reflections in light of these visits.

Chicago, Illinois

Lawndale Christian Community Church

Lawndale Christian Community Church, with its various ministries, is located on the west side of Chicago.[28] The church's ministry centers in its

---

26. Mother Teresa, *No Greater Love*, 12.

27. As stated in the Acknowledgments, I am indebted not only to these communities and people, but also to the Luce Foundation and the Association of Theological Schools in the United States and Canada for the opportunity to make these visits.

28. See http://www.lawndalechurch.org.

neighborhood include drug rehabilitation and transitional housing, prison ministry, legal services, sports ministries, health centers that serve more than 200,000 patients annually, a café and restaurant, a fitness center, and more. The church's motto is "Loving God and Loving People," which extends to all its ministries. For example, the Lawndale Christian Legal Center describes itself as "Loving God, Loving People" by "Raising Up Justly Treated Youth" through forms of "restorative justice." Programs include legal representation, case management, mentoring, after-school programs, and more.[29]

Pastor Wayne "Coach" Gordon states that "Everything we do bears the mark (literal and figurative) of the church." That is, both the church's signage and the church's identity can be seen everywhere. Pastor Gordon connects the church's worship life and its missional life in the following Johannine way:

> Each church service ends with a commission to "go" and con-
> tribute to making the neighborhood whole through one of eight
> forms of community development. The world that God loved is,
> for us, our neighborhood; we need to speak up for those who
> cannot speak out. The church is a family that cares for its neigh-
> bors, offering them physical and spiritual life.[30]

Inspired by John Perkins of the Christian Community Development Association (CCDA), "Coach," his ministry colleagues, and the church see multi-dimensional community development as an essential part of the church's mission in the world. This includes direct service, but also preaching, teaching, and even publicly protesting injustice.

Reba Place Fellowship

In Evanston, Illinois, a northern suburb of Chicago, are Reba Place Fellowship and Reba Place Church.[31] Reba Place Fellowship is a large, established intentional Christian community in Evanston with four households (each consisting of both families and single people, or just singles), as well as

---

29. LCLC brochure; see also http://lclc.net/.

30. Personal interview, April 4, 2016.

31. See http://www.rebaplacefellowship.org and http://rebaplacechurch.org. The community's website notes that it is located in both Evanston and Chicago. The church, which separated formally from the community in the early 1980s, is affiliated with the Mennonite Church USA and describes itself on the web site as "a congregation centered on Jesus Christ and the Kingdom of God, rooted in an Anabaptist tradition, catholic in spirit, evangelical in conviction, charismatic in practice, and antiracist in calling" (accessed February 2, 2018).

several other co-housing arrangements, in close proximity on different city blocks. Founded in 1957 by a group of Mennonite Voluntary Service workers, Reba has stood the test of time for such communities in the U.S. Life together generally consists of shared meals, prayer, hospitality, and sometimes shared ministries. Many community members are also members of Reba Place Church or participate in the life of a daughter church, Living Water Community Church, in the Rogers Park neighborhood of north Chicago.

The community understands itself in the following way: "In love, God has called us together at Reba and gifted us for a life of fellowship and service, for our own blessing and to be a blessing in mission to the world."[32] Allan Howe, a longtime leader in the community, has seen many people come to Reba and find it to be a place of refuge, like a large extended (but countercultural) family, in times of need or crisis (such as domestic abuse).[33]

But this hardly means that Reba ignores the outside world. Allan offers this reflection on the connection between centripetal and centrifugal love:

> One of the common transformative patterns we see in people seeking intentional Christian community is loneliness → community life → hospitality/service to others. . . . We have become the city's [Evanston's] largest landlord of affordable housing [Reba Place Development Corporation[34]]. It is one of the ways we love our neighbors. . . . Christian mission naturally creates community, and a healthy Christian community naturally creates mission.[35]

Affordable housing is not the only centrifugal activity at Reba, but it illustrates the community's symbiosis of community and external mission, an extension of the hospitality practiced in community to the larger community. Other outreach activities include food distribution; a second-hand clothing store; Reba Properties, which provides employment opportunities; Community Creations (greeting cards); and Plain and Simple Furniture (Amish furniture). Woven throughout the Reba mindset and practices are values of justice, racial reconciliation, and creation care.

---

32. See https://www.rebaplacefellowship.org/who-we-are/mission-statement, accessed February 2, 2018.

33. Personal interview, April 3, 2016.

34. See https://www.rebaplacefellowship.org/common-work/reba-place-development-corporation-rpdc (accessed February 2, 2018), which says that its projects "grow out of Reba's commitment to God's Kingdom and God's desire for justice, sharing, and reconciliation." According to David Janzen (personal interview, April 3, 2016), the corporation manages a total of more than two hundred units and employs numerous people to operate and care for them.

35. Personal interview, April 3, 2016.

David Janzen, another longtime member and leader, sees John 13:35, "By this everyone will know that you are my disciples, if you have love for one another," as the community's "theme verse." The household is where inner and outer life meet in God's love, he says: "The overflowing of love within the Trinity comes to the Christian community [as part of the church] and from the church to the world."[36] Of course, David continues, this sort of community and love must be authentic, and Reba has not always done—or balanced—everything perfectly, but the vision continues to be practiced and shared with others.[37]

Durham, North Carolina

Rutba House

Rutba House in the Walltown neighborhood of Durham is an intentional community and hospitality house founded by Jonathan and Leah Wilson-Hartgrove after their experience of profound hospitality and medical care while serving with a Christian Peacemaker Team in Rutba, Iraq at the start of the Iraq war in 2003.[38] Associated (though not formally so) with Rutba House is the School for Conversion (SFC),[39] an educational work directed by Jonathan, which describes itself as "a faith-rooted organization that was created and continues to be shaped by God's vision of a beloved community that we see through the life of Jesus."[40] Its primary mission, says Jonathan, is "to interrupt the cradle to prison pipeline" in his neighborhood and elsewhere.[41]

Jonathan is also a minister at the nearby historically African American St. Johns Baptist Church. He, Leah, and other members of the community engage in a variety of ministries, especially prison ministry (including theological education) and racial reconciliation. Leah has also been active in Capital Restorative Justice Project, which seeks to bring together families in North Carolina that have had a family member murdered, have a family member on death row, or had a family member on death row who was executed.

36. Personal interview, April 3, 2016.

37. See, e.g., Janzen, *Intentional Christian Community Handbook*.

38. See https://emerging-communities.com/tag/rutba-house. For the full story, see Wilson-Hartgrove, *To Baghdad and Beyond*.

39. See http://www.schoolforconversion.org.

40. See https://www.schoolforconversion.org/about-us, accessed February 2, 2018.

41. Personal interview, October 28, 2015.

Long-term, short-term, and neighborhood guests are frequently present at Rutba House, and they take part in the community's life of prayer, meals, ministries of peace and justice, and more. Jonathan sees the Johannine vision of participation and life at the center of Rutba House:

> Participation is our great theme—participating in our own rhythm of life. We are a hospitality house inviting our neighbors and guests into the joy of eternal life—something beyond this system called "modern capitalism" that we know does not work. We know a way of being together and sharing that could go on forever.[42]

Jonathan sees hospitality as the opposite of violence; he deliberately echoes Dorothy Day's affirmation of the works of mercy as the opposite of the works of war.

Picking up on the Johannine theme of life, Sarah Jobe of the Rutba community speaks of prison ministry in terms of enabling others to move from death to life, both literally and spiritually. Surprisingly and ironically, she reports, a number of women for whom she is chaplain and teacher have said, "Prison saved my life."[43] Sarah and Jonathan, along with Professor Douglas Campbell of Duke Divinity School, have initiated and taught in a program that brings divinity students and incarcerated persons together in courses held within prison walls, creating an unusual type of Christian unity. One consistent Johannine word offered to those incarcerated, says Sarah, is "You are a beloved child of God."[44]

North Street Neighborhood and Reality Ministries

Not far from Rutba House in Durham are North Street Neighborhood and, a few blocks away, Reality Ministries (RM, or Reality). The mission statement of RM, founded in 2007 (but growing out of a predecessor ministry), is this: "Creating opportunities for teens and adults with and without developmental disabilities to experience belonging, kinship and the life-changing Reality of Christ's love."[45] North Street Neighborhood is an intentional community of sixteen buildings—originally quadriplex apartment buildings, converted into duplexes and apartments—founded in the summer of

---

42. Personal interview, October 28, 2015.
43. Personal interview, October 25, 2015.
44. Personal interview, October 25, 2015.
45. From http://www.realityministriesinc.org, accessed March 28, 2018.

2012.[46] Its hundred or so residents, many of whom are Christians, include people with and without disabilities as well as Duke Divinity School students and other young people as interns or Reality Fellows. Although RM is largely non-residential, it has one residence in the North Street Neighborhood: Corner House, where eight friends with differing gifts and challenges live together in a spirit of mutuality and interdependence. Like North Street as a whole, Corner House is centered around prayer and hospitality.

North Street Neighborhood began when one family from Reality that had a young person with a disability, other families connected to Reality (both with and without a family member with a disability), the RM staff, and others felt the need for more than a daytime ministry. So, through prayer together, the vision of a community was born, and a man the community calls an "angel developer"—Andrew (Drew) Howell of Legacy Real Property Group—renovated the block-and-a-half of former apartment buildings.

Families with and without relatives with disabilities live in community at North Street. Families, divinity school students, and others often share a house or apartment with one or more persons with disabilities. Members of the community from different households eat together on a regular basis, and they pray morning prayer and evening compline daily. Everyone who is able to participate in group prayer is welcome and encouraged to do so.

Nick Funk joined North Street while attending Duke Divinity School and stayed. "If there's one thing I've learned while living at North Street and participating at Reality," says Nick, "it's that Jesus has a body. Many of our friends need help with the most personal of daily activities." Reflecting on helping to meet such needs, he adds:

> This may sound off-putting, but it's actually *glorious*. There's an "incarnation factor" to life with Jesus that cannot be dismissed. Jesus set the example for us when he washed the disciples' feet, and "the servant is not greater than his or her master."[47]

North Street is a community that sees itself as living in and sharing the abundant life and love of God in Jesus. The community members attempt to love one another and their world. Their centripetal love naturally becomes centrifugal, affecting families, neighbors, and more. Margot Starbuck lives in the community with her three children:

---

46. See http://northstreetneighborhood.weebly.com; see also https://www.christianitytoday.com/thisisourcity/7thcity/building-a-beloved-community.html. I am grateful to Margot Starbuck of North Street Neighborhood, and to Jeff and Susan McSwain of both North Street and Reality, for their assistance with these paragraphs.

47. Personal correspondence, April 2, 2018.

When we moved to North Street I was aware that, from the outside, it appeared to others as if mostly able-bodied people like
myself and my family had done some sort of "good" in choosing
to share life with our friends who live with disabilities. But in a
difficult season of my own life, North Street was exactly where
I needed to be. I believe the deep longing of every heart is to be
received, in the words of Brennan Manning, "as we are and not
as we should be." I experienced that palpable grace and acceptance, when I needed it most, from my neighbors in the North
Street Neighborhood.[48]

Another member of the North Street community is Jeff McSwain, who
is also the founder of Reality Ministries. He and his wife Susan, Reality's
current Executive Director, rent a separate apartment unit in their home
to a young man with disabilities who is sufficiently high-functioning to live
semi-independently. Jeff says that he likes describing RM as "a community
of people of all abilities sharing life together in a variety of ways." He adds,
"We build community around the fact that all of us, regardless of belief, are
together at the center of Christ's love." Moreover, "we at RM *really do* feel
that we are being led to Christ by those whom we are 'leading'—all of us
with and without intellectual disabilities are giving to and receiving from
each other."[49] Reality's Director of Community Development David Sittser
says this about the ministry: "John's theme of 'abiding' is the essence of our
ministry. . . . We spent an entire year of our Tuesday services going through
the 'I am' sayings in John one by one. Our summary: 'I am for you.'"[50]

Taizé, France: la communauté

The Taizé community in south central France (Burgundy) is known
around the world for its simple but beautiful chants and prayer. An ecumenical community of about a hundred brothers from many countries,
Taizé was founded in 1940 by Brother Roger Schutz of Switzerland as a
place to pray and work for reconciliation. Its simple, candle-lit Church
of Reconciliation stands at the center of the community, and in the summer it is filled weekly by some 3,000 youth and young adults (fewer, but
still plenty, in the other months) who come for spiritual renewal through

48. Personal correspondence, March 31, 2018.
49. Personal correspondence, March 28, 2018.
50. Personal interview, October 26, 2015.

prayer and study. They participate in the community's rhythm of thrice-daily prayer and simple meals.[51]

Brother Roger, who was murdered in 2005, was known for his very Johannine theology and spirituality: "God is love alone."[52] Brother John of Taizé, an American-born member who has been a Taizé brother for more than forty years, has noted the connections between community and mission that have been part of the community since its founding: first to help reconcile a divided Europe; then to bring the love of God to young people, especially European youth; and now—while continuing the ministry with young people—an expanded, more global mission to both younger and older people and, in light of the current global refugee situation, a return to something of the original vision. By 2016, at the height of global war and refugee crises, the community had welcomed two Christian families from Iraq; a Muslim family (mother, father, four children) from Syria who had been in a camp in Lebanon for four years; and twelve young men from South Sudan and Afghanistan. Brother John interprets the community's work in this way:

> Mission has been integral to our community from the beginning, even as both the community and the mission have evolved. Our church is of course the Church of Reconciliation. Our founder, Br. Roger, often said and wrote that "Dieu ne peut qu'aimer"—"God can only love." That is certainly the message of John and 1 John. A community of mutual love, as we see in both the Gospel and 1 John, draws people into it; that is the nature of true communion.[53]

He adds:

> I always explain to people that John emphasizes the "love one another," not because the love is exclusive, but because to be perfected (1 John 4:12) it has to be reciprocal, in other words, create a communion. That is what shows the world who God is.[54]

51. See https://www.taize.fr. For a helpful overview, see Santos, *A Community Called Taizé*. There are also numerous books about the community's spirituality and mission (as well as books of its music) written by Br. Roger, Br. John, and the community as whole.

52. Among Brother Roger's many small books is *God Is Love Alone*.

53. Personal interview, July 22, 2016. While I was writing this book, Br. John, who has a Harvard degree in biblical studies, requested my insight on reconciliation in John for the sake of the community leader's (Br. Alois) upcoming speaking engagements. I was privileged to send Br. John chapter 6, which he found convincing and which he shared with Br. Alois and other brothers.

54. Personal correspondence, July 29, 2016.

The community has also embodied its mission of reconciliation and sharing the love of God in the racially divided United States. At the invitation of St. Louis Roman Catholic Archbishop Robert Carlson, some members of the community spent significant amounts of time planning and holding a "Pilgrimage of Trust" to help heal the wounds resulting from the incidents and riots in Ferguson, Missouri. The first pilgrimage occurred in May 2017,[55] but the relationship and work continue.

Final Reflections

My visits to various Christian churches and other sorts of communities have reinforced for me many of the conclusions offered above about the nature of missional theosis according to the Gospel of John. Perhaps a few additional reflections, in light of these vignettes, are appropriate to conclude this work in "the Bible and the church."[56] These include reflections both on the mission and unity of the church and on theological education and formation for the church's unity and mission.

1. Christian community, the "centripetal" experience of the church, including corporate worship and other forms of corporate spirituality, creates the ethos and space for authentic "centrifugal" Christian mission. That is, authentic centrifugal Christian mission grows out of centripetal Christian community and worship.

2. Hospitality—a form of self-giving love—is a fundamental practice of both Christian community and Christian mission.[57] Paradoxically, because hospitality is inherently missional, centrifugal Christian mission can take place within the centripetal experience of Christian community.

3. Christian mission and Christian unity are mutually nourishing realities, not merely in the larger scheme of "ecumenical relations," but in the nitty-gritty of small Christian communities.

4. The missional practices of Christian communities are a function both of the community's corporate identity and of the individual gifts of the various members of the community.

55. See https://pilgrimageoftruststl.com/.

56. That was the category of the Luce Fellows grant that enabled the writing of this volume.

57. See Jipp, *Saved by Faith and Hospitality*; Pohl, *Making Room*; Sutherland, *I Was a Stranger*; Wilson-Hartgrove, *Strangers at My Door*. On hospitality in John specifically, and in the African context, see Kunene, *Communal Holiness*.

5. The church has, but needs to draw more deeply from, a rich reservoir of biblical, patristic, Reformation, and recent writing and practice that combines spirituality and mission. Such resources need to be made available to faculty, seminarians, pastors, and people in the pew.

6. In particular, the rich tradition of intentional Christian community that is also inherently missional needs to be more fully celebrated, imitated, and reimagined for its relevance to more standard forms of being the church. There are too many wonderful things happening that are essentially unknown outside of the immediate circles of influence of such communities. Seminarians need to find ways to experience various forms of Christian community as part of the theological curriculum: in intentional communities, in prisons, and so forth.[58]

7. It is critical that scholars of spirituality and mission, on the one hand, and scholars of mission and Scripture, on the other, be in more regular conversation.[59] This conversation ought to result in more interdisciplinary courses that unite these sub-disciplines and therefore contribute to the blending of these dimensions of Christian existence in the local church.

8. The growing attention to the theme of participation—whether or not that includes the language of theosis—needs further careful study, with special emphasis on its inherent missional character.

9. Theological scholars and pastors need to learn how to articulate a public theology of spirituality and mission that will sustain the church in the challenging times facing the global church today, including such obvious problems as terrorism and the refugee crisis, international problems that are simultaneously also domestic concerns.

10. Christian mission—indeed Christian existence—is fraught with danger. The persecuted church around the world can be an example of Johannine spirituality in terms of its experience of abiding and going, even in the face of hostility.

58. Important resources for understanding intentional Christian communities include Janzen, *The Intentional Christian Community Handbook*; Wilson-Hartgrove, *New Monasticism*; and Rutba House, *School(s) for Conversion*.

59. I found this enormously enriching in several visits to seminaries to give lectures related to the writing of this book, especially at Fuller Theological Seminary.

Conclusion

Much, much more could and should be said about John's missional spirituality, his missional theosis. Nevertheless, what I have articulated in these chapters will perhaps help encourage a "New Perspective" on John, to borrow a phrase from my other life (in Paul). This new perspective means that John offers us a spiritual, ethical, and missional gospel from and for a spiritual, ethical, and missional community of disciples who participate in the *missio Dei* and thereby both exhibit their character—their DNA—as God's children and become more like God.

Neither theologians nor practitioners need fear misunderstandings of the terms "mission" and "theosis," and now also "missional theosis"; rather, we need to hear John's witness on its own terms, and then incorporate it with a kind of creative fidelity into our own understanding and practice of the church in community and in mission to the world.

Modern Works Cited

An, Keon-Sang. "Response to Gorman." Paper presented at Fuller Theological Seminary, April 6, 2016.

Anatolios, Khaled. *Athanasius: The Coherence of His Thought*. New York: Routledge, 2004.

Anderson, Cynthia Peters. *Reclaiming Participation: Christ as God's Life for All.* Minneapolis: Fortress, 2014.

Anderson, Paul N. "Anti-Semitism and Religious Violence as Flawed Interpretations of the Gospel of John." In *John and Judaism: A Contested Relationship in Context*, edited by R. Alan Culpepper and Paul N. Anderson, 265–311. Resources for Biblical Study 87. Atlanta: SBL, 2017.

———. *The Riddles of the Fourth Gospel: An Introduction to John*. Minneapolis: Fortress, 2011.

Ashton, John. *Understanding the Fourth Gospel*. 2nd ed. Oxford: Oxford University Press, 2007.

Attridge, Harold, Warren Carter, and Jan G. van der Watt. "Quaestiones disputatae: Are John's Ethics Apolitical?" *New Testament Studies* 62 (2016) 484–97.

Aus, Roger David. *Simon Peter's Denial and Jesus' Commissioning Him as His Successor in John 21:15–19: Studies in Their Judaic Background*. Studies in Judaism. Lanham, MD: University Press of America, 2013.

Bakhtin, M. M. *Speech Genres and Other Late Essays*. Edited by Caryl Emerson and Michael Holquist. Translated by Vern M. McGee. Slavic Series 8. 2nd ed. Austin: University of Texas Press, 1986.

Barram, Michael D. "The Bible, Mission, and Social Location: Toward a Missional Hermeneutic." *Interpretation* 61 (2007) 42–58.

———. *Mission and Moral Reflection in Paul*. Studies in Biblical Literature 75. New York: Lang, 2006.

———. *Missional Economics: Biblical Justice and Christian Formation*. Grand Rapids: Eerdmans, 2018.

————. "Reflections on the Practice of Missional Hermeneutics: 'Streaming' Philippians 1:20–30." Paper presented at Gospel and Our Culture Network Forum on Missional Hermeneutics, New Orleans, November 21, 2009.

Barrett, C. K. *The Gospel according to St. John.* Louisville: Westminster John Knox, 1978.

Bauckham, Richard. *Gospel of Glory: Major Themes in Johannine Theology.* Grand Rapids: Baker Academic, 2015.

————. "The Holiness of Jesus and His Disciples in the Gospel of John." In *Holiness and Ecclesiology in the New Testament*, edited by Kent E. Brower and Andy Johnson, 95–113. Grand Rapids: Eerdmans, 2007.

Bauckham, Richard, and Carl Mosser, eds. *The Gospel of John and Christian Theology.* Grand Rapids: Eerdmans, 2008.

Beasley-Murray, G. R. *The Gospel of Life: Theology in the Fourth Gospel.* Peabody, MA: Hendrickson, 1991.

Behr, John. *The Mystery of Christ: Life in Death.* Crestwood, NY: St. Vladimir's Seminary Press, 2006.

Bennema, Cornelis. *Encountering Jesus: Character Studies in the Gospel of John.* 2nd ed. Minneapolis: Fortress, 2014.

————. "The Giving of the Spirit in John's Gospel—A New Proposal?" *Evangelical Quarterly* 74 (2002) 195–213.

————. *Mimesis in the Johannine Literature: A Study in Johannine Ethics.* Library of New Testament Studies 498. London: Bloomsbury T. & T. Clark, 2017.

————. "One or Two Pentecosts? The Giving of the Spirit in John 20 and Acts 2." In *Holy Spirit: Unfinished Agenda*, edited by Johnson T. K. Lim, 97–101. Singapore: Word N Works, 2014.

Bennett, Thomas Andrew. *Labor of God: The Agony of the Cross as the Birth of the Church.* Waco, TX: Baylor University Press, 2017.

Beutler, Johnannes. "Faith and Confession: The Purpose of John." In *Word, Theology, and Community in John*, edited by John Painter, R. Alan Culpepper, and Fernando F. Segovia, 19–31. St. Louis: Chalice, 2002.

Blackwell, Ben C. *Christosis: Engaging Paul's Soteriology with His Patristic Interpreters.* Grand Rapids: Eerdmans, 2016. [Original: *Christosis: Pauline Soteriology in Light of Deification in Irenaeus and Cyril of Alexandria.* Wissenschaftliche Untersuchungen zum Neuen Testament 2/314. Tübingen: Mohr Siebeck, 2011.]

————. "Immortal Glory and the Problem of Death in Romans 3.23," *JSNT* 32 (2010): 285–308.

Bosch, David J. *Transforming Mission: Paradigm Shifts in Theology of Mission.* American Society of Missiology Series 16. 20th anniversary ed. Maryknoll, NY: Orbis, 2011.

Brother Roger of Taizé. *God is Love Alone.* Chicago: GIA, 2003.

Brower, Kent. *Holiness in the Gospels.* Kansas City: Beacon Hill, 2005.

Brower Latz, Andrew. "A Short Note toward a Theology of Abiding in John's Gospel." *Journal of Theological Interpretation* 4 (2010) 161–68.

Brown, Raymond E. *The Community of the Beloved Disciple: The Lives, Loves, and Hates of an Individual Church in New Testament Times.* New York: Paulist, 1979.

————. *The Gospel according to John.* 2 vols. Anchor Bible 29–29A. Garden City, NY: Doubleday, 1966, 1970.

Brown, Sherri. "Believing in the Gospel of John: The Ethical Imperative to Becoming Children of God." In *Johannine Ethics: The Moral World of the Gospel and Epistles of John*, edited by Sherri Brown and Christopher W. Skinner, 3–24. Minneapolis: Fortress, 2017.

———. *God's Promise: Covenant Relationship in John*. Mahwah, NJ: Paulist, 2014.

Brown, Sherri, and Christopher W. Skinner, eds. *Johannine Ethics: The Moral World of the Gospel and Epistles of John*. Minneapolis: Fortress, 2017.

Brownson, James V. "A Response at SBL to Hunsberger's 'Proposals . . .' Essay." Paper presented at the Gospel and Our Culture Network Forum on Missional Hermeneutics, Boston, November 22, 2008. http://www.gocn.org/resources/articles/response-sbl-hunsbergers-proposals-essay.

———. *Speaking the Truth in Love: New Testament Resources for a Missional Hermeneutic*. Harrisburg, PA: Trinity, 1998.

Bultmann, Rudolf [K.]. *The Gospel of John: A Commentary*. Translated by George R. Beasley-Murray et al. Philadelphia: Westminster, 1971.

———. *Theology of the New Testament: Complete in One Volume*. 2 vols. Translated by K. Grobel. Reprint. New York: Scribner, 1969. [Original: 1951, 1955.]

Burridge, Richard. *Imitating Jesus: An Inclusive Approach to New Testament Ethics*. Grand Rapids: Eerdmans, 2007.

Byers, Andrew J. *Ecclesiology and Theosis in the Gospel of John*. Society for New Testament Studies Monograph Series 166. Cambridge: Cambridge University Press, 2017.

Byrne, Brendan. *Life Abounding: A Reading of John's Gospel*. Collegeville, MN: Liturgical, 2014.

Caragounis, Chrys C. "'Abide in Me': The New Mode of Relationship between Jesus and His Followers as a Basis for Christian Ethics (John 15)." In *Rethinking the Ethics of John: "Implicit Ethics" in the Johannine Writings*, edited by Jan van der Watt and Ruben Zimmerman, 250–63. Kontexte und Normen neutestamentlicher Ethik / Contexts and Norms of New Testament Ethics Vol. 3; Wissenschaftliche Untersuchungen zum Neuen Testament 1/291. Tübingen: Mohr Siebeck, 2012.

Carriker, Tim. "The Bible as Text for Mission." In *Bible in Mission*, edited by Pauline Hoggarth et al., 29–39. Regnum Edinburgh Centenary Series 18. Oxford: Regnum, 2013.

Carter, Warren. *John and Empire: Initial Explorations*. London: T. & T. Clark, 2008.

Chennattu, Rekha M. *Johannine Discipleship as a Covenant Relationship*. Peabody, MA: Hendrickson, 2006.

Christensen, Michael J., and Jeffery A. Wittung, eds. *Partakers of the Divine Nature: The History and Development of Deification in the Christian Traditions*. Grand Rapids: Baker Academic, 2008.

Collins, Paul M. *Partaking in Divine Nature: Deification and Communion*. London: T. & T. Clark, 2010.

Coloe, Mary L. *Dwelling in the Household of God: Johannine Ecclesiology and Spirituality*. Collegeville, MN: Liturgical, 2007.

———. *God Dwells with Us: Temple Symbolism in the Fourth Gospel*. Collegeville, MN: Liturgical, 2001.

———. "Welcome into the Household of God: The Foot Washing in John 13." *Catholic Biblical Quarterly* 66 (2004) 400–415.

Cooper, Jordan. *Christification: A Lutheran Approach to Theosis*. Eugene, OR: Wipf & Stock, 2014.

Crump, David. "Re-examining the Johannine Trinity: Perichoresis or Deification?" *Scottish Journal of Theology* 59 (2006) 395–412.

———. "Who Gets What? God or Disciples, Human Spirit or Holy Spirit in John 19:30." *Novum Testamentum* 51 (2009) 78–89.

Culpepper, R. Alan. *Anatomy of the Fourth Gospel: A Study in Literary Design.* Philadelphia: Fortress, 1983.

———. "Designs for the Church in the Gospel Accounts of Jesus' Death." *New Testament Studies* 51 (2005) 376–92.

———. "Nicodemus: The Travail of New Birth." In *Character Studies in the Fourth Gospel: Narrative Approaches to Seventy Figures in John,* edited by Steven A. Hunt, D. François Tolmie, and Ruben Zimmerman, 249–59. Grand Rapids: Eerdmans, 2016. [Original: Tübingen: Mohr Siebeck, 2013.]

———. "The Pivot of John's Prologue." *New Testament Studies* 27 (1980) 1–31.

———. "The Johannine Hypodeigma: A Reading of John 13." *Semeia* 53 (1991) 133–52.

Danker, Frederick William, ed. *A Greek-English Lexicon of the New Testament and Other Early Christian Literature* [BDAG]. 3rd ed. Chicago: University of Chicago Press, 2000.

de Villiers, Pieter G. R., and Lloyd K. Pietersen, eds. *The Spirit That Inspires: Perspectives on Biblical Spirituality. Acta Theologica* Supplementum 15. Bloemfontein, South Africa: University of the Free State Press, 2011.

Dodd, C. H. *The Interpretation of the Fourth Gospel.* Cambridge: Cambridge University Press, 1953.

Dokka, Trond Skard. "Irony and Sectarianism in the Gospel of John." In *New Readings in John: Literary and Theological Perspectives: Essays from the Scandinavian Conference on the Fourth Gospel in Århus,* edited by Johannes Nissen and Sigfred Pedersen, 83–107. Journal for the Study of the New Testament Supplement Series 182. Sheffield, UK: Sheffield Academic Press, 1999.

Donovan, Mary Ann. "Alive to the Glory of God: A Key Insight in St. Irenaeus." *Theological Studies* 49 (1988) 283–97.

Dunn, James D. G. "'The Lord the Giver of Life': The Gift of the Spirit as Both Life-giving and Empowering." In *The Spirit and Christ in the New Testament and Christian Theology: Essays in Honor of Max Turner,* edited by I. Howard Marshall, Volker Rabens, and Cornelis Bennema, 1–17. Grand Rapids: Eerdmans, 2012.

Eco, Umberto. *The Open Work.* Translated by Anna Cancogni. Reprint. Cambridge: Harvard University Press, 1989. [Original: 1962.]

Edwards, Mark. *John.* Blackwell Bible Commentaries. Malden, MA: Blackwell, 2004.

Elowsky, Joel C., ed. *John 11–21.* Ancient Christian Commentary on Scripture 4b. Downers Grove, IL: IVP Academic, 2014.

Fairbairn, Donald. *Grace and Christology in the Early Church.* Oxford Early Christian Studies. Oxford: Oxford University Press, 2003.

Fiddes, Paul S. *Participating in God: A Pastoral Doctrine of the Trinity.* Louisville: Westminster John Knox, 2000.

Finlan, Stephen, and Vladmir Kharlamov, eds. *Theōsis: Deification in Christian Theology.* Princeton Theological Monograph Series. Eugene, OR: Pickwick, 2006.

Finn, Nathan A., and Keith S. Whitfield, eds. *Spirituality for the Sent: Casting a New Vision for the Missional Church.* Downers Grove, IL: InterVarsity, 2017.

Flemming, Dean. *Recovering the Full Mission of God: A Biblical Perspective on Being, Doing and Telling.* Downers Grove, IL: InterVarsity, 2013.

———. *Why Mission?* Reframing New Testament Theology. Nashville: Abingdon, 2015.

Flett, John G. *The Witness of God: The Trinity, Missio Dei, Karl Barth, and the Nature of Christian Community.* Grand Rapids: Eerdmans, 2010.

Fowl, Stephen E. "Theological Interpretation of Scripture and Its Future." *Anglican Theological Review* 99 (2017) 671–90.

Gaventa, Beverly R. "The Archive of Excess: John 21 and the Problem of Narrative Closure." In *Exploring the Gospel of John: In Honor of D. Moody Smith*, edited by R. Alan Culpepper and C. Clifton Black, 240–52. Louisville: Westminster John Knox, 1996.

Goheen, Michael W., ed. *Reading the Bible Missionally.* Grand Rapids: Eerdmans, 2016.

Gorman, Mark C. "On the Love of God." ThD diss., Duke Divinity School, 2015.

Gorman, Michael J. *Becoming the Gospel: Paul, Participation, and Mission.* The Gospel and Our Culture Series. Grand Rapids: Eerdmans, 2015.

———. *The Death of the Messiah and the Birth of the New Covenant: A (Not So) New Model of the Atonement.* Eugene, OR: Cascade, 2014.

———. *Elements of Biblical Exegesis: A Basic Guide for Students and Ministers.* Rev. and exp. ed. Grand Rapids: Baker Academic, 2009.

———. "The Gospel according to John" [introduction and notes]. In *Wesley Study Bible NRSV*, edited by Joel B. Green and William H. Willimon, 1285–1320. Nashville: Abingdon, 2009.

———. *Inhabiting the Cruciform God: Kenosis, Justification, and Theosis in Paul's Narrative Soteriology.* Grand Rapids: Eerdmans, 2009.

———. "Paul's Corporate, Cruciform, Missional Theosis in Second Corinthians." In *'In Christ' in Paul: Explorations in Paul's Theology of Union and Participation*, edited by Michael J. Thate, Kevin J. Vanhoozer, and Constantine R. Campbell, 181–208. Reprint. Grand Rapids: Eerdmans, 2018. [Original: Tübingen: Mohr Siebeck, 2014.]

———. "The Spirit, the Prophets, and the End of the 'Johannine Jesus.'" *Journal of Theological Interpretation* 12 (2018) 1–23.

———. "The This-Worldliness of the New Testament's Other-Worldly Spirituality." In *The Bible and Spirituality: Exploratory Essays in Reading Scripture Spiritually*, edited by Andrew T. Lincoln, J. Gordon McConville, and Lloyd K. Pietersen, 151–70. Eugene, OR: Cascade, 2013.

Green, Joel B. "Modern and Postmodern Methods of Biblical Interpretation." In *Scripture and Its Interpretation: A Global, Ecumenical Introduction to the Bible*, edited by Michael J. Gorman, 187–204. Grand Rapids: Baker Academic, 2017.

Gundry, Robert H. *Jesus the Word according to John the Sectarian: A Paleofundamentalist Manifesto for Contemporary Evangelicalism, Especially Its Elites, in North America.* Grand Rapids: Eerdmans, 2002.

Habets, Myk. *The Anointed Son: A Trinitarian Spirit Christology.* Princeton Theological Monograph Series 129. Eugene, OR: Pickwick, 2010.

———. "Theosis, Yes; Deification, No." In *The Spirit of Truth: Reading Scripture and Constructing Theology with the Holy Spirit*, edited by Myk Habets, 124–49. Eugene, OR: Pickwick, 2010.

———. "Walking *in mirabilibus supra me*: How C. S. Lewis Transposes Theosis." *Evangelical Quarterly* 82 (2010) 15–27.

Hallonsten, Gösta. "*Theosis* in Recent Research: A Renewal of Interest and a Need for Clarity." In *Partakers of the Divine Nature*, edited by Michael J. Christensen and Jeffrey A. Wittung, 281–93. Grand Rapids: Baker Academic, 2007.

Harris, R. Geoffrey. *Mission in the Gospels*. Eugene, OR: Wipf & Stock, 2014.

Hastings, Ross. *Missional God, Missional Church: Hope for Re-evangelizing the West*. Downers Grove, IL: InterVarsity, 2012.

Hauerwas, Stanley. *Unleashing the Scripture: Freeing the Bible from Captivity to America*. Nashville: Abingdon, 1993.

Hays, Richard B. *Echoes of Scripture in the Gospels*. Waco, TX: Baylor University Press, 2016.

———. *Reading Backwards: Figural Christology and the Fourfold Gospel Witness*. Waco, TX: Baylor University Press, 2016.

Heil, John Paul. *The Gospel of John: Worship for Divine Life Eternal*. Eugene, OR: Cascade, 2015.

Hengel, Martin. "The Prologue of the Gospel of John as the Gateway to Christological Truth." In *The Gospel of John and Christian Theology*, edited by Richard Bauckham and Carl Mosser, 265–94. Grand Rapids: Eerdmans, 2008.

Holder, Arthur, ed. *The Blackwell Companion to Christian Spirituality*. Oxford: Blackwell, 2005.

Holmes, Stephen R. "Trinitarian Missiology: Towards A Theology of God as Missionary." *International Journal of Systematic Theology* 8 (2006) 72–90.

Humble, Susan Elizabeth. *A Divine Round Trip: The Literary and Christological Function of the Descent/Ascent Leitmotif in the Gospel of John*. Contributions to Biblical Exegesis and Theology 79. Leuven: Peeters, 2016.

Hunsberger, George R. "Proposals for a Missional Hermeneutic: Mapping a Conversation." *Missiology: An International Review* 39 (2011) 309–21.

Janzen, David. *The Intentional Christian Community Handbook: For Idealists, Hypocrites, and Wannabe Disciples of Jesus*. Brewster, MA: Paraclete, 2013.

Jipp, Joshua. *Saved by Faith and Hospitality*. Grand Rapids: Eerdmans, 2017.

Johnson, Andy. *Holiness and the* Missio Dei. Eugene, OR: Cascade, 2016.

Kanagaraj, Jey J. *"Mysticism" in the Gospel of John: An Inquiry into Its Background*. Journal for the Study of the New Testament Supplement Series 158. Sheffield, UK: Sheffield Academic Press, 1998.

Käsemann, Ernst. *The Testament of Jesus: A Study of the Gospel of John in the Light of Chapter 17*. Translated by Gerhard Krodel. Philadelphia: Fortress, 1968.

Keating, Daniel A. *Deification and Grace*. Naples, FL: Sapientia, 2007.

———. "Typologies of Deification." *International Journal of Systematic Theology* 17 (2015) 267–83.

Keener, Craig S. *The Gospel of John: A Commentary*. 2 vols. Reprint. Grand Rapids: Baker Academic, 2012. [Original: Peabody, MA: Hendrickson, 2003.]

Knoppers, Gary N. *Jews and Samaritans: The Origins and History of Their Early Relations*. New York: Oxford University Press, 2013.

Koester, Craig R. *Symbolism in the Fourth Gospel: Meaning, Mystery, Community*. 2nd ed. Minneapolis: Fortress, 2003.

———. *The Word of Life: A Theology of John's Gospel*. Grand Rapids: Eerdmans, 2008.

Kok, Kobus. "As the Father Has Sent Me, I Send You: Toward a Missional-Incarnational Ethos in John 4." In *Moral Language in the New Testament: The Interrelatedness of Language and Ethics in Early Christian Writings*, edited by Ruben Zimmermann, Jan G. van der Watt, and Susanne Luther, 168–93. Kontexte und Normen neutestamentlicher Ethik / Contexts and Norms of New Testament Ethics, Vol. 2. Wissenschaftliche Untersuchungen zum Neuen Testament 2/296. Tübingen: Mohr Siebeck, 2010.

Koshy, Asish Thomas. *Identity, Mission, and Community: A Study of the Johannine Resurrection Narrative.* Biblical Hermeneutics Rediscovered 11. New Delhi: Christian World Imprints, 2018.

Köstenberger, Andreas J. *John.* Baker Exegetical Commentary on the New Testament. Grand Rapids: Baker Academic, 2004.

———. *The Missions of Jesus and the Disciples according to the Fourth Gospel, with Implications for the Fourth Gospel's Purpose and the Mission of the Contemporary Church.* Grand Rapids: Eerdmans, 1998.

———. "Sensitivity to Outsiders in John's Gospel and Letters and Its Implications for the Understanding of Early Christian Mission." In *Sensitivity toward Outsiders: Exploring the Dynamic Relationship between Mission and Ethics in the New Testament and Early Christianity,* edited by Jakobus (Kobus) Kok et al., 171–86. Wissenschaftliche Untersuchungen zum Neuen Testament 2/364. Tübingen: Mohr Siebeck, 2014.

———. *A Theology of John's Gospel and Letters.* Grand Rapids: Zondervan, 2009.

Köstenberger, Andreas J., and Scott R. Swain. *Father, Son and Spirit: The Trinity and John's Gospel.* New Studies in Biblical Theology. Downers Grove, IL: InterVarsity, 2008.

Kunene, Musa Victor Mdabuleni. *Communal Holiness in the Gospel of John: The Vine Metaphor as a Test Case with Lessons from African Hospitality and Trinitarian Theology.* Langham Monographs. Carlisle, UK: Langham Partnership, 2012.

Kysar, Robert. *John: The Maverick Gospel.* 3rd ed. Louisville: Westminster John Knox, 2007.

———. *John's Story of Jesus.* Reprint. Eugene, OR: Wipf and Stock, 2003. [Original: Philadelphia: Augsburg Fortress, 1984.]

Lamb, David A. *Text, Context and the Johannine Community: A Sociolinguistic Analysis of the Johannine Writings.* Library of New Testament Studies 477. London: Bloomsbury T. & T. Clark, 2014.

Le Grys, Alan. *Preaching to the Nations: The Origins of Mission in the Early Church.* London: SPCK, 1998.

Legrand, Lucien. *Unity and Plurality: Mission in the Bible.* [Original: *Le Dieu qui vient: la mission dans la Bible.*] Translated by Robert R. Barr. Maryknoll, NY: Orbis, 1990.

Lee, Dorothy A. *Flesh and Glory: Symbolism, Gender, and Theology in the Gospel of John.* New York: Crossroad, 2002.

———. *Hallowed in Truth and Love: Spirituality in the Johannine Literature.* Eugene, OR: Wipf & Stock, 2012.

Leithart, Peter J. *Traces of the Trinity: Signs of God in Creation and Human Experience.* Grand Rapids: Brazos, 2015.

Lewis, C. S. *Screwtape Letters.* London: Bles, 1942.

Lincoln, Andrew T. *The Gospel according to St. John*. Black's New Testament Commentary 4. Peabody, MA: Hendrickson, 2005.

———. "The Johannine Vision of the Church." In *The Oxford Handbook of Ecclesiology*, edited by Paul Avis, 99–118. Oxford: Oxford University Press, forthcoming 2018.

Lincoln, Andrew T., J. Gordon McConville, and Lloyd K. Pietersen, eds. *The Bible and Spirituality: Exploratory Essays in Reading Scripture Spiritually*. Eugene, OR: Cascade, 2013.

Litwa, M. David. *Becoming Divine: An Introduction to Deification in Western Culture*. Eugene, OR: Cascade, 2013.

Lossky, Vladimir. *The Mystical Theology of the Eastern Church*. Reprint. Crestwood, NY: St. Vladimir's Seminary Press, 1976. [Original: *Essai sur la théologie mystique de l'Eglise d'Orient*. Paris: Éditions Montaigne, 1944. ET, London: James Clarke, 1957.]

Lunn, Nicholas P. *The Original Ending of Mark: A New Case for the Authenticity of Mark 16:9–20*. Eugene, OR: Pickwick, 2014.

Macaskill, Grant. *Union with Christ in the New Testament*. Oxford: Oxford University Press, 2014.

Manning, Gary T. Jr. *Echoes of a Prophet: The Use of Ezekiel in the Gospel of John and in Literature of the Second Temple Period*. Journal for the Study of the New Testament Supplement Series 270. London: T. & T. Clark, 2004.

Marrow, Stanley B. "Κόσμος [*Kosmos*] in John." *Catholic Biblical Quarterly* 64 (2002) 90–102.

Martyn, J. Louis. *History and Theology in the Fourth Gospel*. Nashville: Abingdon, 1968.

Matson, Mark A. "To Serve as Slave: Footwashing as Paradigmatic Status Reversal." In *One in Christ Jesus: Essays on Early Christianity and "All That Jazz," in Honor of S. Scott Bartchy*, edited by David Lertis Matson and K. C. Richardson, 113–31. Eugene, OR: Wipf & Stock, 2014.

McGuckin, John. "The Strategic Adaptation of Deification in the Cappadocians." In *Partakers of the Divine Nature*, edited by Michael J. Christensen and Jeffrey A. Wittung, 95–114. Grand Rapids: Baker Academic, 2008.

McKinzie, Greg. "Missional Hermeneutics as Theological Interpretation." *Journal of Theological Interpretation* 11 (2017) 157–79.

McPolin, James. "Mission in the Fourth Gospel." *Irish Theological Quarterly* 36 (1969) 113–22.

Meeks, Wayne A. "The Ethics of the Fourth Evangelist." In *Exploring the Gospel of John: In Honor of D. Moody Smith*, edited by R. Alan Culpepper and C. Clifton Black, 317–26. Louisville: Westminster John Knox, 1996.

———. "The Man from Heaven in Johannine Sectarianism." *Journal of Biblical Literature* 91 (1972) 44–72.

Meier, John P. "Love in Q and John: Love of Enemies, Love of One Another." *Mid-Stream* 40 (2001) 42–50.

———. *A Marginal Jew: Rethinking the Historical Jesus*. Vol. 4, *Law and Love*. Anchor Yale Bible Reference Library. New Haven: Yale University Press, 2009.

Michaels, J. Ramsey. *The Gospel of John*. New International Commentary on the New Testament. Grand Rapids: Eerdmans, 2010.

Minear, Paul S. "The Original Functions of John 21." *Journal of Biblical Literature* 102 (1983) 85–98.

Moloney, Francis J. "The Function of John 13–17 within the Johannine Narrative." In *The Gospel of John: Text and Context*, edited by R. Alan Culpepper, Rolf Rendtorff, and Ellen Van Wolde, 260–83. Biblical Interpretation Series 72. Leiden: Brill, 2005.

——. *The Gospel of John*. Sacra Pagina 4. Collegeville, MN: Liturgical, 1998.

——. *Love in the Gospel of John: An Exegetical, Theological, and Literary Study*. Grand Rapids: Baker Academic, 2013.

——. "To Make God Known: A Reading of John 17:1–26." In *The Gospel of John: Text and Context*, 284–312. Leiden: Brill, 2005.

Mosser, Carl. "The Greatest Possible Blessing: Calvin and Deification." *Scottish Journal of Theology* 55 (2002) 36–57.

Motyer, Stephen. *Your Father the Devil? A New Approach to John and "the Jews."* Paternoster Biblical and Theological Monographs. Carlisle, UK: Paternoster, 1997.

Nellas, Panayiotis. *Deification in Christ: Orthodox Perspectives on the Nature of the Human Person*. Translated by Norman Russell. Crestwood, NY: St. Vladimir's Seminary Press, 1987.

Newbigin, Lesslie. *The Light Has Come: An Exposition of the Fourth Gospel*. Grand Rapids: Eerdmans, 1982.

Nissen, Johannes. *New Testament and Mission: Historical and Hermeneutical Perspectives*. Frankfurt: Lang, 1999.

O'Grady, John F. "The Prologue and Chapter 17 of the Gospel of John." In *What We Have Heard from the Beginning: The Past, Present, and Future of Johannine Studies*, edited by Tom Thatcher, 215–28. Waco, TX: Baylor University Press, 2007.

Oakman, Douglas. "The Political Meaning of a Cipher—John 21:11." *Biblical Theology Bulletin* 47 (2017) 87–94.

Okure, Teresa. *The Johannine Approach to Mission: A Contextual Study of John 4.1–42*. Wissenschaftliche Untersuchungen zum Neuen Testament 2/31. Tübingen: Mohr Siebeck, 1988.

Parsenios, George L. *Departure and Consolation: The Johannine Farewell Discourses in Light of Greco-Roman Literature*. Novum Testamentum Supplements 117. Leiden: Brill, 2005.

Peterson, Brian Neil. *John's Use of Ezekiel: Understanding the Unique Perspective of the Fourth Gospel*. Minneapolis: Fortress, 2015.

Phillips, Peter M. *The Prologue of the Fourth Gospel: A Sequential Reading*. London: T. & T. Clark, 2006.

Pohl, Christine D. *Making Room: Recovering Hospitality as a Christian Tradition*. Grand Rapids: Eerdmans, 1999.

Rabens, Volker. "Johannine Perspectives on Ethical Enabling in the Context of Stoic and Philonic Ethics." In *Rethinking the Ethics of John: "Implicit Ethics" in the Johannine Writings*, edited by Jan G. van der Watt and Ruben Zimmermann, 114–39. Kontexte und Normen neutestamentlicher Ethik / Contexts and Norms of New Testament Ethics Vol. 3. Wissenschaftliche Untersuchungen zum Neuen Testament 1/291. Tübingen: Mohr Siebeck, 2012.

Rakestraw, Robert V. "Becoming Like God: An Evangelical Doctrine of Theosis." *Journal of the Evangelical Theological Society* 40 (1997) 257–69.

Rensberger, David. "Spirituality and Christology in Johannine Sectarianism." In *Word, Theology, and Community in John*, edited by John Painter, R. Alan Culpepper, and Fernando F. Segovia, 173–88. St. Louis: Chalice, 2002.

Rossé, Gérard. *The Spirituality of Communion: A New Approach to the Johannine Writings*. Hyde Park, NY: New City, 1998.

Russell, Brian D. *(re)Aligning with God: Reading Scripture for Church and World*. Eugene, OR: Cascade, 2016.

Russell, Norman. *Cyril of Alexandria*. The Early Church Fathers. New York: Routledge, 2000.

———. *The Doctrine of Deification in the Greek Patristic Tradition*. Oxford Early Christian Studies. Oxford: Oxford University Press, 2004.

———. *Fellow Workers with God: Orthodox Thinking on Theosis*. Foundations Series 5. Crestwood, NY: St. Vladimir's Seminary Press, 2009.

Rutba House, ed. *School(s) for Conversion: 12 Marks of a New Monasticism*. Eugene, OR: Cascade, 2005.

Sánchez M., Leopoldo A. *Receiver, Bearer, and Giver of God's Spirit: Jesus' Life in the Spirit as a Lens for Theology and Life*. Eugene, OR: Pickwick, 2015.

Sanders, Jack T. *Ethics in the New Testament: Change and Development*. Philadelphia: Fortress, 1975.

Scheffler, Eben. "Jesus' Non-violence at His Arrest: The Synoptics and John's Gospel Compared." *Acta Patristica et Byzantina* 17 (2006) 312–26.

Schneiders, Sandra M. *Jesus Risen in Our Midst: Essays on the Resurrection of Jesus in the Fourth Gospel*. Collegeville, MN: Liturgical, 2013.

———. *Written That You May Believe: Encountering Jesus in the Fourth Gospel*. New York: Crossroad, 1999.

Schnelle, Udo. *Das Evangelium nach Johannes*. Theologischer Handkommentar zum Neuen Testament 4. Leipzig: Evangelische Verlagsanstalt, 1998.

———. *Theology of the New Testament*. Translated by M. Eugene Boring. Grand Rapids: Baker Academic, 2009.

Segovia, Fernando F. "John 1:11–18 as Entrée into Johannine Reality: Representation and Ramifications." In *Word, Theology, and Community in John*, edited by John Painter, R. Alan Culpepper, and Fernando F. Segovia, 33–64. St. Louis: Chalice, 2002.

Skinner, Christopher W. "The Good Shepherd Lays Down His Life for the Sheep" (John 10:11, 15, 17): Questioning the Limits of a Johannine Metaphor." *Catholic Biblical Quarterly* 80 (2018) 97–113.

———. "Introduction: (How) Can We Talk About Johannine Ethics? Looking Back and Moving Forward." In *Johannine Ethics: The Moral World of the Gospel and Epistles of John*, edited by Sherri Brown and Christopher W. Skinner, xvii–xxxvi. Minneapolis: Fortress, 2017.

———. "Love One Another: The Johannine Love Command in the Farewell Discourse." In *Johannine Ethics: The Moral World of the Gospel and Epistles of John*, edited by Sherri Brown and Christopher W. Skinner, 25–42. Minneapolis: Fortress, 2017.

———. "Virtue in the New Testament: The Legacies of John and Paul in Comparative Perspective." In *Unity and Diversity in the Gospels and Paul: Essays in Honor of Frank J. Matera*, edited by Christopher W. Skinner and Kelly R. Iverson, 301–24. Society of Biblical Literature Early Christianity and Its Literature 7. Atlanta: Society of Biblical Literature, 2012.

———. "The World: Promise and Unfulfilled Hope." In *Character Studies in the Fourth Gospel: Narrative Approaches to Seventy Figures in John*, edited by Steven A. Hunt,

D. François Tolmie, and Ruben Zimmerman, 61–70. Reprint. Grand Rapids: Eerdmans, 2016. [Original: Tübingen: Mohr Siebeck, 2013.]

Skreslet, Stanley H. *Picturing Christian Witness: New Testament Images of Disciples in Mission*. Grand Rapids: Eerdmans, 2006.

Smit, Peter-Ben. "The Gift of the Spirit in John 19:30? A Reconsideration of παρέδωκεν τὸ πνεῦμα [*paredōken to pneuma*]" *Catholic Biblical Quarterly* 78 (2016) 447–62.

Smith, D. Moody. "Ethics and the Interpretation of the Fourth Gospel." In *Word, Theology, and Community in John*, edited by John Painter, R. Alan Culpepper, and Fernando F. Segovia, 109–22. St. Louis: Chalice, 2002.

———. *The Theology of the Gospel of John*. New Testament Theology. Cambridge: Cambridge University Press, 1995.

Spohn, William V. *Go and Do Likewise: Jesus and Ethics*. New York: Continuum, 1999.

Stare, Mira. "Ethics of Life in the Gospel of John." In *Rethinking the Ethics of John: "Implicit Ethics" in the Johannine Writings*, edited by Jan G. van der Watt and Ruben Zimmerman, 213–28. Kontexte und Normen neutestamentlicher Ethik / Contexts and Norms of New Testament Ethics Vol. 3; Wissenschaftliche Untersuchungen zum Neuen Testament 1/291. Tübingen: Mohr Siebeck, 2012.

Stube, John Carlson. *A Graeco-Roman Rhetorical Reading of the Farewell Discourse*. Library of New Testament Studies 309. London: T. & T. Clark, 2006.

Sunquist, Scott W. *Understanding Christian Mission: Participation in Suffering and Glory*. Grand Rapids: Baker Academic, 2013.

Sutherland, Arthur. *I Was A Stranger: A Christian Theology of Hospitality*. Nashville: Abingdon, 2006.

Swartley, Willard M. *Covenant of Peace: The Missing Peace in the New Testament Theology and Ethics*. Grand Rapids: Eerdmans, 2006.

———. *Health, Healing and the Church's Mission: Biblical Perspectives and Moral Priorities*. Downers Grove, IL: InterVarsity, 2012.

Talbert, Charles H. "The Fourth Gospel's Soteriology between New Birth and Resurrection." In *Getting "Saved": The Whole Story of Salvation in the New Testament*, edited by Charles H. Talbert and Jason A. Whitlark, 176–91. Grand Rapids: Eerdmans, 2011.

———. *Reading John: A Literary and Theological Commentary on the Fourth Gospel and Johannine Epistles*. Reading the New Testament 4. Rev. ed. Macon, GA: Smyth & Helwys, 2013.

Tam, Josaphat C. *Apprehension of Jesus in the Gospel of John*. Wissenschaftliche Untersuchungen zum Neuen Testament 2/399. Tübingen: Mohr Siebeck, 2015.

Teresa, Mother. *No Greater Love*. Edited by Becky Benenate and Joseph Durepos. Novato, CA: New World Library, 1989.

Thatcher, Tom. "Cain the Jew the AntiChrist: Collective Memory and the Johannine Ethics of Loving and Hating." In *Rethinking the Ethics of John*, edited by Jan van der Watt and Ruben Zimmerman, 350–73. Kontexte und Normen neutestamentlicher Ethik / Contexts and Norms of New Testament Ethics Vol. 3. Wissenschaftliche Untersuchungen zum Neuen Testament 1/291; Tübingen: Mohr Siebeck, 2012.

———. *Greater than Caesar: Christology and Empire in the Fourth Gospel*. Minneapolis: Fortress, 2009.

Thomas, John Christopher. *Footwashing in John 13 and the Johannine Community*. 2nd ed. Cleveland, TN: CPT, 2014.

Thompson, Marianne Meye. *The God of the Gospel of John*. Grand Rapids: Eerdmans, 2001.

———. *John: A Commentary.* The New Testament Library. Louisville: Westminster John Knox, 2015.

———. "Response to Gorman." Paper presented at Fuller Theological Seminary, April 7, 2016.

———. "'They Bear Witness to Me': The Psalms in the Passion Narrative of the Gospel of John." In *The Word Leaps the Gap: Essays on Scripture and Theology in Honor of Richard B. Hays,* edited by J. Ross Wagner, C. Kavin Rowe, and A. Katherine Grieb, 267–83. Grand Rapids: Eerdmans, 2008.

van der Watt, Jan G. "Ethics and Ethos in the Gospel according to John." *Zeitschrift für die neutestamentlich Wissenschaft und die Kunde der älteren Kirche* 97 (2006) 147–76.

———. *Family of the King: Dynamics of Metaphor in the Gospel of John.* Leiden: Brill, 2000.

———, ed. *Identity, Ethics, and Ethos in the New Testament.* Beihefte zur *Zeitschrift für die neutestamentliche Wissenschaft und die Kunde der älteren Kirche* 141. Berlin: de Gruyter, 2006.

———. *An Introduction to the Johannine Gospel and Letters.* T. & T. Clark Approaches to Biblical Studies. London: T. & T. Clark, 2008.

———. "Radical Social Redefinition and Radical Love: Ethics and Ethos in the Gospel according to John." In *Identity, Ethics, and Ethos in the New Testament,* edited by Jan G. van der Watt, 107–33. Beihefte zur Zeitschrift für die neutestamentliche Wissenschaft 141. Berlin: De Gruyter, 2006.

van der Watt, Jan G., and Ruben Zimmerman, eds. *Rethinking the Ethics of John: "Implicit Ethics" in the Johannine Writings.* Kontexte und Normen neutestamentlicher Ethik / Contexts and Norms of New Testament Ethics, Vol. 3. Wissenschaftliche Untersuchungen zum Neuen Testament 1/291. Tübingen: Mohr Siebeck, 2012.

Van Gelder, Craig, and Dwight J. Zscheile. *The Missional Church in Perspective: Mapping Trends and Shaping the Conversation.* Grand Rapids: Baker Academic, 2011.

Vellanickal, Matthew. *The Divine Sonship of Christians in the Johannine Writings.* Analecta Biblica 72. Rome: Biblical Institute, 1977.

Waaijman, Kees. *Spirituality: Forms, Foundations, Methods.* Translated by John Vriend. Leuven: Peeters, 2002.

Wells, Samuel. *Incarnational Ministry: Being with the Church.* Grand Rapids: Eerdmans, 2017.

———. *Incarnational Mission: Being with the World.* Grand Rapids: Eerdmans, 2018.

Williams, Peter J. "Not the Prologue of John." *Journal for the Study of the New Testament* 33 (2011) 375–86.

Williams, Rowan. "Deification." In *The Westminster Dictionary of Christian Spirituality,* edited by Gordon S. Wakefield, 106–8. Philadelphia: Westminster, 1983.

Williamson, Lamar Jr. *Preaching the Gospel of John: Proclaiming the Living Word.* Louisville: Westminster John Knox, 2004.

Wilson-Hartgrove, Jonathan. *New Monasticism: What It Has to Say to Today's Church.* Grand Rapids: Brazos, 2008.

———. *Strangers at My Door: A True Story of Finding Jesus in Unexpected Guests.* New York: Convergent, 2013.

———. *To Baghdad and Beyond: How I Got Born Again in Babylon.* Eugene, OR: Cascade, 2005.

Yong, Amos. *The Missiological Spirit: Christian Mission Theology in the Third Millennium Global Context*. Eugene, OR: Cascade, 2014.

Zimmermann, Ruben. "The 'Implicit Ethics' of New Testament Writings: A Draft of a New Methodology for Analysing New Testament Ethics." *Neotestamentica* 43 (2009) 399–423.

Zimmerman, Ruben, Jan G. van der Watt, and Susanne Luther, eds. *Moral Language in the New Testament: The Interrelatedness of Language and Ethics in Early Christian Writings*. Kontexte und Normen neutestamentlicher Ethik / Contexts and Norms of New Testament Ethics, Vol. 2. Wissenschaftliche Untersuchungen zum Neuen Testament 2/296. Tübingen: Mohr Siebeck, 2010.

Zizioulas, John D. *Being as Communion: Studies in Personhood and the Church*. Crestwood, NY: St. Vladimir's Seminary Press, 1985.

Index of Names

Subject Index

Scripture Index

CPSIA information can be obtained
at www.ICGtesting.com
Printed in the USA
BVHW080237150620
581352BV00004BA/96